Issues in Historiogr...

The Debate on the Cr...

1824

Manchester University Press

Issues in Historiography
General editor
R. C. RICHARDSON
University of Winchester

Already published

Issues in Historiography

The Debate
on the Crusades

CHRISTOPHER TYERMAN

MANCHESTER
UNIVERSITY PRESS
MANCHESTER AND NEW YORK

distributed in the United States exclusively by Palgrave Macmillan

Copyright © Christopher Tyerman 2011

The right of Christopher Tyerman to be identified as the author of this work has been asserted by him in accordance with the Copyright, Designs and Patents Act 1988.

Published by Manchester University Press
Oxford Road, Manchester M13 9NR, UK
and Room 400, 175 Fifth Avenue, New York, NY 10010, USA
www.manchesteruniversitypress.co.uk

Distributed in the United States exclusively by
Palgrave Macmillan, 175 Fifth Avenue, New York,
NY 10010, USA

Distributed in Canada exclusively by
UBC Press, University of British Columbia, 2029 West Mall,
Vancouver, BC, Canada V6T 1Z2

British Library Cataloguing-in-Publication Data
A catalogue record for this book is available from the British Library

Library of Congress Cataloging-in-Publication Data applied for

ISBN   978 0 7190 7320 5 hardback
ISBN   978 0 7190 7321 2 paperback

First published 2011

The publisher has no responsibility for the persistence or accuracy of URLs for any external or third-party internet websites referred to in this book, and does not guarantee that any content on such websites is, or will remain, accurate or appropriate.

Typeset by Action Publishing Technology Ltd, Gloucester
Printed in Great Britain by TJ International

For

Imogen and William

CONTENTS

GENERAL EDITOR'S FOREWORD

History without historiography is a contradiction in terms. The study of the past cannot be separated from a linked study of its practitioners and intermediaries. No historian writes in isolation from the work of his or her predecessors nor can the commentator – however clinically objective or professional – stand aloof from the insistent pressures, priorities and demands of the ever-changing present. In truth there are no self-contained academic 'ivory towers'. Historians' writings are an extension of who they are and where they are placed. Though historians address the past as their subject they always do so in ways that are shaped – consciously or unconsciously as the case may be – by the society, cultural ethos, politics and systems of their own day, and they communicate their findings in ways which are specifically intelligible and relevant to a reading public consisting initially of their own contemporaries. For these reasons the study of history is concerned most fundamentally not with dead facts and sterile, permanent verdicts but with highly charged dialogues, disagreements, controversies and shifting centres of interest among its presenters, with the changing methodologies and discourse of the subject over time, and with audience reception. *Issues in Historiography* is a series designed to explore such matters by means of case studies of key moments in world history and the interpretations, reinterpretations, debates and disagreements they have engendered.

Tyerman's subject – the crusades – is only the second medieval topic to join the Issues series. Like its predecessor on the Norman Conquest by Marjorie Chibnall it has a long and complex historiography. In Christopher Tyerman's densely crowded but clearly argued pages the reader will find a perceptive and challenging survey which brings out the shifting centres of interest among the many writers who have engaged with this subject, the different agendas which underpinned their various offerings, the kind of sources they used and relied on, and the impact of their particular religious, political and cultural contexts. Early chroniclers such as William of Tyre and his changing posthumous reputation come under scrutiny. Reformation perspectives such as John Foxe's *History of the Turks* (1566) are examined and as Tyerman's survey progresses through the seventeenth and eighteenth centuries writers such as Thomas Fuller, Voltaire and Edward Gibbon are drawn into the discussion. The cultural as well as political significance of Napoleon's late eighteenth-century Egyptian and Syrian campaigns is considered as is a nineteenth-century predilection to view crusaders as well-intentioned missionaries. When we reach the twentieth century Lawrence of Arabia receives a passing mention. Sir Steven Runciman's multi-volume history of the crusades, however, is accorded a full, but certainly not reverential, treatment. Modern American contributions to crusade historiography – some of them far from illuminating – are rehearsed. Claude Cahen, 'a rare marxist', and the Egyptian Aziz Suryal Atiya find a place here. Tyerman casts his net very widely; his subject dictates that he should.

Present-day relations between the West and Islam help to make Tyerman's book a highly relevant text for students and their teachers. The author's account of the historiography of the crusades emphatically rejects easy modern parallels. Nonetheless by virtue of its subject matter this volume does more than unpack the many layers of a particular topic which has continued to exert its fascination on generations of commentators over the centuries. Revealingly this study opens a window on to a broader landscape of deep-rooted, uneasy and often brutal international relations.

R. C. Richardson
July 2010

PREFACE

The history of history is increasingly fashionable. All history is revisionist, a response to what others have written. Thus, at its simplest, reading other historians will help any writer of history clarify their own views of the past. Writing history is not a neutral revelation but a malleable, personal, contingent, cultural activity. History examines the past by translating it into the present. The role of the translator – the historian – is thus instrumental, never a passive recorder or neutral interrogator but always a controlling producer. Study of the work of historians – historiography – becomes part of the way any historical subject is apprehended. Consequently, this book acts as a necessary pendant to my previous work on the crusades themselves. It is a negotiable analysis of predecessors and contemporaries.

This is not an entirely abstract exercise. Attitudes to the past are often conditioned by early perceptions, even, perhaps especially, if these are subsequently revised or rejected. My acquaintance with crusading began with images of heroic but misguided knights in the marvellously vivid, tendentious, but far from unintelligent, illustrated Ladybird History series of the 1950s and 1960s. Such pictures stay etched on the retina of memory. Intellectual engagement was later stimulated at school by exposure to the set-piece rhetorical arias of Edward Gibbon, Ernest Barker and Steven Runciman, embodiments of the very English tradition of astonished rational condescension that, although I did not then know it, reached back to Thomas Fuller in the seventeenth century. The bruising literary power of their historical imaginations failed to disguise that these were no objective summings up. From the very start, it was clear that the crusades were and remained controversial. They and their interpretations continue to be so in circles both academic and not. Why this should and continues to be so is a question that has long engaged me and provides the excuse for this book.

Inevitably, surveying historians across almost a thousand years is the labour of the magpie inviting error, superficiality and omission. No doubt the alert reader will spot examples of all three, for which I alone am responsible. That there are not more can be attributed to the work of other scholars, not least some of those discussed in what follows. The enterprise has been equally dependent on the resources and friendliness of the libraries in Oxford where I have principally worked on the book, the still incomparable Bodleian, the History Faculty and those of my two colleges. To my colleagues at Hertford and New College, I owe a continuing debt of companionship and intellectual stimulation. I have tried out some of these ideas on my pupils in Oxford and on audiences in Oxford and Dublin. I thank them for their comments, generosity and tolerance as I do the MUP's anonymous reader. The editor and publishers of this series have combined patience and encouragement in rare measure. Lest proper perspective not be lost, the book is dedicated to two as yet innocent of the strange games historians play.

CJT
Oxford
7 July 2010

INTRODUCTION

Few events of European history have captured the sentiments of contemporaries and the imaginations of later observers more vividly than the series of Christian wars now known as the crusades. At least from the capture of Jerusalem by an army of western Europeans in July 1099, if not before, this particular exercise in holy violence has attracted diverse interpretations from promoters, historians and theologians, from religious enthusiasts and from their critics. As wars regarded by their instigators as religious acts nonetheless directed at securing temporal space for Christendom and Christianity, they inescapably exposed the compromises of pragmatic idealism, the tension between rhetoric and experience, transcendent hope with present fear, the promise of eternal rewards with the immediacy of military conflict. Consequently, crusading was always controversial, a forum where moral absolutes jostled with material contingency.

There have been no centuries since the eleventh when books on the crusades have not been published and secured wide readership. At its simplest this has reflected crusading's protean nature. Over more than five centuries after the First Crusade (1095–99), armies under the banners of the cross and sustained by special offers of forgiveness of sins associated with that first campaign to win Jerusalem, reached all corners of Europe and the littoral of the Near East, touching some seminal political events of the age: the reordering of the Near East and the frontiers between Islamic and Christian rulers in the Mediterranean; the German and Christian conquest of the southern and eastern Baltic; the repression of religious dissent in Christendom; the assertion of papal authority. Although this book is not about the historical crusades as such, the briefest of surveys may help set the scene.

Large armies from western Europe attacked Syria, Palestine and Egypt in a series of massive campaigns by land and sea to some of which later commentators attached numbers: the First (1095–99 with a second wave 1101–2); Second (1146–49); Third

(1187–92); Fourth (1198–1204); Fifth (1217–21). Other substantial assaults on the eastern Mediterranean included the crusades of Frederick II of Germany (1228–29) and Louis IX of France (1248–54) who also briefly invaded Tunisia (1270). Louis's invasion of Egypt in 1249 was the last such from western Europe until Bonaparte's in 1798. Between grand assaults, many substantial but lesser expeditions followed similar routes, such as the crusades of the count of Champagne and the earl of Cornwall in 1239–41. Settlements were established along the Levantine littoral that lasted in various guises and extent from 1098 to 1291. Cyprus was captured in 1191 and held by western rulers until 1571. Jerusalem was in western Christian hands from 1099 to 1187 and, less securely, 1229–44. The next western European conqueror in the Holy City was General Allenby in December 1917 at the head of a polyglot army including a significant proportion of Muslims. In 1204 the Fourth Crusade had been diverted to capture the Greek capital of Constantinople (lost in 1261), an outrage for Greek Christians that irrevocably sealed the church schism with the Latin church of the west.

Traditions, ideology and institutions grew up thickly around these wars. Distinctive among these were the wearing of a cross to signal the taking of a vow; the consequent grant of spiritual privileges, remission of penalties of sins and later full indulgences for sin; the perception of this war as a sort of armed pilgrimage; temporal privileges such as avoidance of law suits or repayment of debts; and the protection of crusaders' families and property by the church. From the late twelfth century, taxes on laymen and especially the clergy were instituted to pay for these expeditions. Specific techniques and systems of propaganda and recruitment were honed to raise troops. While rhetorically, legally and emotionally retaining a connection with the Jerusalem war, if only as a reference point, this form of warfare proved easily exportable to other areas of conflict that involved the perceived interests of the official Latin church. These included the conquest of Muslim al-Andalus by the Christian kingdoms of Spain in the twelfth and thirteenth centuries; the German penetration and annexation of the pagan eastern Baltic from the mid-twelfth to the fifteenth centuries; the suppression of heresy, notably in Languedoc in southern France in wars known as the Albigensian crusades (1209–29); the defence of papal temporal interests in Germany and Italy in the thirteenth and fourteenth centuries, the so-called political crusades. Together, these wars produced their own literature, liturgy and religious communities, notably the military orders, such as the Templars, Hospitallers and Teutonic Knights. Clearly associated, if lacking official support, were popular uprisings ostensibly aimed at the recovery of Jerusalem, such as the Children's Crusade (1212) and the Shepherds' Crusades (1251 and 1320). In places, even those attacked by crusaders countered by adopting the cross – such as anti-papalists in Germany in 1240 or rebels in England in 1263–65.

Crusading became culturally normative, even if active participation always remained a minority activity. The practice, aspiration and ideals of crusading persisted throughout the later middle ages, on occasion igniting military action, as against the Ottoman Turks in the Balkans in 1396, 1444 or 1456. The dying fall of active crusading, even if more in word than deed, lingered long into the sixteenth century and beyond. The attendant religious propaganda and economic necessities reached far beyond military recruitment into parish churches and taxpayers' pockets throughout the Latin Christian world; into the mechanics of salvation, the liturgy of penance and the ideology of kingship. At once a symptom and an encouragement of western Europe's engagement with its neighbours, crusading promoted the interests of international commerce while defining cultural differences, notably in the alienation of the Greek orthodox tradition. Alternatively or simultaneously imagined as wading through blood to the foot of the Cross, as an assertion of Christian identity, or as a moral and morale-boosting focus for resistance to enemies of church, faith or nation, the crusades coloured the texture of medieval politics, religion and society. Even after the reality of these wars faded into collective memory from the sixteenth century, their particular quality continued to exert a hold, on confessional and rationalist critics no less than religious or sentimental supporters.

However, unlike other familiar aspects of the medieval past, such as the Vikings, Charlemagne's empire, or the Norman Conquest, the crusades never fitted easily into later cultural patterns. As historians from the seventeenth century increasingly rejected religiously inspired providential interpretations of past events, they looked in the crusades for the origins of their own times in the development of nations, institutions of government, the growth of commerce and, above all, the progress of 'manners' or civilisation. The crusades sat awkwardly between secular and religious history in periods when the distinction was taken as axiomatic. They received the lofty condescension of the Enlightenment as they had the doctrinal disapproval of Protestants. Their inextricable weave of idealism and materialism, inconvenient for materialist and idealist historians alike, produced a near-ubiquitous rush to judgement, one of the most persistent and prominent features in histories of the crusades. Even today, writers on the crusades are routinely interrogated by reviewers and readers as to whether they regard the crusades in a positive or negative light. While some still oblige, experts on few other medieval events are expected to provide such moral opinions.

This uniqueness also represented a challenge to the tradition of historians seeking to chronicle national development, especially after the Reformation. Except in special cases such as early modern or Franco's Spain, the crusades rarely conformed to any straightforward projection of nationalism or national identity, their role in the emergence of nation states, for long of deep historical and cultural interest, apparently obscure or equivocal. The intrinsic internationalism of crusading rendered the spatchcocking of the crusades into narratives of national progress or pride an uneasy business. Richard I, good crusader but absent king, provided one classic example of the difficulties; the embarrassment of Philip II of France abandoning the Third Crusade and the pious failures of Louis IX two more. This did not result in the crusades being ignored in cultic national histories. Rather they were incongruously recruited to serve under national flags. In the nineteenth century, the simultaneous developments of colonial politics and critical history combined with its spurious nationalism to consolidate crusading's popularity as a subject for entertainment and moralising. The European dash for empire happily recruited the crusades as exemplars of cultural virtues, occasionally vices, or superiority over conquered peoples and societies. Where Enlightenment critics had concentrated their fire on the moral, religious and cultural aspects of crusading, the debate in the nineteenth and early twentieth centuries revolved around essentially materialist interpretations, the crusades as wars of conquest, motors of economic expansion and expressions of colonialism. Thus crusading became reconciled with prevailing politico-historical fashions.

The twentieth century appeared to reinforce this. The creation of the State of Israel (1948) seemed initially to feed into the colonial model, certainly stimulating research into the westerners' settlement of Syria and Palestine. In Israel itself, new forms of national perspective were developed while the state's very existence ignited new forms of malign historical parallelism that continue to resonate loudly across contemporary political and cultural debates. Away from the Near East, the ideological wars that engulfed or threatened twentieth-century Europe encouraged new engagement with the ideology of crusading. At the same time, the intellectual as well as physical retreat from European imperialism was matched by root and branch critical reappraisal of the old model of crusading colonialism. Historians continue to mould the subject according to their own interests. Yet however viewed, the crusades constitute one of the great subjects of European history. They conjure issues of the manifestation of systems of transcendent belief; cultural and religious identity; economic and political expansion; imperialism and colonisation; the ideology, legitimacy and pathology of public violence; the experience of war; the impact of militarism on noncombatants, host societies and victim communities; inter-ethnic and inter-faith relations; the nature of popular political and religious action; state-building; and the use of propaganda. The crusades remain one of the few subjects of professional history that carry wide popular recognition even if little serious understanding.

This alone would merit examination. However, perhaps to the surprise of those who regarded the crusades as merely a clash of arms for remote, ultimately futile, inexplicable or hypocritical territorial or ideological goals, in the past half-century the crusades have become an increasingly prominent aspect of serious medieval study and research around the academic world, embracing some of the newest historiographical, techniques. This development also deserves study. The object of this book is to give some account of how such interest has been created, developed and sustained. It investigates the ways in which the crusades have been observed by historians from the 1090s to the present day. Especial emphasis is placed on the academic after-life of the crusades from the sixteenth to twenty-first centuries.

This will not be another contribution to the debates on the nature of the phenomenon or to the major interpretive problems that continue to arouse professional controversy and research. It merely attempts to describe the history of these different opinions, how they have been adopted and their historical contexts. It is a book about books. Unlike some recent scholarship, this will not include detailed consideration of the wider post-medieval cultural reception of the crusades and the use of the images and language of crusading in art, literature and popular culture except insofar as these affected historians' approaches to the subject and what they wrote. Over thirty generations and more, the crusades have occupied simultaneous parallel worlds of past events and present imagination, a duality that provides the substance for what follows.

1

'The greatest event since the Resurrection': some medieval views of the crusades

The very first narrative accounts of the crusades were composed by participants on the First Crusade itself. They were contained in letters sent to the west in 1097–99, culminating in the carefully edited and pointed version prepared for the pope by the crusade leadership in September 1099, the first surviving history.[1] Although composed by eyewitnesses, these letters were formal exercises designed to construct didactic stories to explain to their audience the providential significance of the events experienced. They certainly did not contain simple or unadorned still less objective accounts of 'what really happened'. The military campaign was insistently rendered as a divinely instigated and directed mission that operated in the double contexts of history and scripture, this world and the next. Setting the tone for much subsequent historicising, from the start the First Crusade was a literary construct.

Medieval writers knew from the classical past that history differed from annals or chronicles on the one side, and satire, drama or other literary genres on the other. History was deliberately stylish, interpretive and didactic. Specifically Christian historiography, a legacy of the late Roman Empire and writers such as Augustine of Hippo, concerned itself with the significance of terrestrial events in relation to divine providence, sin and the march of the world to the Day of Judgement. Individuals could become merely patterns of conduct and free will. The narrative of events contained a moral purpose, presented rhetorically, in order to persuade. The Biblical tradition differed in that it purported to present a divinely inspired account of God's relations with his Creation, especially Man, culminating in the revelation of the Crucifixion and Resurrection and the prophecy of Christ's return at the end of time. Its truth was many-layered, including literal, allegorical, metaphorical and mystical, but it was Revealed Truth, testament of Faith itself.

The First Crusade, Latin chronicles and their legacy

The drama of the First Crusade provoked a uniquely heavy literary response in the immediate production of histories trying to make sense of it. These shared some distinctive features. Whether conceived as *Gesta* (i.e. deeds, of an individual, such as Ralph of Caen's *Gesta Tancredi*, or a people, the *Gesta Francorum* or *Gesta Dei Per Francos*) or *Historia*, the earliest written histories of the First Crusade are essays in interpretation, not mere recitation of events, not Annals or Chronicles. Despite often romantic wishful thinking of later readers, they are all compilations of memories of participants and other written accounts; there are no single-author memoirs. Each account is shot through with precise biblical allusions aimed at establishing specific interpretive parallels between the crusaders and the Israelites of Exodus or the Maccabees. Urban II's call to arms evoked Christ's own injunction to believers to take up their crosses and follow him. Events attracted biblical language; the fall of Jerusalem in 1099 could be recalled in words from the Book of Revelation. The great significance of the success of the first Jerusalem journey was unmistakable. In the words of the most popular history of the First Crusade, written within a decade of its conclusion, 'since the creation of the world what more miraculous undertaking has there been (other than the mystery of the redeeming Cross) than what was achieved in our own time by the journey of our own people to Jerusalem?'[2] Just as the First Crusade was depicted as a sign of God's immanence, so its story was crafted as if it were a continuation of holy scripture defining a new chapter in God's revelation to man. From the start, the historiography of crusading was conceived as a branch of theology.

Although the First Crusade remained central to all later understanding of what crusading meant, its interpretation seemingly rested on a very narrow tradition. The dominant Latin version of the events of 1095–99 derived from a sequence of related texts, the most influential and possibly earliest of which was the anonymous *Gesta Francorum* (before 1104, possibly as early as 1099/1100, perhaps derived from a previous compilation in circulation). Although composed as if by a participant as a linear narrative, in an apparently artless style, the *Gesta* shows signs of careful construction. Embracing a number of simultaneous perspectives, evidently from different sources, its clear didactic intent reveals itself in albeit mangled scriptural references and, not least, in placing the most direct interpretation of this form of holy war in the mouth of the mother of the Muslim ruler of Mosul: 'the Christians alone cannot fight with you ... but their god fights for them every day'. The scene is close to vernacular epic.[3] The *Gesta* provided or shared material used by three other veterans of the campaign, Raymond of Aguilers, canon of Le Puy (pre-1105), Fulcher of Chartres, chaplain to Baldwin I of Jerusalem (first redaction pre-1105), and, most closely related, the Poitevin Peter Tudebode (before 1111).[4] Although Raymond's and Fulcher's accounts were used by other writers, the primacy of the *Gesta* version was assured through its reworking, in particular by Robert of Rheims (c. 1106/7). The *Gesta* survives in seven medieval manuscripts; Raymond in at least ten; Fulcher in sixteen; Tudebode in four; Robert in ninety-four, thirty-seven from the twelfth century alone. Of the works of Robert's two sophisticated Benedictine colleagues who also decided to improve the *Gesta*'s relatively unadorned account, Baldric of Bourgueil's (c. 1107) and Guibert of Nogent's (1109) survive respectively in seven and eight medieval manuscripts. The contrasting Rhineland *Historia* of Albert of Aachen (first six books possibly soon after 1102) survives in thirteen manuscripts, but is genuinely independent of both the *Gesta* tradition and its propagation by the northern French Benedictine mafia, although like them reliant on participants' testimony. Among the Latin histories, Albert provided the only substantial challenge to the papalist, northern French tradition and only came into his own via the mediation of the cosmopolitan Jerusalemite historian, William of Tyre (c. 1130–86). The other Latin literary accounts and the scattered monastic and urban chronicles scarcely competed.[5]

At least for the twelfth century, Robert of Rheims was pervasive. Apart from the French version of William of Tyre's *Historia*, Robert's was the only medieval prose crusade history known to have been directly translated into a vernacular language (German) during the middle ages. With his embellishments, Robert's use of the *Gesta* confirmed a specific narrative scheme: the fulfilment of God's direct will; Urban II and papal authority; and the unity of crusaders as 'Franks', the new Chosen People. Others said much the same. Fulcher of Chartres has a Turk warn Kerboga of Mosul before the battle of Antioch in 1098: 'Behold the Franks are coming; flee now or fight bravely for I see the banner of the mighty Pope advancing.' Robert's view was cemented by wide dissemination of manuscripts. Emperor Frederick Barbarossa of Germany received a copy before he embarked on the Third Crusade in 1189. It was put into Latin verse in Alsace, also in the 1180s. Many twelfth-century chroniclers and poets across Latin Christendom relied on Robert.[6]

The need for such an establishment view became clear, as the details of what had happened on the First Crusade were contested from the start. Writing in the very first years of the twelfth century, Raymond of Aguilers, possibly disingenuously, claimed to have been prompted to compose his account of the eastern expedition by the lies being spread by deserters.[7] The weight of enthusiastic commentary suggests a desire to reconcile this new form of holy war with traditional ecclesiastical views on the sinfulness of violence, a task lent topicality by the contemporary controversies surrounding papally approved war against its opponents in western Europe. The earliest accounts of the First Crusade therefore adopted a tone of advocacy, a register that never entirely left medieval, and some modern, descriptions of crusading. Success needed to be justified with reference to God's will; so too, and increasingly frequently, did failure. While both its sources and influence reached deep into lay society, the creation of a recognisable and generally accepted crusade myth rested with these clerical authors, most of whom circled a strongly self-referential core. They set the pattern of understanding of the events that subsequently defined the whole.

Their academic justification for this warfare covered a wide swathe of intellectual terrain that included more overtly secular interpretations of crusading to match the theological, legal and evangelical. The English monk William of Malmesbury, whose extensive account (c. 1125) was based on Fulcher of Chartres, chose classical virtues against which to assess the heroic crusaders. He avoided the language of penance and pilgrimage almost entirely and stressed secular motives. The First Crusade was ascribed to a deal between Urban II and Bohemund of Taranto designed to use the ensuing commotion to secure Rome for one and a Balkan principality for the other.[8] Material incentives were recognised in some of the earliest reworkings of the eyewitness compilations, such as Robert of Rheims.[9] The values and aspirations of the godly warrior appeared not just in vernacular poems, epics and romances, stories first sketched around the camp-fires of the First Crusade itself. Elite Latin writers as much as the authors of *chansons* balanced the will of God and the agency of man, terrestrial glamour, honour, bravery, profit and excitement, the worth of man, being set against a fairly two-dimensional backcloth of religious virtue; theology was dressed up as adventure – and vice versa.

This is unsurprising. Raymond of Aguilers's original co-author of his account of the First Crusade was a knight, Pons of Balazun, killed at the siege of Arqah in 1099.[10] Many of the tales incorporated in the earliest accounts derived from participants in the fighting. The language and images of epic and romance are rarely far from the elbows of the clerical authors; histories and *chansons* shared common sources and common milieux. Baldric of Dol had Urban II urge his audience at Clermont to cast aside the 'belt of knighthood' (*militiae cingulum*) to become knights of Christ (*milites Christi*).[11] The qualities of the two knighthoods were clearly the same. The fusion of the sacred and profane is evident in the earliest histories: Raymond of Aguilers's excited pride in describing battles; the breathless immediacy of the *Gesta Francorum*'s account of the daring night-time escalade that delivered Antioch to the crusaders in June 1098; or Albert of Aachen's penchant for the exotic anecdote, such as Godfrey de Bouillon's encounter with a bear in Anatolia or the heroic deaths of Sven of Denmark and his intended, Florina of Burgundy. Praise of battle was intrinsic to the whole concept of crusading; the letters of Stephen of Blois and Anselm of Ribemont from the crusader camps in 1097–98 make this very clear. So, too, did Urban II when writing to monks at Vallombrosa in October 1097: 'we were stimulating the minds of knights to go on this expedition, since they might be able to restrain the savagery of the Saracens by their arms'. Ralph of Caen's biography of one of the stars of the First Crusade, Tancred of Lecce (before 1118), contained the classic account of how the crusade released the young, violent Tancred from the burden of sin through the offer of penitential warfare. No longer need Tancred choose 'the Gospels or the world? His experience in arms recalled him to the service of Christ.'[12] The martial flavour was picked up in all the earliest reconstructions of the pope's Clermont speech and remained unavoidably prominent in all clerically composed Latin histories and chronicles of subsequent crusades, supported by substantial theological underpinning in works such as Bernard of Clairvaux's famous 1130s apologia for the military order of the Templars, *De Laude Novae Militiae*.[13]

The vernacular relationship

The same traits coursed through the increasingly sophisticated and varied vernacular crusade literature in the twelfth century, particularly in Francophone regions, from Norman England to Languedoc. They were also vividly caught in a German text, the *Millstätter Exodus*, which drew parallels between the biblical Israelites' invasion of Canaan and the First Crusade.[14] In French, cycles of often closely related crusade poems, surviving from the later twelfth century, were almost certainly based on much earlier works. These included an epic account concentrating on the siege of Antioch in 1097–98, the *Chanson d'Antioche*, that purported to be based on eyewitness testimony, a poem by a veteran; it certainly incorporated material derived from Latin descriptions of the events. Of the even more fanciful poems, *Les Chetifs*, about the 1101 crusade, was perhaps written at Antioch c. 1149, and the *Chanson* or *Conquête de Jérusalem*, composed by the mid-1130s, concentrated on the capture of the Holy City. By 1200, verse chivalric epic was used in Ambroise's history of the deeds of Richard I and the Third Crusade, the *Estoire de la guerre sainte*.[15] Within a generation of Ambroise, vernacular prose genres, both epic and romance, not only incorporated crusading motifs but were also applied to describing contemproary crusades, such as the early thirteenth-century French vernacular accounts of the Fourth Crusade by Geoffrey of Villehardouin and Robert of Clari or, later, Jean of Joinville's famous late thirteenth-century life of Louis IX.

Like the Latin authors a century before, Villehardouin and Clari appeared to be deliberately using a form – prose – that was connected with truth, whose content was similarly geared to inspire confidence: the identity of author/narrator with participant/witness; the careful use of the third-person narration. It had been suggested that each were in some ways composing apologia, Villehardouin for the controversial turn the Fourth Crusade took in attacking and conquering Constantinople rather than Egypt; Clari to validate his own and his compatriots' exploits and the looted relics he had brought back to Picardy.[16] Like verse epics and romances, they were highly crafted for effect. Similarly, Joinville's life of Louis IX is part hagiography, part adventure, part mirror of princes, the narrative in this case being, where the author is a witness, carefully in the first person. This bears some similarity to the device of first-person narrative that characterised some of the earliest accounts of the First Crusade, lending the text fabricated authenticity. Joinville was trying to make Louis a saint.[17] Joinville's first person was paralleled by Odo of Deuil, whose story of the Second Crusade, *De Profectione Ludovici VII in Orientem*, also praised the religious example set by his hero, Louis VII.[18] The use of the vernacular by Villehardouin, Clari or Joinville, or in the thirteenth-century translation and continuations of William of Tyre's Jerusalem *Historia* (c. 1170–84), may have been designed to make their texts more widely accessible, but was far from demotic. It enabled authors to borrow motifs and techniques from secular literature appropriate to tales of martial glory, confirming the combination of religious conviction with admiration for martial virtue in order to justify the ways of God to man.

Vernacular histories possessed a long pedigree. The relationship between vernacular poems and songs and the more formal media of prose histories and chronicles is well attested. Behind many passages of the *Chanson d'Antioche* lies Robert of Rheims. The exchange of ideas and images was reciprocal not antithetical.

The mingling of legend and supposed historical fact, a modern not medieval conceptual distinction, could present problems. The great Jerusalem historian William of Tyre (c. 1130–86) rejected the story of Godfrey of Bouillon's descent from a swan knight, the 'cigni fabulam' as he dismissively called it, which was contained in the popular epic cycle of the *Chevalier au Cygne*. A generation earlier, Geoffrey Gaimar, writing in French verse, displayed no such fastidiousness. He suggested that Duke Robert of Normandy had been offered the crown of Jerusalem (which he had not) in 1099 because of his prowess in killing the sultan of Mosul (which he did not), exploits illustrating Robert's performance of 'much good chivalry' (*mainte bele chevalerie*). Yet Gaimar could have derived these fancies from the hugely scholarly historian William of Malmesbury, writing as early as 1125, when Robert was still alive.[19] Throughout the process of retelling the story of the First Crusade, Latin/clerical invention and interpretive tropes readily cross-pollinated with vernacular literature.

Much of this exotically imagined wedding of piety and thrills circulated orally, without finding written permanence. A monk living on the Franco-Flemish border in the 1130s was sufficiently confident of his audience's knowledge of the First Crusade through songs and hymns as well as books that he forbore to provide a detailed account of it in his chronicle.[20] Even if elements in the *Chanson d'Antioche* cannot definitively be traced to a participant in the First Crusade, verse accounts did circulate alongside the Latin prose histories, sharing a common pool of information and imagery. Robert of Rheims and perhaps Raymond of Aguilers seem to have used a Latin poem in their histories of the First Crusade. Another such, by Gilo of Paris, based on the *Gesta*, survives from before 1120. Guibert of Nogent even went so far as to suggest that he would not include 'anything which was not already being sung publicly', whether vernacular or Latin is unclear.[21] The geographic and social spread of the vernacular interpretations was extensive. Besides the northern French epic, an Occitan version on the siege of Antioch, the *Canso d'Antioca*, perhaps by an educated Limousin knight, Gregory Bechada, may well have been commissioned within a decade of the siege itself, 'so that', a local reader noted later in the century, 'the populace might fully comprehend it'. The surviving fragment of the *Canso* is far from artless. It echoes the *Song of Roland* in glorying in the gaudy accoutrements and bloody combat of war. Riches are regarded as the legitimate reward for victory by 'due process of law'. The crusading dead return as a celestial regiment to aid their fellows defeat the Turks.[22] Songs, sometimes scabrous or slanderous, could pack a clear political or historical message and were clearly not without impact. Gerhoh of Reichersberg, in the mid-twelfth century, even claimed songs by and about crusaders had contributed to an improvement in public morals.[23]

The conundrum of Peter the Hermit and William of Tyre

The interplay of clerical exposition and vernacular adventure stories produced one major historiographical peculiarity. The prevalent northern French, Benedictine Latin version of the First Crusade existed in parallel to a very different tradition embodied in the vernacular verse crusade cycles and the history of the Rhinelander Albert of Aachen. One obvious contrast lay in the treatment of Peter the Hermit and Urban II. Robert of Rheims dismissed Peter as a hypocrite, a covert gourmand who projected an image of sobriety and asceticism. By contrast, Albert of Aachen and the tradition that later formed the *Chanson d'Antioche* placed him at the centre of the origins of the crusade, the *primus auctor* in Albert's phrase, whose bad experiences on pilgrimage to the Holy Sepulchre and a vision of Christ inspired him to rouse western Christendom on his return. This was not the only alternative version doing the rounds. At least two more stories, similar to the account of Peter's pilgrimage but with different dramatis personae, circulated in southern France and Italy.[24] Different accounts had different central characters to gain narrative cohesion and local appeal. Godfrey of Bouillon, central to the Lorraine tradition of Albert, provided an especially convincing focus as he became the first Latin ruler of Jerusalem in 1099. Away from the papalist tradition, a different interpretation of the origins and essence of the crusade was possible, less theologically refined but perhaps more vivid, although Robert of Rheims was no slouch in coining a good story. Contemporaries appeared content with a variety of stories, many giving prominence to favoured locals. In this way, by 1140, in the words of the Franco-English Henry of Huntingdon put into the mouth of the bishop of the Orkneys at the battle of the Standard (1138), the First Crusade had became a manifestation of Norman imperialism: after France, England and Apulia, 'Jerusalem the celebrated and famous Antioch both submitted to you.'[25]

More surprising than regional diversity was the way in which Robert's popular version was rapidly superseded after c. 1200 even in academic circles. This was largely due to the French translations of William of Tyre's Jerusalem *Historia* (finished perhaps in 1184). Only nine manuscripts, and a fragment of a tenth of William's original Latin text, survive, confined to France and England, while at least fifty-nine manuscripts of the thirteenth-century French translation, often with continuations, exist.[26] William's *Historia* was the first scholarly crusade history to combine research in earlier chronicles and, from the 1170s, contemporary commentary with a considered academic reflection on both. It is also the most impressive, possibly the brightest jewel of the twelfth-century renaissance of historical writing, William himself a product of the best academic training western Europe could offer.[27] William's approach to the crusade became the one most widely circulated, replacing Robert's almost totally, except perhaps in parts of Germany.

On the seminal First Crusade, unlike the Franco-papal version, William, following an early redaction of Albert of Aachen as his source, afforded Peter the role of chief instigator, with Godfrey of Bouillon and his family presented as a holy line of monarchs, divinely ordained protectors of William's own holy *patria* of Jerusalem. William integrated Urban II as responding to Peter's initiative. The contrast between the morality, discipline and spiritual goodness of the founding crusaders and the travails of their flawed successors established a clear pattern of political development and causation that retained its force both as narrative and as exemplar against which people and events could be judged. Because William provided a history of events in the generations after 1099, for audiences c. 1200 and beyond, his completeness made his history more satisfying than Robert's, and his coherent analysis more powerful in establishing a coherent vision of the whole enterprise. The legendary First Crusade provided the reference point for the failures of the Second Crusade and the Egyptian campaigns of the 1160s or the internal bickering of the kingdom of Jerusalem in the 1170s and 1180s. The tension between the providential and the human was intrinsic to William's portrait of Christian Outremer as a warrior state, a garrison to protect the holiest of Christian relics, under the leadership of a blessed dynasty. Pen portraits of successive kings of Jerusalem in the manner of Suetonius's *Lives of the Caesars* pointed the kingdom's changing fortunes. The grim, disruptive reality of King Baldwin IV's (1174–85) leprosy was rendered heroic. Acutely aware of material causation, William's famous account of the growing Muslim unity, Saladin's power and the encirclement of the Latin kingdom of Jerusalem after 1150 (Book 21; c.7) combined masterly historical analysis with potent commentary on human frailty and the consequence of sin.

Both in Latin and French, William's work lay behind important later histories. The great English chronicler Matthew Paris of St Alban's (d. 1259) used a Latin copy. Even by the time of the Fifth Crusade (1217–21) William's *Historia* was known to Jacques de Vitry and Oliver of Paderborn, the former incorporating large sections of William into his influential *Historia Orientalis* (c. 1220). In his letters from the Fifth Crusade's camp at Damietta, James even used William's phrases for the First Crusade to describe circumstances in the later crusaders' camp.[28] Both James and Oliver were practising crusade preachers as well as historians. William's image of the charismatic Peter the Hermit suited the emphasis on apostolic poverty, evangelism to the laity and moral rearmament characteristic of the polemics of crusading's second century.

William's populist account of the First Crusade not only suited the academic agenda of thirteenth-century crusade promoters. It exerted a profound influence on all subsequent interpretations of crusading until the last 150 years or so. Excerpts from William's history found their way into encyclopaedic compendia, such as Vincent of Beauvais's *Speculum Historiale* (1246–59), another medieval bestseller with 100 surviving manuscripts. By 1300, William's interpretation had become standard, for example in the widely disseminated crusade history of the Venetian Marino Sanudo Torsello (c. 1320), who may have received it via Vincent of Beauvais. The French translation was known by some simply as the *Livre dou conqueste*. It was translated into Spanish in the later thirteenth century and Italian in the fourteenth. William Caxton put extracts into English a century later. William's influence persisted through early printed editions of the Latin text (1549, 1564, 1611).[29] The humanist Benedetto Accolti's history of the First Crusade, *De Bello a Christianis Contra Paganos* (1463/64), made critical use of William (in this case the French translation) regarding him as a reliable if unrefined source. This pre-eminence continued for another four centuries, including the then apparently definitive works of Friedrich Wilken and Joseph-François Michaud in the first third of the nineteenth century.[30]

The creation and testing of a cultural tradition

As he admitted, William of Tyre's history relied on strands of oral and literary traditions.[31] The gap between Latin or vernacular histories, verse, songs, liturgy or sermons was more of form than content. The 'affabulation' or creation of the legend of the crusade perhaps began even before the first contingents of Peter the Hermit's armies left western Europe in 1096. Central and repeated themes unified ecclesiastical and secular observers and, if they are to be believed, responses: revenge for wrongs committed to Christ; obligation to God and honour amongst men; the direct, inescapable yet beneficent immanence of God in worldly affairs; status, both spiritual and secular; reputation and the fear of temporal shame; the destiny of the eternal soul; the desire for physical expression of faith and contact with the divine through the greatest of relics, the land where Christ trod the earth; the greater responsibilities and hierarchical position of the *ordo pugnatorum* in a society whose public values were defined by an increasingly self-conscious coalition of clergy and military aristocracy. In its written record, crusading provided a symbolic and actual moral test and example, interlacing secular and religious preoccupations, the transcendent quality of the activity presented in vignettes of temporal heroism and the assurance of rewards, temporal fame and eternal salvation.

Latin crusade histories appear to fall into two categories: one academic, overtly intellectual, showy and didactic; the other seemingly artless, lacking self-conscious inter-textual references. The subsequent embellishment of the *Gesta Francorum* would appear to demonstrate the point. It is the first of a number of crusade accounts that adopt a linear narrative scheme adorned with only the simplest scriptural lexicon: Odo of Deuil's description of the French crusade in 1147–48; Raoul's portrayal of the siege of Lisbon in 1147; the 'pseudo-Ansbert' chronicle of the German crusade to the east in 1188–90; or Henry of Livonia's memoir of the German conquest and conversion of Livonia from the 1190s to the 1220s.[32] Yet these 'simple' narratives are no such thing. They form as much part of the production of a coherent case for crusading as their more elaborate peers, their very directness a tool of instruction and persuasion. They contain no more and no less 'authenticity' or immediacy of record – of facts or feelings – than more clearly refined texts. Any assessment of impact comes with the obvious caveat of the accident of survival. The fragments still being unearthed in modern libraries and archives indicate how much was written and how much has been lost. The two most detailed accounts of the Second Crusade, Odo of Deuil's *De Profectione Ludovici in Orientem* and Raoul's *De Expugnatione Lyxbonensi*, both, in good classical fashion, composed as if by witnesses to the events they describe, only survive in a single manuscript each. Yet they, in common with the fragmentary chronicles, confirm the coherence of the literary message.

We have seen how writers on the First Crusade cannibalised each other's work. Odo of Deuil admitted to reading an account of the First Crusade in preparation for his own. The sole manuscript of *De Profectione* was at some point in the library of Clairvaux, the abbey run by the major preacher of the Second Crusade, Bernard. The *De Expugnatione* contains formal sermons that echo with some accuracy the theological arguments that Bernard used in his preaching in 1147. Similar literary and theological cohesion has been argued for Baltic crusade texts at the end of the twelfth century.[33] Certain networks of transmission are obvious, such as the northern French Benedictine abbeys that produced the major histories of the First Crusade. The chain of Cistercian houses provided similar likely channels of transmission as members of the order led successive preaching campaigns from the Second to the Fifth Crusade, a role that passed to the friars in the thirteenth century. The Cistercians were also heavily involved in promoting the crusade to the eastern Baltic lands, the context of Henry of Livonia's chronicle.

Some histories, such as Oliver of Paderborn's description of the Fifth Crusade, the *Historia Damiatina*, seemed to have begun life as letters, which again could be circulated though existing channels of communication. Letters of members of the First Crusade, for instance, were published by bishops back in western Europe.[34] The increasing centralisation of crusade organisation under the direction of the papacy provided another focus, as did the increasingly extensive exchange of scholars between universities and cathedral schools, such as the super-educated William of Tyre. One, possibly most, important motor for creating, copying and circulation of crusade histories seems to have been secular patronage: the courts of nobles, princes and kings, crusaders in fact or imagination. The circulation of histories itself formed an active part of crusading, from providing material for sermons to exciting courtly armchair enthusiasm. This almost holistic quality of received memory across many media and social contexts suggests that, although much has been lost, at least the general shape of crusade historiography may be traced with some confidence.

Yet, despite – or perhaps because of – becoming a cultural norm of almost uncontested moral worth, debate over the practice of crusading was rarely stilled. A Wurzburg monk could describe the preachers of the disastrous eastern Mediterranean campaigns of 1147–48 as 'pseudo-prophets, sons of Belial and witnesses of anti-Christ' who managed to recruit tourists, adventurers, mercenaries, debtors, criminals, escaped convicts and defaulters on tenancy obligations.[35] A few, such as Ralph Niger at the time of the Third Crusade, launched more root and branch criticisms, based on a traditional anxiety that spiritual struggles should first be won within individual souls rather than on distant battlefields.[36] The expansion of crusading targets in the thirteenth century witnessed lively if inevitably partisan discussions on the value or legitimacy of the various campaigns and their leaders. Arguments beyond those of the elites, which may have been rather different, fell largely beyond the chronicler's vision or purpose. However, the literary topos of mass enthusiasm and cross-taking consistently concealed an intricate web of prosaic and not always supportive reactions in the context of normal patterns of social control and community. The outbreaks of non-elite crusade enthusiasm, such as the Children's Crusade of 1212 or the Shepherds' Crusades of 1251 and 1320 or the popular crusade of 1309, threw up further evidence of a contested acceptance of official propaganda. While displaying deep-seated acceptance of the crusade myth, they represented a public critique of the crusader credentials of their rulers. In wishing to recreate a heroic, pristine unencumbered form of crusading, they seemed more influenced by the myths of crusade literature and revivalist rhetoric than some of those involved in developing actual crusade strategy.[37]

Complete rejection of crusading, like overt pacifism, was rare. The Cistercians, one of the more austere of the new closed monastic orders, were in the forefront of crusade preaching between the 1140s and 1220s. They were succeeded by the mendicant orders of Friars whose official abandonment of materialism did not extend to the wars of the cross, which they mostly regarded as acceptable adjuncts to their missionary strategies towards non-Christians.[38] Even on the exotic fringes of orthodoxy, the prophetic mystic Joachim of Fiore once regarded the Third Crusade as part of the divine scheme for the end of time, although, after its failure, he and later followers turned decisively against the crusade in their scheme of the predicted Apocalypse. While eschatological imaginings may have helped excite support for the First and even the Second Crusades, here one strand of thirteenth-century apocalyptic prophecy and exegesis turned decisively against crusading.[39] The only consistent anti-crusade pacifists were to be found amongst those decisively outside official Roman Catholic orthodoxy. The Waldensian heretics appear to have maintained an absolute abhorrence and condemnation of homicide. While amongst the Dualist Cathars possibly only the *perfecti* shared this absolutist position, their tradition of anti-materialist thought as much as their experiences at the hands of crusaders in Languedoc (1209–29) encouraged visceral opposition.[40]

Taming the crusade: pilgrimage and law

One of the odder fallacies of later historiography assumed crusading possessed theoretical consistency. While conceived by some as a new phenomenon, the crusade was simultaneously associated with real or imagined precedent. In secular and vernacular literature, heroes remote in time, such as Charlemagne or Arthur, were decked out in unmistakably crusading clothing. Together with the holy warriors of the Old Testament, they created an impression that crusading had always existed. Underpinning crusade language and the popularity of Holy Land expeditions lay a form of collective religio-historical nostalgia that made biblical Palestine as familiar (and malleable) as Arthur's Britain, Charlemagne's Francia or even Frankish Jerusalem. Yet this link with an imagined past failed to conceal what witnesses such as Guibert of Nogent saw as startlingly new.[41] In response to their degree of novelty, Urban II's ideas came in for interpretation and, in a sense, dilution. Within months of the Clermont speech, although Urban continued to emphasise the warlike aspects of the mission, clergy across western Europe began unsystematically to interpret the call as one for an armed pilgrimage. The objective, Jerusalem, and the promise of remission of the penalties of confessed sin made the association straightforward, confining the crusade within a traditional religious exercise, even though Urban had distanced his war from other religious actions by the institution of the new liturgical rite of taking the cross.[42] However closely crusading became related to pilgrimage, the two rites remained free-standing, crusaders (e.g. the French monarchs Louis VII, Philip II and Louis IX) taking the cross and receiving the scrip and staff of pilgrimage separately.

The contrast between pilgrimage and Urban's penitential war was recognised. Robert of Rheims invented an exchange between Egyptian ambassadors and the crusader leaders during the siege of Antioch early in 1098. The Egyptians declared themselves 'amazed' that the Christians 'should seek the Sepulchre of your Lord as armed men, exterminating their people from long-held lands – indeed butchering them at sword point, something pilgrims should not do'. The ambassadors then offered access to Jerusalem provided the Christians advanced as pilgrims only, 'carrying staff and scrip'. This allowed Robert to put into the mouths of the crusade leaders a formal justification for the holy war itself: 'Nobody with any sense should be surprised at us coming to the Sepulchre of Our Lord as armed men.' The justice of their cause is based on the mistreatment of unarmed pilgrims, the prior Christian ownership of Palestine – both traditional Augustinian just war defences – and the direct agency of God: 'Since God has granted us Jerusalem, who can resist?'[43] Such apologia, which became standard fare, indicates that there may have been something that needed justification.

The fusion of crusade and pilgrimage was rapid. Although some monastic communities who accepted property in return for subsidising First Crusaders ignored pilgrimage, stressing the object of the campaign 'to fight and to kill', and the crusaders' own letters of 1096–99 contained very few references to their being pilgrims, impetus came from monks as well as chroniclers such as the author of the *Gesta* or Fulcher of Chartres, trying to make sense of these remarkable events. The extent to which they echoed the immediate opinions of crusaders remains unclear; the crusade leaders' report to Paschal II of the capture of Jerusalem that described the previous two years' campaign made no mention of pilgrimage.[44] Soon, however, holy wars and pilgrimage became almost inseparable, *militia* and *peregrinatio* tightly braided together. The association was confirmed in the preaching of the Second and Third Crusades. By the thirteenth century, crusaders marching to fight Frenchmen in Languedoc or pagans in the Baltic could be described as pilgrims.[45] Rituals of crusaders' departures often revolved around visits to pilgrim shrines.[46] The most sought-after crusade booty was relics. Although the legal distinction remained firm, whatever Urban II's intentions, the analogy of crusade and pilgrimage had proved too tempting and powerful.

The legal status of crusading presented more scope for debate. The First Crusade had been envisaged as unique, a flash of divine intervention reordering the world, operating outside existing and developing theories of legitimate violence, a religious duty not a legal category, demanding possibly unrealistic constancy of spiritual purity and devotion. As this form of war was applied to further campaigns in the east, then to wars in

Iberia and then the Baltic, the awkwardness of having a religious activity that defied definition except as God's will became apparent. Crusading continued to disturb ecclesiastical norms. As interest in just war arguments grew amongst twelfth-century canon lawyers, the crusade needed to be tamed. In the great collection of canon law first compiled at Bologna c. 1139–40 known as Gratian's *Decretum*, a whole section, Causa 23, was devoted to just war waged against heresy. Despite some modern assumptions to the contrary, no mention was made of crusading holy war.[47] Thereafter, lawyers spent some time trying to extrapolate Gratian's just war texts to suit crusading, with only partially convincing results. Gratian's authorities for war against heretics were massaged to validate wars against Muslims even though legal nicety was a possibly inappropriate response to 'God wills it!' Canonists seemed uncomfortable with such a transcendent command as it bore no mechanism for human validation beyond acceptance of, in this case, the interpretive power of the papacy. Given that papal apologists sought to explain papal authority in terms of law, precedent, scriptural authority and reason, the lack of an equivalent objective apparatus for the crusade might have appeared anomalous despite the clear biblical precedents.

Nonetheless, the corralling of the crusade into just war theory was a logical extension of an original polemic that had included right intent, restitution for the Muslims' violent occupation of Christian lands and, almost immediately, revenge for infidel atrocities. In the last quarter of the twelfth century the characterisation of crusading as a just war became more apparent, in the work of the Bologna-educated William of Tyre or the canonist Huguccio of Pisa. A generation later, the exchange between holy and just war was most evident, for example in Henry of Livonia's creation myth for Latin Christian Livonia. By the end of the thirteenth century, crusading was customarily fitted into schemes of canon law, natural justice and the *ius gentium* or the 'law of nature', not just the eleventh-century reliance on the blanket sanction of holiness. Crusade theory began to move towards a rights-based model that later underpinned most European attitudes to warfare in general.[48] At the end of the fourteenth century, Honoré Bouvet's *Tree of Battles* (1387) illustrated how far views on crusading could go yet remain within the generally approved tradition. Bouvet argued that Christians had no automatic right to make war on infidels, unless the pope acted to remedy offences against the law of nature, which included occupation of Christian lands but also seemed to include persecution of Christian residents in lands that had never been ruled by believers. It was accepted that Muslims possessed rights and that their expulsion from the Holy Land was based on law as much as faith.[49] Whatever he said at Clermont, this was not exactly the message of Urban II.

Fitting crusading into a rational frame invited criticism of a kind not possible if all was simply put down to God's wishes. Repeated failures, culminating in the loss of the Holy Land in 1291, made questioning the crusade, genuine debate, inevitable. Every major crusade after 1099 had attracted some hostile comment. Medieval society was far less deferential than many – then and now – liked to believe. In the later thirteenth century, when Christian holdings in the Holy Land were crumbling, preachers of crusades against Christians, for example, encountered sharp criticism certainly in some hostile literary witnesses, probably on the ground as well. Repeated failure to secure the Holy Land raised doubts about God's intent and provoked concern at papal efforts being diverted to other theatres of holy war. Crusades to the Holy Land tended to be controversial because of their inadequacies. Crusades elsewhere were more domestically politically partisan, eliciting responses to match. On top of doubts over leadership and strategy, issues surrounding crusade finance – taxation, proceeds from redemptions and, later, indulgence sales – matched the niceties of natural law in provoking scrutiny, qualification, questioning, debate and criticism.[50]

Some later medieval perspectives

The greatest incentive to doubt and criticism was failure. Attitudes followed events. The inability to recapture any part of the Holy Land after 1291, the effective abandonment of the Jerusalem crusade after the Cypriot–Egyptian treaty of 1370, the rise of the Ottoman Turks in the Balkans from the 1350s and the simultaneous distraction of ceaseless warfare in Italy and between France and England, forced a reassessment of crusading, not in theory so much as in practice. In all sorts of ways, crusading became more peripheral, its moral image replacing personal experience. To emphasise the slightly other-worldly virtue of his Knight in the *Canterbury Tales*, Chaucer depicted him as having fought in wars for Christendom, not the more immediate, preoccupying Hundred Years' War.[51] Increasingly, crusade imagery, ideology, scriptural precedents and rhetoric were appropriated by secular national rulers, notably in fourteenth-century France and England, and late fifteenth-century Spain, each intent on casting themselves as monarchs of holy lands, new Israels worthy of protection by God and their subjects. Even in his poem praising the crusader attack on Alexandria in 1365, Guillaume de Machaut, possibly to save Charles V of France's blushes, pointedly argued for the moral primacy of defending the *patria*: 'a man's truly valiant who defends his own inheritance; no castle stormed, no battle in the field can equal this'.[52] Soon, national holy war competed with crusading for more than men or money; it secured the enthusiasm of national churches and provided a new source of glorious chivalric anecdotes. The Arthur of Geoffrey of Monmouth in the 1130s was a sort of crusader against pagan Saxons; the Arthur of the fourteenth-century Middle English poem *Morte d'Arthur* was a sort of an Edward III, hammer of the French.[53]

The emotions of holy war were divorced from the monogamy of crusading. Although continuing to flourish as a social ideal, religious duty and formal political ambition, in the fourteenth century mass involvement in the crusade was restricted to paying money, chiefly through taxes from church property, and buying indulgences. Crusading troops tended to be professional, some *soi-disant* experts explicitly arguing against volunteers who had taken the cross being involved in the early stages of any crusade.[54] The numerous small campaigns against Mamluks and Turks in the fourteenth and fifteenth centuries, with a very few exceptions such as the defence of Belgrade (1456), attracted very little cross-taking or mass recruitment. Crusading ceased to be something the faithful did, merely something they supported, like modern charity donations. Wars of the cross were tailored to confused frontlines, such as the competition for political space between Greeks, Latins, Slavs, Hungarians and Ottomans in the Balkans.

The clear imperatives of twelfth – or thirteenth-century Palestine or Egypt were hard to recreate. In any case, while the crusade remained a source of good stories and a moral yardstick, Christendom lacked sufficient cohesion to use it as a weapon. By 1452, Jean Germain, bishop of Chalons, could refer nostalgically to: 'the old *voyages* and *passages* of Outremer which are called *croisiez*'.[55] The later middle ages offered different historical perspectives. The unredeemed failure of 1291 encouraged acute soul-searching and reassessment of objectives and methods. Although there is little sign of a complete rejection of holy war, at least when aimed at securing the Holy Land, some doubts were expressed at its current efficacy. Those interested in converting Muslims, such as the Franciscan polymath Roger Bacon (*Opus Majus*, 1266–68) or the Dominican preacher William of Tripoli (*De Statu Saracenorum*, 1273), claimed that crusading would not, as Innocent IV had argued, assist evangelism and, in an argument reminiscent of the Joachites, suggested that Islam was on the verge of internal collapse.[56] Such an approach was not widespread. Most commentators were more pragmatic; that crusades had failed because of sin, inadequate resources and incompetence.

Between the Second Council of Lyons in 1274 and the outbreak of the Hundred Years' War in the late 1330s, a welter of advice and comment flowed to and from the courts of church and state in western Europe. Some works provided information about the east from travellers, merchants, members of military orders or pilgrims. Others were more closely allied to specific projects or plans. Governments sought information and advice from potential carriers of troops such as Venice or Marseilles. There were detailed schemes to repopulate the Near East with Christians (from the French provincial lawyer Pierre Dubois) or to conquer North Africa en route to the Holy Land (from the Catalan mystic and missionary Ramon Lull). Many adopted a possibly spurious air of expertise, such as the Venetian Marino Sanudo Torsello whose substantial and widely circulated *Secreta Fidelium Crucis* (1306–21) gave precise details of shipping, recruitment, strategy, tactics and finance.[57]

Three elements stood out from this 'recovery literature': the assumption that crusading was a redemptive act; a concentration on the mechanics of war and conquest; and a keen sense of the lessons to be drawn from the past. Both the Armenian Hayton of Gorgios's advice to the pope in 1307 and Sanudo's proposals came with extensive histories attached.[58] All writers sought to explain how old mistakes could be rectified. Many extended the intellectual and conceptual reach of crusade planning. Dubois considered matters of western and eastern demography. Hayton's historical sections covered geography and ethnography. Sanudo's plan, that included an initial commercial blockade of Egypt, rested on an appreciation of Mediterranean economics as well as attempting to calculate the financial implications of any campaign. These writers were placing the crusade in a much wider context beyond the religious imperatives of thirteenth-century promoters such as James of Vitry or Humbert of Romans, who had been hidebound by western academic preoccupations and operated within the conventions of crusade preaching. It is notable that, in contrast to most previous crusade analysis, few pieces of 'recovery' literature came from preachers or academics, and many from laymen.

However, 'recovery' literature proved abortive in the face of European politics, notably the Hundred Years' War (1337–1453) and the papal schism (1378–1417). Prospects for a mass crusade – in the 1360s, 1390s, 1450s and 1460s – were hopelessly compromised by divisions, rivalries, self-interest and inadequate finance. The difficulties of planning any such major campaign were now well understood. Within the traditional genre of crusade writing, the theoretical treatises of the early fourteenth century gave way to two contrasting types. On the one hand, in visionary tracts from the eastern Mediterranean veteran utopian Philippe de Mézières (1327–1405) or the poet and courtier Eustace Deschamps (c. 1346–1406), the crusade provided a moral context within which to address domestic issues. For all his apparent awareness of political reality, the prolific Mézières, for instance, was much more interested, especially as he got older, with spiritual redemption and regeneration than with fighting Muslims. Support for the ideals of crusading would produce peace and reform within Christendom. In works such as *Le songe du vieil pèlerin* (1386) or the *Epistre lamentable* (1397), Mézières pedalled not crusade advice but a prose form of 'devotional romance', full of allegory and personified Virtues and Evils, distanced by form and content from actual crusade planning. Even his scheme for a new military order that would conduct any putative crusade had no very serious substance, its final regulations (1395) even forbidding fighting anywhere except the Holy Land despite the advancing Ottomans on the Danube and before the walls of Constantinople. For Mézières and many other crusade-infected writers of the later middle ages, crusading was essentially a utopian metaphor, at times a fairly whimsical one at that.[59]

In apparent contrast, a number of factual descriptions of the Levant were produced in the second quarter of the fifteenth century that at first sight seem to point to a more practical approach, notably Emanuele Piloti's description of Egypt (c. 1439) and the accounts of their Levantine travels by the Burgundian agents Ghillbert de Lannoy (1420) and Bertrandon de la Broquière (c. 1455). Even Jean Germain's heatedly imaginative *Discours du voyage d'Oultremer* (1452), addressed to Charles VII of France, purported to be a blueprint for a Christian counter-attack in the eastern Mediterranean.[60] In fact none of these presented any serious crusade plans. All were spiced with wishful thinking. The concentration on Egypt was hardly relevant; their use of crusade history as romantic as any versifier's. The works of Lannoy and Broquière fitted the fashion for travel literature realised in the extraordinary popularity of the fictitious *Travels* of John Mandeville, one of the most copied and circulated works of the later middle ages which began with a ringing if wholly traditional endorsement of the Holy Land crusade. The stereotype of the exotic and corrupt east is already apparent in Broquière's description of portly Sultan Murad II.[61] However, there was little of practical use. Even one of the most vociferous self-proclaimed crusade enthusiasts, Duke Philip the Good of Burgundy (1419–67), despite repeatedly protesting his eagerness to combat the Ottomans, possessed a library full of books concerning the Holy Land but bereft of volumes about the Turks.[62]

Only where active crusading persisted, at least in name and legal theory, was the crusade actually debated as a material weapon of policy. At the Council of Constance (1414–18), the legitimacy of the Teutonic Knights' hold on Prussia and their war against the now Christian Lithuanians were challenged and defended on grounds of principle. The Polish advocate Paul Vladimiri argued that only in the Holy Land did Christians have the right to contest the right of non-Christians to rule, thereby undermining the original *raison d'être* of the Teutonic Knights' rule in Prussia and Livonia. He quoted Thomas Aquinas in support of the idea that infidels had natural rights to possession just as strong as Christians, the Holy Land excepted, and that forceful conversion was unlawful. He noted that the conversion of the Lithuanians had been achieved (in 1386) peacefully by the Poles not through the violence of the Teutonic Knights. Vladimiri based his case on theories of just war and natural rights. By contrast, the Knights' case rested on papal plenitude of power, even over infidel lands, and a characteristically sentimental self-seeking version of history in which the blood of Christian warriors had sanctified the holy land of Prussia. The Knights were new Maccabees who had defended Christendom (including Poland) from pagans and against whom the Poles had allied with the infidel Lithuanians. Although Vladimiri was grandstanding, his arguments showed how crusading could be regarded, as Bouvet had a generation earlier, as just one category of war, legal or not, rather than as a unique, transcendent and universal obligation.[63]

This did not mean that crusading had ceased to find cultural traction or political appeal. Popes went on granting crusading status to wars against the Ottomans, not just in the fifteenth century but far beyond, at least until 1689. Spanish monarchs in the century after Ferdinand (1479–1516) and Isabella (1474–1504) placed the crusade near the rhetorical centre of their expansionist national monarchic messianism. In response to the Ottoman threat, a whole new genre of crusade historiography emerged that, in volume, possibly surpassed what had gone before. From Petrarch in the 1330s, self-consciously classicising humanist commentators concerned themselves with the crusade for two related reasons. They faced the obvious threat posed by the Turks to what they regarded as the civilised – that is, their own – world. Fifteenth-century Italy stood at the centre of Christendom, the focus of humanist interest but also on the frontline against the Turks across the Adriatic. Alone of the countries of western Europe, mainland Italy suffered Ottoman occupation – of Otranto, briefly in 1480–81. Episodes from the crusading past could also be held up as moral exemplars of the classical virtues of selflessness, cooperation, civic responsibility and Christian patriotism, crusaders, as it were, standing in for classical heroes of the Roman Republic. It is sobering to realise that more crusade writing survives from the period 1451–81 than for the whole of the preceding centuries. However, although linked to the anti-Ottoman agenda of Renaissance popes such as Calixtus III (1455–58) and Pius II (1458–64) in the reaction to the fall of Constantinople, it must be wondered whether the works of the likes of Francesco Filelfo, Flavio Biondi, Cardinal Bessarion, Pius II himself, the millenarian George of Trebizond or Benedetto Accolti went very far beyond rhetorical exercises. Humanist rhetoric may have defined both man and his message; however, Filelfo, for example, switched his position from calling for an anti-Turkish crusade to a distinctly philo-Turkish stance, as his Florentine patrons swung against plans for a crusade led by Venice. Even Accolti's great work on the First Crusade, *De Bello a Christianis Contra Paganos* (1463/64) may have been composed as much with an eye to establishing his intellectual credentials as chancellor of Florence as in aiding Pius II's crusade plans. It was hardly pragmatic and an odd descent into unreason for Pius II himself to brand the Ottomans as barbarians and inhuman (*immanis*); he knew better.[64]

The trajectory of Pius II's views on the crusade reveals how far it had became diffused within a whole range of other interests and attitudes. From being an acute and rational observer of the Turkish threat, after his election as pope Pius degenerated into symbolism and polemic. His motives for supporting crusading had always been bound up with asserting humanist principles of civilisation as much as the Turkish threat *per se*, yet after 1453 he resorted to the old mirage of Jerusalem and the language of demonisation. His crusade scheme of 1463–64, the propaganda for which far exceeded its modest dimensions, was as an assertion of papal authority, a gesture to restore its reputation which, Pius observed, had been damaged by, among other things, its failed crusade policies: 'we are in a position of insolvent bankers ... we have no credit'. However realistic as to the selfish motives of would-be allies, Pius's view of the crusade and its ideology was solipsistically western, tapping into ubiquitous communal imprints of shared historical myths and legends, sustained by a vigorous liturgical tradition that maintained Jerusalem, the Holy Land and even a demonised Turk in an extended metaphor for godliness and the Christian life.[65]

The use of the crusade and its history, by humanists and other contemporary writers, occupied a world of polemic, serving parochial religious, cultural and political functions. By affecting to address actual immediate temporal issues, the logistical work of Sanudo, the topographical researches of Lannoy, Piloti or Broquière, the cosmic fantasies of Mézières or Germain, the rhetoric of the humanists, projected an idealised vision of human affairs, comfortingly familiar rather than challengingly fresh. They signally failed to address the politics of the Balkans and the Mediterranean or any other theatre of religious holy war. Of course, that in itself was one of the oldest traditions of crusade histories. Ever since the *Gesta Francorum*, most crusade commentators, even, it could be argued, William of Tyre, had the obsessions and expectations of a western European audience firmly in mind. Conceptually, the crusade was a creation of western European religious culture not of the frontiers with Islam or paganism. Its histories both reflected and reinforced this. Medieval crusade historiography, like other historical writing of the period, was less concerned to recite information than in illustrating didactic lessons conjured from an invented universe of optimism, virtue, evil, punishment for sin, reward for goodness; a world defined by memories of past glory. For many generations, these images bore simultaneous witness to the crusade as cultural habit and moral exemplar. Its histories created an accessible past while addressing the concerns of the present, a theme at the heart of this book.

Notes

1 H. Hagenmeyer, *Die Kreuzzugsbriefe aus de Jahren 1088–1100* (Innsbrück, 1901); for the Sept. 1099 letter, Letter XVIII, pp. 102–14, 167–74; trans. E. Peters, ed., *The First Crusade* (2nd edn Philadelphia PA, 1998), pp. 292–6 (and pp. 283–97 for others); it survives in at least ten twelfth-century manuscripts alone.

2 Trans. C. Sweetenham, *Robert the Monk's History of the First Crusade*

(Aldershot, 2005), p. 77. In general, J. Riley-Smith, *The First Crusade and the Idea of Crusading* (London, 1986), esp. chaps 4 and 6.

3 *Gesta Francorum et Aliorum Hierosolymitanorum*, ed. R. Hill (London, 1962), quotation at p. 53; J. Rubinstein, 'What is the *Gesta Francorum* and Who was Peter Tudebode?', *Revue Mabillon*, n.s. 16 (2005), 179–204. The literature on the *Gesta* is considerable, reflecting its apparent chronological immediacy and subsequent influence; for a recent summary, with references to the central articles by C. Morris, J. France and J. B. Wolf, see Y. N. Harari, 'Eyewitnessing in Accounts of the First Crusade: The *Gesta Francorum* and Other Contemporary Narratives', *Crusades*, 3 (2004), 77–99, esp. notes 43, 47 and 63.

4 Raymond of Aguilers, *Historia Francorum qui ceperunt Jerusalem*, trans. J. H. and L. L. Hill (Philadelphia PA, 1968); Fulcher of Chartres, *A History of the Expedition to Jerusalem*, trans. H. S. Fink and F. R. Ryan (Knoxville TN, 1969); Peter Tudebode, *Historia de Hierosolymitano Itinere*, trans. J. H. and L. L. Hill (Philadelphia PA, 1974).

5 R. Hiestand, 'Il cronista medieval e il suo pubblico', *Annali della facolta di lettere e filosofia dell'università di Napoli*, 27 (n.s. 15), (1984–85), 207–27; J. France, 'An Unknown Account of the Capture of Jerusalem', *English Historical Review*, 87 (1972), 771–83; the versions by Baldric and Guibert are, among other places, in *Recueil des historiens des croisades* (hereafter *RHC*): *Historiens occidentaux* (Paris, 1844–1905), iv, 1–111; 115–263; Albert of Aachen, *Historia Ierosolimitana*, ed. and trans. S. Edgington (Oxford, 2007); intro. pp. xxi–xxxvii for rel. with William of Tyre.

6 Sweetenham, *Robert, passim*; intro. esp. p. 9; Fulcher, p. 105.

7 Raymond of Aguilers, p. 15.

8 William of Malmesbury, *De Gestis Regum Anglorum*, ed. W. Stubbs, Rolls Series (London, 1887–89), ii, 390; cf. R. Thomson, 'William of Malmesbury, Historian of Crusade', *Reading Medieval Studies*, 23 (1997), 121–34.

9 Sweetenham, *Robert*, pp. 80–1.

10 Raymond of Aguilers, p. 15.

11 *RHC Occ.*, iv, 14.

12 Raymond of Aguilers, pp. 32–5, 45–6, 60–4 etc.; *Gesta Francorum*, pp. 45–7; Albert of Aachen, pp. 142–5, 222–5; Peters, *First Crusade*, pp. 44–5, 284–91; Ralph of Caen, *Gesta Tancredi*, trans. B. S. and D. S. Bachrach (Aldershot, 2005), p. 22.

13 *In Praise of the New Knighthood*, trans. M. Barber and K. Bate, *The Templars* (Manchester, 2002), pp. 215–27.

14 D. H. Green, *The Millstätter Exodus: A Crusading Epic* (Cambridge, 1966).

15 S. Duparc-Quioc, *Le cycle de la croisade* (Paris, 1955); eadem, *La chanson d'Antioche* (Paris, 1977); but see R. Cook, '*Chanson d'Antioche, chanson de geste: Le cycle de la croisade est-il épique?* (Amsterdam, 1980); cf. Sweetenham, *Robert*, pp. 35–42 and Albert of Aachen, esp. p. xxvii; Ambroise, *The Crusade of Richard the Lion-Heart*, trans. M. J. Hubert and J. L. La Monte (New York NY, 1976).

16 Geoffrey of Villehardouin, *The Conquest of Constantinople*, trans. M. R. B. Shaw, *Chronicles of the Crusades* (London, 1963), pp. 29–160; Robert of Clari, *The Conquest of Constantinople*, trans. E. H. McNeal (New York NY, 1966).

17 John of Joinville, *Life of St Louis*, trans. M. R. B. Shaw, *Chronicles of the Crusades* (London, 1963), pp. 163–353.

18 Odo of Deuil, *De Profectione Ludovici VII in Orientem*, ed. and trans. V. G. Berry (New York NY, 1948).

19 William of Tyre, *Historia*, ed. R. B. C. Huygens as *Chronicon* (Turnhout, 1986), i, p. 427; Geoffrey Gaimar, *Lestoire des Engleis*, ed. T. Duffus Hardy and C. T. Martin, Rolls Series (London, 1888–89), i, pp. 244–5, l. 5750 for quotation; William of Malmesbury, *Gesta Regum*, ii, pp. 460–1.

20 C. Tyerman, *God's War: A New History of the Crusades* (London, 2006), p. 244 and note 4 and, generally, pp. 244–7.

21 Gilo of Paris, *Historia Vie Hierosolimitane*, ed. and trans C. W. Grocock and J. E. Siberry (Oxford, 1997); *RHC Occ.*, iv, 121.

22 *The Canso d'Antiocha*, ed. and trans. L. M. Paterson and C. Sweetenham (Aldershot, 2003), pp. 5–6, 201, 217, 229.

23 C. Morris, 'Propaganda for War', *Studies in Church History*, xx, ed. W. J. Shields (Woodbridge, 1983), 93.

24 Sweetenham, *Robert*, p. 83; Albert of Aachen, pp. 2–9 (p. 4 for *primus auctor*), 13–45; the thirteenth-century Spanish *Gran Conquesta de Ultramar* may preserve one early version; the Genoese Caffaro another, *Canso d'Antiocha*, p. 41; *Annali Genovesi di Caffaro*, ed. L. T. Belgrano (Genoa, 1890), i, 99–101.

25 Henry of Huntingdon, *Historia Anglorum*, ed. D. Greenway (Oxford, 1996), pp. 714–15. For one local hero, Raimbold Croton, C. Tyerman, *The Invention of the Crusades* (London, 1998), p. 11 and note 16, p. 129.

26 P. W. Edbury and J. G. Rowe, *William of Tyre: Historian of the Latin East* (Cambridge, 1988), pp. 3–5; P. Edbury, 'The French Translation of William of Tyre's *Historia*', *Crusades*, 6 (2007), 69–105.

27 *Chronicon*, ed. Huygens; *A History of Deeds Done Beyond the Sea*, trans. E. A. Babcock and A. C. Krey (New York NY, 1941); for William's own account of his education, R. B. C. Huygens, 'Guillaume de Tyr étudiant', *Latomus*, 21 (1962), 811–29.

28 Tyerman, *God's War*, p. 641 and refs note 82.

29 For the transmission of William's text, *Chronicon*, ed. Huygens, pp. 3–34, 76–91; Edbury and Rowe, *William of Tyre*, pp. 3–5; Marino Sanudo Torsello, *Secreta Fidelium Crucis*, ed. J. Bongars, *Gesta Dei Per Francos* (Hanau, 1611), ii, 98.

30 R. Black, *Benedetto Accolti and the Florentine Renaissance* (Cambridge, 1985), pp. 299–315; below, Chapter 4.

31 Babcock and Krey, *Deeds*, i, p. 56.

32 Odo of Deuil, as in note 18 above; *De Expugnatione Lyxbonensi*, ed. and trans. C. W. David (New York NY, 1976); *Historia de Expeditione Friderici Imperatoris*, ed. A Chroust (Berlin, 1928); Henry of Livonia, *Chronicon Livoniae*, ed. L. Arbusow and A. Bauer (Hanover, 1955); trans J. A. Brundage, *The Chronicle of Henry of Livonia* (New York NY, 2003).

33 K. V. Jensen, 'Introduction', in *Crusade and Conversion on the Baltic Frontier 1150–1500*, ed. A. V. Murray (Aldershot, 2001), p. xxi.

34 Oliver of Paderborn, *The Capture of Damietta*, trans. J. J. Gavigan, in *Christian Society and the Crusades 1198–1229*, ed. E. Peters (Philadelphia

PA, 1971), pp. 48–139; for evidence of compilation, see chap. 34 p. 89; Tyerman, *God's War*, p. 172 and note 9 p. 933.

35 *Annales Herbipolensis, Monumenta Germaniae Historica, Scriptores*, ed. G. H. Pertz *et al.* (Hanover, 1826–1934), xvi, 5.

36 Ralph Niger, *De Re Militari et Triplici Via Peregrinationis Ierosolimitano*, ed. L. Schmugge (Berlin, 1977).

37 G. Dickson, *The Children's Crusade* (London, 2008); *idem, Religious Enthusiasm in the Medieval West: Revivals, Crusades, Saints* (Abingdon, 2000); Tyerman, *God's War*, pp. 607–11, 802–4, 880–1.

38 On this see B. Z. Kedar, *Crusade and Mission* (Princeton NJ, 1984).

39 E. R. David, 'Apocalyptic Conversion: The Joachite Alternative to the Crusades', *Traditio*, 125 (1969), 127–54; Kedar, *Crusade and Mission*, pp. 112–16, 219–23.

40 M. Barber, *The Cathars* (Harlow, 2000); M. Lambert, *Medieval Heresy* (Oxford, 2002).

41 *RHC Occ.*, iv, 124.

42 J. M. Jensen, 'War, Penance and the First Crusade', in *Medieval History Writing and Crusading Ideology*, ed. T. M. S. Lehtonen and K. V. Jensen (Helsinki, 2005), pp. 51–63; J. Flori, *La guerre sainte* (Paris, 2001), pp. 316–20; Tyerman, *God's War*, pp. 64–74; Urban's letters, Peters, *First Crusade*, pp. 42, 44–6.

43 Sweetenham, *Robert*, pp. 136–8.

44 Tyerman, *God's War*, pp. 72–3 and refs.

45 Tyerman, *Invention*, p. 52; Henry of Livonia, *Chronicle, passim*.

46 E.g. John of Joinville, *Life of St Louis*, p. 195.

47 Gratian, *Decretum*, ed. A. Frieberg, *Corpus Iuris Canonici*, i (Leipzig, 1879), Causa XXIII; cf. E.-D. Hehl, *Kirche und Krieg im 12 Jahrhundert* (Stuttgart, 1980); J. Riley-Smith review, *Journal of Ecclesiastical History*, 33 (1982), 290–1; J. A. Brundage, *Medieval Canon Law and the Crusader* (Madison WI, 1969), esp. p. 190; in general, F. H. Russell, *The Just War in the Middle Ages* (Cambridge, 1975).

48 H. E. J. Cowdrey, 'Christianity and the Morality of Warfare during the First Century of Crusading', in *The Experience of Crusading*, ed. N. Housley and M. Bull, i (Cambridge, 2003), 175–92; J. Muldoon, *Popes, Lawyers and Infidels* (Liverpool, 1979); Kedar, *Crusade and Mission*.

49 Honoré Bonet (*recte* Bouvet), *Tree of Battles*, ed. G. W. Coopland (Liverpool, 1949), esp. pp. 126–8.

50 P. Throop, *Criticism of the Crusades* (Amsterdam, 1940); E. Siberry, *Criticism of Crusading* (Oxford, 1985); Tyerman, *Invention*, pp. 3–4, 88–98; H. E. Mayer, *The Crusades* (Eng. trans. 2nd edn Oxford, 1988), pp. 312–13, 320–1.

51 G. Chaucer, *Canterbury Tales*, ed. W. Skeat (Oxford, 1894–97), General Prologue ll. 43–78; M. H. Keen, 'Chaucer's Knight, the English Aristocracy and the Crusade', in *English Court Culture in the Later Middle Ages*, ed. V. J. Scattergood and J. W. Sherbourne (London, 1983), pp. 45–63; in general N. Housley, *The Later Crusades* (Oxford, 1992).

52 Tyerman, *God's War*, pp. 906–12; Guillaume de Machaut, *The Capture of Alexandria*, trans. J. Shirley and P. Edbury (Aldershot, 2001), p. 35.

53 Geoffrey of Monmouth, *Historia Regum Britanniae*, ed. A. Griscom and R. Ellis Jones (London, 1929), esp. pp. 437–8; *Alliterative Morte Arthure*, ed. E. Brock, Early English Text Society, o.s. 8 (London, 1871).

54 Sanudo, *Secreta*, Book II; in general Tyerman, *God's War*, pp. 826–915.

55 Jean Germain, *Discours du voyage d'oultremer*, ed. C. Schefer, *Revue de l'Orient Latin*, 3 (1895), 339.

56 Kedar, *Crusade and Mission*, pp. 177–83.

57 In general, A. Leopold, *How to Recover the Holy Land* (Aldershot, 2000).

58 *RHC Documents arméniens* (Paris, 1869–1906), ii, 113–363; Sanudo, *Secreta*, Book III, *Gesta Dei Per Francos*, ii.

59 N. Iorga, *Philippe de Mézières (1327–1405) et la croisade au xive siècle* (Paris, 1896); Philippe de Mézières, *Songe du vieil pèlerin*, ed. G. Coopland (Cambridge, 1969); C. Tyerman, 'New Wine in Old Skins: The Crusade and the Eastern Mediterranean in the Later Middle Ages', in *The Eastern Mediterranean in the Later Middle Ages*, ed. C. Holmes and J. Harris (Oxford, forthcoming); Housley, *Later Crusades*, pp. 377–93.

60 Notes 55 and 59 above.

61 Bertrandon de la Broquière, *Le voyage d'outremer*, ed. C. Schefer, *Recueils des voyages* (Paris, 1896), pp. 176–7, 181–6.

62 J. Paviot, *Les ducs de Bourgogne, la croisade et l'Orient* (Paris, 2003), p. 238.

63 For a summary, E. Christiansen, *The Northern Crusades* (2nd edn London, 1997), pp. 231–41.

64 Housley, *Later Crusades*, pp. 99–100, 384–9; N. Bisaha, *Creating East and West* (Philadelphia PA, 2004); M. Meserve, 'Italian Humanists and the Problem of the Crusade', in *Crusading in the Fifteenth Century*, ed. N. Housley (Basingstoke, 2004), pp. 13–38; J. Hankins, 'Renaissance Crusaders', *Dumbarton Oaks Papers*, 49 (1995), 111–207, esp. 121–2; Tyerman, 'New Wine'; Black, *Benedetto Accolti*.

65 Note 64 above; A. Linder, *Raising Arms: Liturgy in the Struggle to Liberate Jerusalem in the Late Middle Ages* (Turnhout, 2003); N. Bisaha, 'Pope Pius II and the Crusade', in *Crusading in the Fifteenth Century*, pp. 39–52; *Memoirs of a Renaissance Pope*, trans. F. A. Gragg, ed. L. C. Gabel (London, 1960), pp. 237, 239, 241–59, 327–8, 340–3, 347, 351–2, 354, 357, 358, 369; Pius II, *Commentaria*, i, ed. M. Meserve and M. Simonetta (Cambridge MA, 2003), 99, 132–5, 160, 210–11, 266–7; Housley, *Later Crusades*, pp. 105–9; Tyerman, *God's War*, pp. 870–1.

2

'The *rendez vous* of cracked brains'?[1]
Reformation, revision,
texts and nations 1500–1700

Two of the mainstays of fifteenth-century writing on the crusades were challenged and recast in the century that followed. Responses to holy war, past and present, to regain Jerusalem or repulse the Ottoman, were compromised by new religious divisions that reconfigured much of the intellectual as well as political and confessional map of Christendom, leading, in Fernand Braudel's terms, to a transition from a period of 'external' wars of faith, such as the crusades, to one of 'internal' wars of faith, such as the wars of religion and, later, the Thirty Years' War. Braudel placed the key period of transformation as the 1570s, but the process was gradual and uneven.[2] These developments were paralleled by and contributed to an undermining of the humanist approach to the study of history in general and of crusading in particular. The emphasis on classical style, rhetoric, the morality of individual actions and the great deeds of warriors and courtiers was increasingly complemented by a fragmentation of literary genres and a novel attempt to collect, collate and study the primary sources. Humanists had little time for textual, as opposed to philological, scholarship: Accolti's history of the First Crusade, for all its learned classical elegance, had relied on a poor French translation of William of Tyre. A century and a half later, the often frustrating attempts by the great Huguenot editor, Jacques Bongars, to seek out manuscripts of William of Tyre's Latin speak of a different world.[3]

Printing and new generations of antiquarian scholars revolutionised the availability of crusade texts and hence the range and depth of historical understanding. Attitudes to the continuing warfare against the Turks and interpretations of past conflicts fought under the Cross became adjuncts to antagonistic religious polemic. For the first time, a genuinely distinct social model of crusading was presented in which the motives of leaders and led were squeezed into fresh deterministic typologies. New romantic visions of the past, pre-eminently those of Torquato Tasso, while leading crusade fiction even further from historical let alone contemporary experience, established such a firm hold on the imaginative tradition as to provide almost a counter-history to the dry debates of the *savants*. Chivalry was not dead, but traditional knightly values stood increasingly as signifiers of cultural status and self-image rather than as drivers of public policy. Castiglione's *Il Cortegiano* (1528) might have seen the crusade still as the duty of princes, but by 1550 the very basis of crusading in papal authority and the Roman Catholic penitential system had been contested (and not just by evangelicals or Protestants) and widely rejected. By the early seventeenth century the whole idea of justifying war on religious grounds found powerful and increasingly influential critics. While wars for defence and recovery of lost territory never lost general approbation, the realpolitik of Catholic France, for many the cradle of crusading, and Protestant England forming alliances with the Turks stretched ideas of a specifically holy war beyond even sophistical resuscitation. And looming above and, literally, beyond debates on the merits of crusading, in unnerving commentary, part extension, part confutation of past crusading certainties, stood the European experience in confronting the pagan natives of the New World, the greatest conceptual as well as material revolution of the age.

Texts and religion

Scholars from the early nineteenth century to the early twenty-first have noticed that at no time was crusade historiography free from confessional debate, sentimental approval or rational and ideological disdain. Most of these competing elements can be located in the period of the Reformation, driven not only by the radical and permanent fragmenting of religious orthodoxies but also by the need to cope with the actual and perceived threat of the Ottomans and the expansion of scholarly exchange and literary market consequent on the increasing use of the printing press. The continued context of a political conflict with the Turks cast an unavoidable shadow across all attitudes to the crusades, whether French and German Catholic apologists calling for a new holy war to resist the Ottomans, the English Protestant martyrologist John Foxe including a *History of the Turks* in his great catalogue of persecution, or Francis Bacon casting his dialogue on holy war in the double mould of wars against infidels in the Mediterranean and against pagans in America. The sixteenth century, although not the last to see papally authorised crusades, was probably the last to witness popular – if local – enthusiasm for taking the cross and unforced familiarity with crusade institutions, language and physical trappings. From the defence of Hungary and Austria in the 1520s, the Pilgrimage of Grace in England in 1536, to the battle of Lepanto in 1571, the Spanish Armada in 1588 or the Toulousain Roman Catholic *crucesignati* receiving papal indulgences to kill Huguenots in 1568, the crusade was more than an engrossing image from the past or academic by-road, although it had become those as well.[4]

The umbilical link between current events and crusade history was amply demonstrated by the *De Bello Sacro* (1549) of Johannes Herold (1514–67), a continuation of William of Tyre that took the story of the crusades from the Third and Fourth Crusades, through the fall of Acre to events in the Mediterranean and Near East in the later middle ages, including the invasions of Tamburlaine (d. 1405), ending with the Ottoman Sultan Selim the Grim's conquest of Syria and Egypt (1516–17) and the accession of Suleiman the Magnificent in 1520. The narrative has random appendages of a Florentine account of the fall of Acre, two letters regarding the Albigensian Crusade and one concerning the Spanish reconquista. The nod to the past was underscored by Herold's history being bound and distributed together with an edition of William of Tyre's original *Historia* (in the 1560 Basel edition). The awareness of the present was paraded in Herold's preface (of 1549) which repeatedly alludes to contemporary circumstances, as well as drawing attention to the good humanist notion of history as a reservoir of edifying examples.

Herold lamented current religious divisions, 'dissensione animorum'.[5] Soon the crusades were being examined through that filter of religious controversy. However, the historiographical battle-lines were neither clear nor impermeable. In certain pre-Reformation reformist Catholic circles, the idea that wars could be lawful if possessed of religious motives such as conversion was challenged; only secular motives, such as defence of rightfully held lands, could justify fighting Muslims, an attitude that became standard among Lutherans and later Protestant intellectuals.[6] This formed part of a general move towards the complete replacement of concepts of holy war with those of just war as criteria for legitimizing public warfare, a process that had begun in the twelfth and thirteenth centuries and found fruition in the theories of Gentili and Grotius in the early seventeenth. Although papal bulls still thundered with the language of holy war and a united Christendom, some near the frontline with Islam were less tied to traditional rhetoric. Roman Catholics, well versed in crusade history, emphasised the necessity for those fighting to obey the legitimate authority of the Holy Roman Emperor, to hold the right intent, namely to defend Christians and Christendom, and to display humility. They praised the crusades not so much as demonstrations of faith but as ways of protecting Christianity, avoiding the traditional weight placed on indulgences. Many of these non-sectarian justifications for war were shared by Lutheran and other Protestant advocates of armed resistance to the Turks.[7]

A classic evangelical stance to the crusade was that adopted by John Foxe (1516–87) in his *History of the Turks* (1566), which included a brief conspectus of crusade history as well as sustained commentary on crusading ideology and effectiveness. The laudable desire and sincere efforts of the faithful to combat the infidel had been subverted by their own sins, the central explanatory device throughout the middle ages, and by 'the impure idolatry and profanation' of the Roman church. 'We war against the Turk with our works, masses, traditions and ceremonies: but we fight not against him with Christ ... He that bringeth St George or St Denis, as patrons, to the field ... leaveth Christ, no doubt, at home.' The crusades failed because of impure religion; the Turk will only be defeated if Catholics turn to 'pure' religion. The papacy was responsible for the failure of the crusades, the loss of Constantinople and the continuing rise of the Ottomans. The pope should devote his energies in uniting Christendom not attacking Protestants; Vienna was saved in 1529 through the presence of some good Lutherans among its defenders. However, Foxe holds out little hope. Historically, the Roman church had abandoned scriptural religion; 'the pope's crossed soldiers' had even attacked those who, in the eyes of Foxe and most reformers, had maintained the purity of faith, the Albigensians and Waldensians (whose beliefs Protestant historians habitually lumped together).[8]

Foxe used crusade history as a weapon to further his wider polemical purpose. However, the crusades furnished convenient analogies for both sides. Just as Foxe charted the corruption of the western church through the failures of crusading, so a partisan equation regularly made by Catholic apologists, particularly when religious differences bled into rebellions and civil wars, identified evangelical reformers with Muslims and Turks. Thus, in his preface to his edition of Jacques de Vitry's *Historia Orientalis* of 1597, François Moschus of Armentières compared the wars against Islam and those against 'Lutherans and other Evangelical pseudo-prophets', explaining at length the similarities between the religions of Luther and Muhammed. However, Moschus was not just a polemical pamphleteer or sermoniser. In preparing his edition of Jacques de Vitry, he had searched for manuscripts, confessional pugilists on all sides seeking to lend such academic weight to their blows on their opponents.[9] Increasingly, from the 1550s, as much interest was shown in the use of crusades or religious war against rival Christians as in struggles against Islam. In the competition to assert ownership of the medieval past to support Catholic or Protestant visions of the present and future, crusade history provided rich examples alternatively of the power of Catholic faith or the contradiction between popular devotion and ecclesiastical abuse. The survival of manuscripts and early printed editions of so many important and vivid primary sources in libraries across western Europe supplied unrivalled ammunition as well as a cover of academic respectability for the religious combatants. This helps explain the initially perhaps surprising popularity of crusade textual scholarship among opponents of the church of Rome who explicitly rejected crusading's theology of penance and ecclesiastical trappings.

Foxe's theme of the corruption of a good cause was pursued

with greater learning and subtlety by the Lutheran scholar Matthew Dresser (1536–1607): 'This war had a double cause: one by the Roman popes, the other by Christian soldiers.' Dresser held a number of professorial chairs of classical languages, rhetoric and history in northern Germany. A protégé of the duke of Brunswick, he was also alert to the public potential of history as the official historiographer to the elector of Saxony. In his academic circle, the editing of classical and medieval texts was flourishing, allowing historians to write, as they thought authoritatively, about the remote past. One of his acquaintances, the editor, historian, genealogist and antiquarian Reiner Reineck (1541–95), persuaded him to write a commentary on the causes and course of the crusades for an edition of what he thought was an anonymous compendium of crusade texts, in fact Albert of Aachen's account of the First Crusade and the reign of Baldwin I of Jerusalem, *Chronicon Hierosolymitanum* (Helmstedt, 1584). Dresser's central interpretation revolved around the repeated contrast between the piety of the crusaders and the materialism of the papacy. The First Crusaders were compared to the classical Argonauts for their steadfast faith, but Urban II launched the expedition primarily as part of his campaign against Henry IV of Germany. Papal avarice and duplicity, buttressed by the profanity of monks and friars, negated the honesty of the ordinary crusaders. Dresser did extend his analysis to more mundane causation. Although Outremer may have been lost through papal pursuit of temporal power in Europe, it had nonetheless been undermined by lack of settlers and a high mortality rate. Crusaders may have been ignorant but were misled rather than mischievous. This extended into the sixteenth century, when, according to Dresser, Hungary was lost through ecclesiastical interference. At root, the very goals of the crusaders were flawed; despite the piety, virtue and just, honest effort of many, earthly Jerusalem was not, as their priests told them, blessed but cursed, the whole idea of restoring the physical Holy Places nothing but 'detestable superstition'.[10]

Crucially for the continued study of the crusades, its critics did not dismiss them as irrelevant. Dresser conducted his commentary as a sort of dialogue with the medieval past to portray reformed evangelical Christianity as a continuum rather than, as his confessional adversaries would see it, a destructive break. Both sides vied for the essentials of crusade history, but the task for Protestants appeared even more urgent as they sought to establish bridges to the medieval Christian heritage, even as critics. The use of medieval texts, reflecting a cross-denominational fashion for antiquarianism, served their critique of contemporary Catholicism; thus Matthew Parker, Elizabeth I's Anglican archbishop of Canterbury, collected insular writers such as the anti-papal thirteenth-century Matthew Paris. Dresser's coadjutor, Reiner Reineck, was prominent in a similar endeavour. Although making his reputation as a historian of Ancient Greece in the 1570s, his editorial work on medieval texts in the 1580s and 1590s, like Parker's collection of manuscripts, regularly focused the universal religious debate within a national frame, his editions including the *Annals* of Charlemagne, Helmold of Bosau's *Chronica Slavorum* and the chronicles of Widukind of Corvey and Thietmar of Merseberg. His editor's introduction to the *Chronicon Hierosolymitanum*, like Dresser's commentary, reveals an unmistakable German bias, Reineck declaring to his patron, the duke, that the crusades brought glory to the house of Brunswick, an appeal to dynastic association that featured regularly in crusade historiography well into the nineteenth century. Apart from the *Chronicon Hierosolymitanum*, Reineck's editions of crusade texts included Hayton's *Flowers of the East*, an early fourteenth-century narrative of Near Eastern history and crusade advice widely popular in the sixteenth century. Reineck, who operated within an extensive network of antiquarians, collectors, scholars and historians, claimed he had collated and compared his *Chronicon Hierosolymitanum* with William of Tyre and Robert of Rheims, and made reference to Otto of Freising's remarks on the Second Crusade and various Greek sources, including Nicetas Choniates.[11]

The desire to reconcile the present with a possibly controversial past was evident in the work of Jacques Bongars (1554–1612), one of the greatest editors of crusade texts. Bongars was a Huguenot bibliophile, historian and diplomat, employed from 1585 by King Henry of Navarre, later Henry IV of France (1589–1610). In his twenties he had visited the Vatican Library and began publishing texts in 1581. Usefully, his cousin

Paul Petau (1568–1614) was a collector of medieval manuscripts, including crusade texts such as Albert of Aachen and the anonymous *Gesta Francorum*. Fluent in French, Latin, German and, unusually for this time, English, Bongars travelled widely across Europe from England (which he visited at least twice) to Constantinople. He had studied at Jena shortly before Dresser had taken the chair of rhetoric and history there and, at various times, had helped Reineck with his researches. When he came to publish his own collection of crusade chronicles, the only text Bongars was content to reprint rather than re-edit was Reineck's Albert of Aachen. As resident ambassador to the Holy Roman Empire 1593–1610, he acted as Henry IV's agent with the German Lutheran princes, including Dresser's and Reineck's patron, the duke of Brunswick. Wherever he went, Bongars searched archives and libraries, collecting material, corresponding with and meeting fellow scholars, such as the antiquarian Sir Henry Savile in England in 1608. At his death, Bongars left between five and six hundred manuscripts and a library of over three thousand printed books. As with his German associates, Bongars saw the past as informing the present. Not a violent sectarian, he nonetheless declined to follow his master in converting to Rome, retaining a dislike of 'la superstition papistique' which he described as contrary to God, the king and France: 'contre la crainte et le service de Dieu, l'amour du roi et de la patrie'.[12]

Bongars's great edition of crusade texts, in the light of his association of God, king and country, significantly appropriated Guibert of Nogent's title *Gesta Dei Per Francos* (Hanau, 1611). It proved a milestone in crusade historiography, used until the early nineteenth century by most serious subsequent crusade historians – Gibbon possessed a copy – and, for some texts, still used today.[13] Bongars's was a Herculean achievement. The two parts comprised 1,500 closely printed pages, almost a million words, representing scrutiny of variant manuscripts in libraries from Rome to Cambridge. The thirteen texts and fragments in Part I include most of the main narratives of the First Crusade: Robert of Rheims, Baldric of Bourgueil, Raymond of Aguilers, Albert of Aachen, Guibert of Nogent and, for the first time, the anonymous *Gesta Francorum* (from a copy lent him by his cousin Petau) and

Fulcher of Chartres; the histories of William of Tyre and Jacques de Vitry; Oliver of Paderborn's account of the Fifth Crusade; a selection of papal bulls, letters; and, tellingly for the national frame Bongars sought to erect around the crusades, documents on the canonisation of Louis IX in 1297. Part 2 printed, from a unique Vatican manuscript, the strongly anti-papal, pro-French monarchy *De Recuperatione Terra Sanctae* of 1307 by the Norman legist Pierre Dubois and, from two manuscripts now in the Vatican, one probably supplied by Petau, a version of the bulky compendium of crusade advice, commercial analysis and Outremer history by the Venetian Marino Sanudo Torsello, *Secreta Fidelium Crucis* (this redaction 1321), along with maps prepared for Sanudo by Pietro Vesconte and some of Sanudo's correspondence. Bongars's editions were far from perfect, being uncritical, for example not distinguishing the relationship between the content of First Crusade sources or their precise chronological sequence of composition; partial, in the employment of a limited range of manuscripts; and inaccurate in transcription and textual omissions, perhaps a function of haste or reliance on amanuenses. However, for all these faults, Bongars strove, in the words of one of his English associates, to produce 'the most correct' editions.[14] In doing so, he offered what was, in effect, an exhaustively complete history of the Holy Land crusades from Urban II to the early fourteenth century told exclusively through primary sources, the most significant single contribution towards providing the foundations for writing crusade history before the nineteenth century.

However, as with other editors of crusade texts, such academic objectivity could also serve to deliver a pointed argument more subtly but perhaps more crushingly than the pyrotechnics of polemicists such as Foxe. Bongars's prefatory remarks and dedications suggest a purpose not confined to academic purism. The diplomat, courtier and Calvinist compete for attention. Part 2's dedication to Venice dwells not only on the Republic's role in the crusades but on its contemporary independence and support for Henry IV. Bongars's description of the crusades as 'most dangerous and most glorious' neatly summed up the tension between religious disapproval and historical admiration. He acknowledged that readers would find details of impiety, superstition and shame yet slid past crude confessional diatribe by commenting that such things are the common experience of mankind to which history is but a mirror. Calvin had argued that there was a difference between resistance to the Turks based on papal self-interest and legitimate opposition in the hands of divinely ordained lay magistrates. This neat equation of service to God and obedience to ruler echoed Bongars's preferences, revealed in the title, *Gesta Dei Per Francos*, the prayer at the end of his introduction and the dedication to Part 1. In Bongars's hands Guibert of Nogent's title assumed a more explicitly national tinge; for the medieval abbot *Franci* meant western Europeans; for Bongars it meant Frenchmen. The prayer looked to princes to implement God's commands as being next to Him in power. The dedication to Louis XIII associated the young king with his crusading ancestors, especially Louis IX, a line of kings pre-eminent in pursuing the crusade.

The intellectual context of Bongars's work was hardly neutral, nor were his choice of texts. Pierre Dubois's *De Recuperatione Terra Sanctae*, as well as talking of a grand scheme for a general attack on Islam, an idea circulating in France around 1600, argued that, as a prerequisite, Christendom needed radical reform, including ecclesiastical disendowment, an end to clerical celibacy and educational reform, with the French monarch controlling Europe through administration of papal temporalities and dominance over the empire.[15] Much of this programme would have appeared precisely topical at the court of Henry IV. In the humanist tradition of using history to hold up moral examples, Bongars presented his crusade texts, rather in the manner of Dresser and Reineck, almost as commentaries on the power of faith and the consequences of abuse, sin and division. Avoiding direct religious polemic allowed Bongars to extract the good in holy war even where corrupted by papal dogma. In this way, both Catholic and Protestant could demonstrate their lineal descent from a medieval past that embraced both traditions, a process eased by associating crusading with national pride. The point was especially clear when made in a book published in Germany by a diplomat with a cosmopolitan background and career who considered himself almost a naturalised German. The national appeal – to France or, as in Book 2, Venice – allowed each region

of Christendom to appropriate its own crusading past confession-
ally or ecumenically according to circumstance, a tradition that
was to have a long history.

Secularism: the French tradition

Bongars's work was fashionable and, given the limits of such a
bulky and expensive work, popular, judging from the number of
copies still littered across European libraries. Interest in the
crusade was a feature of the courts of Henry IV and Louis XIII,
fuelled by a recrudescence of what has been described as
Turcophobia bordering on mania, particularly in France at the
time of the Turco-imperial war of 1593–1606. Amongst those
who published works on crusading and the eastern question were
two panegyrists of Henry IV, Jean-Aimes de Chavigny and Jean
Godard, and Francois de la Noue, a relative of Bongars's wife.
The issue had clear continuing political resonance; Catholics in
Toulouse became *crucesignati* and received papal indulgences to
fight Huguenots as late as 1568. Some Roman Catholic writers,
both lay and clerical, still equated Protestants with Turks well
after the accession of Henry IV.[16] By portraying crusading as a
matter of national pride, Bongars was aping his master's policy of
attempting to escape the politically destructive vice of theological
debate. His efforts found parallels in attempts on the other side of
the confessional divide to create a form of Gallicanism, a distinctively French narrative of ecclesiastical history emphasising
France's special, providential quality and independence, for
example from papal control, a strand in political commentary
that reached back at least to Philip IV and writers such as Pierre
Dubois.[17] The title of a French translation of William of Tyre by
Gabriel du Préau published in 1574 was unequivocal: *Histoire de
la Guerre Sainte, dite proprement, La Franciade orientale*. Even
where other nations' involvement was acknowledged, as in Yves
Duchet's history published in Paris in 1620, precedence was
obvious: *Histoire de la guerre sainte faite par les francais et autres
chrétiens*. Prominent among such Gallican interpreters of France's
medieval past was the Catholic Parisian lawyer Etienne Pasquier
(1529–1615) whose remarks on the crusades, written in the
1590s and incorporated into his massive historical compendium

Recherches de la France (begun 1560) stands at the head of what would become a long procession of distinctively French writing on the crusades that stretched to the twentieth century. The relevance of his work was made clear: wars based on religious causes had devastated France for over thirty years (since 1562) persuading Pasquier that for all the zeal of the combatants, no benefit accrued for the church.[18]

Pasquier's moderate Catholic stance (for instance, he was a hammer of the Jesuits' attempts to infiltrate the university of Paris) provides the narrative obverse to Bongars's textual antiquarianism: wide-ranging, critical, topical. He used and cited medieval sources, for example Guibert of Nogent and Nicetas Choniates. He was one of the earliest writers to number the Holy Land expeditions: he counted six, perhaps reflecting usage already commonplace. There were echoes of the Protestant critique in his central assertion that the piety of the first crusades was later diverted by popes to fight their enemies within Europe whom they declared heretics, offering indulgences and forgiveness of sins to those who helped fight them. Some have suggested that Pasquier may have had in mind papal hostility to Henry IV before his translation to Roman Catholicism. The victims of papal aggression down to the fourteenth century are listed, the wars against Frederick II coming in for especial criticism. The anti-papal tone is sustained throughout the chapter devoted to the crusades (Book VI, chapter 25) as well as in references elsewhere in the *Recherches*.[19] The sale of indulgences and taxation of the church degenerated into money-making schemes for popes and those princes who appropriated the income. Pasquier was careful to deny direct papal control over French affairs, arguing that the First Crusade was the consequence of Peter the Hermit's evangelism and Urban II acting in concert with the Council of Clermont comprised of French clerics. Philip I of France was seen as lending his approval via the council held in Paris where he authorised his brother Hugh's involvement. Like Bongars, Pasquier associated the wars in the Holy Land with 'la grandeur de nostre France'.[20] (It is no coincidence that the *Recherches*, unusually for a contemporary academic work, was written in the vernacular not Latin.) Given the equivocal role he judged was played by religion, Pasquier took a consistently secular view of the impact of the crusades in trying to identify winners and losers. Those who gained were primarily those who stayed at home or acquired lands from the expeditions themselves or from their domestic consequences. The losers were the faithful, who were increasingly cast as dupes, most participants losing money, property or reputation. In pursuit of his secular theme, Pasquier considered the long-term social and political consequences of the crusades for France, which fitted his wider interests in the development of French social and legal institutions, an approach that formed a major element of crusade study during the Enlightenment. Pasquier argued that by draining France of many of its leading nobles, kings were better able to assert their power over lesser aristocrats thus beginning the rise of a strong monarchy in medieval France.

Pasquier's critique was fundamentally hostile. The crusades to the Holy Land had comprehensively failed, making the Levant 'the tomb of Christians'; Islam had emerged triumphantly more powerful than before.[21] Thanks to abuse and corruption, primarily down to the papacy, the crusades had caused ruin and desolation to the church, Pasquier tracing a direct link from the sale of crusade indulgences to Martin Luther's rebellion. His reconciliation of the contrast of genuine faithful zeal of the crusaders and the harm inflicted on themselves and their cause was bleak. Scarred by the experience of religious warfare in France, that contradicted religious belief, Pasquier concluded that religion could not be advanced through arms. Regarding the crusades as an enterprise aimed at converting the infidel, he cited Gregory I in rejecting the use of force to compel faith. This rejection of holy war and religious war looked forward to the ideas of Francis Bacon, Gentili and Grotius. Many of Pasquier's other notions similarly anticipated later discussions as well as following current ones. Above all, in his search in the crusades for the origins of the modern world and particularly modern France, which was why he included them in the *Recherches* in the first place, Pasquier, like Bongars, subjected them to secular assay. He asked not just were they 'good' or 'bad' but precisely how and for whom and, escaping the Augustinian model of *ratione peccati*, why.

Pasquier and Bongars presaged the tone of the succeeding few generations of French crusade scholars for whom texts and national self-applause went arm in arm. The crusades became a favoured topic of Gallican writers, stimulating interest in their surviving memorials. Numerous editions of the vernacular French chronicles of Geoffrey de Villehardouin and Jean de Joinville were produced, beginning in 1601 and 1609 respectively, culminating in editions (1657, 1668) by the great medieval philologist and historian Charles du Fresne du Cange (1610–88), who also wrote a *Histoire de l'empire de Constantinople* (1657) and left an unpublished description of the noble (chiefly French) families of Outremer. Genealogy in a society in which nobility conveyed tangible benefits as well as elevated status soon became a staple support of crusade studies, encouraging the antiquarian and the forger in almost equal measure. The cult of St Louis spilt over from medieval texts, such as Joinville, to biographies (at least five in seventeenth-century France), to prose fiction and epic verse, such as *Saint Louys* by the Jesuit Pierre Le Moyne (1602–71), a farrago of false history and anachronistic characters that went into eight editions between 1653 and 1672. Although his subject was ostensibly historical, Le Moyne's point was cultural, the reverse of Pasquier's; Christian and military virtues easily sat together, between the Devout and the Brave there existed no opposition or contradiction. Christian chivalry came once more to aid the reputation of the crusade.[22]

The debate between regarding the crusades as symbols of medieval superstition, barbarity and decadence or, alternatively, as a source of pride and witness to laudable Christian idealism and heroism had begun, fuelled largely by the contrast between academic dissection and popular invention. Here the highly influential, sentimental, fictive and romantic fantasies of Torquato Tasso's *Gerusalemme Liberata* (first published in Italian in 1581) played a significant part in exciting popular interest and even determining public perceptions. The consequent slough of bad epics shed by the marriage of history and romance even included an unpublished and apparently execrable poem by César de Nostredame (1553–c. 1630), son of the 'prophet' Michel, with the unpromising title *Hippiade ou Godefroi et les chevaliers*.[23]

While a number of crusading heroes, notably Peter the Hermit and Godfrey de Bouillon but also including unlikely candidates such as Simon de Montfort the Elder, established lasting reputations, St Louis occupied a pinnacle of his own, the standard against which his successors were repeatedly judged. Although not exclusively because of his crusading exploits, St Louis's devotion to a higher cause and his identification of his nation with it occupied a central element in his attraction. Kings from Henry III (1574–89) onwards were regularly compared (or contrasted) with the crusader saint, none more than Louis XIV (1643–1715) to whom, unsurprisingly from those in royal circles, such as du Cange, works on the crusade were frequently dedicated. Some of this crusading revivalism was associated with contemporary political issues in which Louis XIV held or was being persuaded to hold an interest, most obviously possible leadership of counter-attacks against the Turks. One of the more unusual associations of Louis, the crusades and the eastern problem came from the German philosopher and mathematician Gottfried Wilhelm Leibniz (1646–1716).

Working for the elector of Mainz, in 1671–72 Leibniz forwarded to the French government a proposal for a new French conquest of Egypt. This, Leibniz claimed, would combine the benefits of dishing the Dutch, destroying the Ottoman Empire, giving mastery of the seas and international commerce to France, and make Louis XIV the arbiter of Christendom and an eastern emperor to challenge Alexander the Great. He may have hoped for a sympathetic hearing. In the same year as he wrote his project, the French Levant trading company was established, the beginning of the creation of French dominance over trade with the Ottoman eastern Mediterranean. However, Leibniz's real motive may have been more prosaically to relieve the Low Countries and the Rhineland of French aggression.[24]

Woven into the very essence of Leibniz's plan was the history of the crusades, in particular the Egyptian strategy of the thirteenth and fourteenth centuries, precedents for his new 'holy war'. Three elements distinguished Leibniz's scheme: France's especial role in the crusades that translated into a continuing destiny; insistence that the crusades were and could again be conducted for the benefit of Christendom and even humanity; and the prophetic notion that a successful new conquest of Egypt could lead to western, mainly French colonisation of the Near

East to 'spread civilisation and ideas of humanity'; Christianity would be extended to Asia and Africa.[25] To back up his colonising theme he drew comparisons with European expansion in North America and India. The crusades failed, Leibniz argued, chiefly because of the crusaders' divisions and mistakes. To support the prospects for Louis XIV's success, Leibniz emphasised, in a manner later made very familiar by European Mediterranean imperialists and colonists, that the Ottoman system was decadent (harems, sodomy, drugs etc.), tyrannical and primitive. More sweeping still, Leibniz drew the contrast between 'the European life, full of calm and dignity and the barbarism (*moeurs barbares*) of Asia'.[26] Morally and materially, holy war itself was admirable and efficacious, even in the recovery of the Holy Sepulchre. Of his own project and by implication its medieval predecessors he remarked that 'no more just or more holy scheme has entered human thought'.[27] The recipients of Leibniz's plan seemed less impressed: 'un peu chimérique', 'un peu extravagant' reported one to Louis XIV; the difficulties surprising and 'quasi-insurmontables' commented another. Louis XIV's foreign minister neatly summed it up with a rather different take on the crusades to the French ambassador to Leibniz's master, the elector of Mainz: 'I say nothing about the schemes for a holy war: but you know that they have ceased to be *à la mode* since St Louis.'[28]

Unsurprisingly, the Leibniz scheme was left to moulder in archives and libraries until rediscovered in 1795, just in time for Bonaparte's invasion of Egypt (1798–99) and the re-emergence of views uncannily similar to Leibniz's on the crusades, Christian colonialism, the superiority of the west and the decadence of the east. Far more popular, far more representative even, if far less unequivocally positive, was the *Histoire des croisades* (1675) of Louis Maimbourg (1610–86). A Jesuit, later expelled from his order in 1682 for his strident Gallicanism, Maimbourg aimed his work at noble patrons and a general educated readership. His success was witnessed by the many contemporary editions and translations in France and abroad; the 1682 French edition even crossed the Atlantic later to find a place in the library of Thomas Jefferson. Although hedging his bets over enthusiasm and disapproval, Maimbourg avoids confessional dialectics. The crusades were lit by 'heroic actions' (particularly by Frenchmen), 'scarcely to be outdone' (except perhaps by his royal patron), deeds that revealed Christian values of steadfastness and courage with French values of honour. From sycophantic praise of Louis XIV, inevitably compared with Louis IX, the national and royal bias is clear. Like Leibniz, there is a hint that Louis XIV is expected to emulate or out-do the great deeds of his predecessors. More commercially, perhaps, Maimbourg insists he had included all the names of nobles mentioned in the primary texts but would welcome information about others, supported by evidence ('des bonnes mémoires').

Despite its nationalist, royalist deference and accessible style, Maimbourg's reading embraced many of the main sources, even if they had been mined uncritically: Robert of Rheims; Guibert of Nogent; Suger of St Denis; William of Tyre; Nicetas Choniates; Matthew Paris; Jean of Joinville. Maimbourg did not doubt that his audience would recognise his subject as 'noble and agreeable', touching the 'Great Concerns and the Principal Estates of Europe and Asia', a cosmic frame rarely missing from general crusade histories. Maimbourg sharpened the point by following the usual pattern of early modern histories in bringing his story into his own age, mentioning resurgent fears of the Ottomans and the plans to combat them, precisely the context of Leibniz's proposal. Above all, Maimbourg's approach was marked by a not untypical vicarious French triumphalism; large-scale narrative based on original sources; and an eye for temporal causation not divine will. His English translator (English edition 1685) and fellow royal enthusiast, John Nalson, paid him what he saw as the compliment of remarking that Maimbourg 'hath the least of that foolish Bigotry, which never fails to render any Profession of Religion ridiculous', a very Anglican sentiment.[29]

However, the attention paid in France to the crusades produced more than eccentric schemes for world domination, grovelling apologia for monarchy, bad verse or populist national history. The temporal emphasis in interpretation produced new conceptual frameworks within which the crusades could be reassessed, ideas that were taken up but hardly discovered or invented by the philosophical historians of the eighteenth century. The Gallicanism that allowed French crusade historians to escape the flail of religious controversy produced a whole new set of interpretive models. Perhaps the most influential writer in the circulation of these ideas was the lawyer turned priest and theologian Claude Fleury (1640–1723), whose massive *Histoire ecclésiastique* (20 volumes, 1691–1737) and his more conceptually concise summary *Discours sur l'histoire ecclésiastique* (1691) directly influenced prominent eighteenth-century writers on the crusades such as Voltaire, Robertson and Gibbon (who owned one copy of the *Histoire* and two of the *Discours*).[30] Like many who wrote on the crusades in seventeenth-century France, Fleury was a royal pensioner, tutor to members of Louis XIV's extended family, an ecclesiastical moderate, or courtly trimmer who largely hid behind academic theology rather than engage in church politics, a position more easily maintained as his *magnum opus* only reached 1414. Yet his views on the crusades were clear enough. Fleury tempered the extravagance of Leibniz's positive vision of crusading by a thoughtful analysis that combined traditional consideration of religious motives and status with a precise assessment of material consequences. Unusually, Fleury employed a modern-seeming historical relativism, when, for instance, having outlined papal justifications for the enterprise, he commented that now in later, calmer times, he found in them neither solid nor just reasoning.[31] In general, Fleury's criticisms of the crusades were temperate, unrhetorical, founded on the discussion of evidence rather than first principles.

In common with many of his predecessors, Fleury typified the crusades as having begun in a spirit of justified spiritual enthusiasm only for the ideal to be corrupted by bad discipline, poor morals and inept leadership. Materialism began to predominate, citing the familiar evidence of papal direction, the Italian crusades, taxes and the sale of indulgences, until the crusades on all fronts degenerated into 'temporal affairs for which religion acted only as pretext'.[32] One of Fleury's bolder strokes, aligning him more with Protestant than Catholic historians, was to criticise the concentration inherent in crusade ideology on associating Christianity with locations rather than the spirit. His analysis of the course and consequences of crusading was refreshingly acute and measured, rehearsing many themes that later become standard interpretations. He attributed the original idea for a crusade to Gregory VII, a feature of early modern historiography that oddly slipped from prominence in later centuries. Saladin's reconquest of Jerusalem in 1187 was conducted in a manner 'plus digne' than the Christians'.[33] The kingdom of Jerusalem was too tiny to be considered an especially fruitful result of the First Crusade. Using the thirteenth-century *Gesta Innocenti*, he noticed that Innocent III had tried to stop the diversion of the Fourth Crusade to Constantinople, but that Byzantium's fall had ultimately led to the success of the Ottomans. The expansion of crusading theatres had weakened attempts to defend the Holy Land in the thirteenth century. In the Baltic, the initial drive to convert had been subverted by the material ambitions of the Teutonic Knights. Not unlike his fellow lawyer Pasquier, Fleury argued for the conversion not destruction of Muslims.

Fleury's historical analysis is moderate, less heated and more academic than Maimbourg, in many ways similar to the stance of the English divine Thomas Fuller's popular *Historie of the Holy Warre* (1639). However, in one crucial respect Fleury goes beyond his contemporaries. He shared with Leibniz a low view of Islamic culture, but went further than the German polymath to trace a precise course in which the crusades contributed directly to the progress of European civilisation and superiority. 'Beyond the conquests of kingdoms and principalities, these enterprises produced results less eye-catching but more solid, the growth of navigation and commerce that enriched Venice, Genoa and the other maritime cities of Italy.' The crusades led to western control of Mediterranean trade. Armed with this 'freedom of trade' ('liberté du commerce'), merchants from Venice, Genoa, Pisa and Florence capitalised on the flow of goods from Greece, Syria and Egypt and, hence, ultimately from the Indies, to the material benefit of their cities and the flourishing of arts and manufactures.[34] In the context of the long-standing legal and academic debate in France about the fate of the medieval 'feudal' regime, the development of trade and industry provided an antithesis to the old rural society and marked a step towards a more modern world. This was the implication of Leibniz's scheme; it is Fleury's clear conclusion. This idea of cultural and social progress based on commerce and economic power became a staple of eighteenth-century thought, whether in the hands of

Voltaire or Adam Smith. Touching on the interpretation of history, economics and social change, it led directly to the positive reinterpretations of the crusades in the later eighteenth century. Usually seen as a distinctive development of the Enlightenment, the idea of progress and the crusades' role in it had been current long before. It was fitting that Fleury cited, in support of these theories, the great work on the commercial implications of the crusade by the fourteenth-century Venetian Marino Sanudo, which he had found in Bongars's *Gesta Dei Per Francos*.[35]

Scepticism: the English tradition

One of the most striking features of crusade historiography over the sixteenth and seventeenth centuries was the manner in which the confessional differences of the early part of the period gave way, on the one hand, to national epics (mainly in France) and, on the other, to a cosmopolitan debate across national and religious boundaries as to the moral or material merits or demerits of the phenomena. Few managed the philosophical detachment of Francis Bacon (1561–1626) in his unfinished fragment *Advertisement Touching an Holy Warre* (1622). According to Thomas Fuller writing a decade and a half after his death, Bacon had planned a full history of the crusades.[36] The surviving fragment is part of an incomplete mock-classical dialogue on holy war conducted by constructed archetypes of opinion: a moderate divine; Protestant and Catholic zealots; a soldier; a courtier; and a politician. The debate turned on whether 'the propagation of the Faith by arms' was legitimate or not. Bacon then uses his characters' discussion of past and contemporary history, from Urban II to the Ottomans and the Incas, to display the contrasting perspectives: the traditional Catholic defence of religious war; nostalgia for wars fought for noble causes; demands for an end to internecine Christian conflict in the greater task of combating infidels; severe Protestant denial of the concept of religious warfare; and cynical dismissal of the whole idea: 'the Philosopher's Stone and an Holy War were but the *rendez vous* of cracked brains that wore their feather in their head instead of their hat'. For Bacon, as he wrote in 1624, offensive religious wars could not be approved unless supported by lawful temporal justification. More obviously than many who considered the crusades, Bacon acknowledged the impact on attitudes to holy and just wars of the experience of the conquest of the Americas, and the debates about the status of native Americans as targets for aggression, conquest and conversion.[37] Prudence and law appeared preferable to religious faith as justification for war.

English writers on the crusades provide a revealing parallel to their French contemporaries in refashioning the medieval conflicts. As in France, contemporary politics and theological debate determined much of the historical commentary. Late fifteenth- and sixteenth-century England shared the continental tradition of interest in the crusading past. In 1481 William Caxton had printed the earliest English translation of William of Tyre (like Accolti basing it on a French version), his introduction encapsulating the three selling points of crusade history: relevance to the current Turkish threat; models of good and bad behaviour, in good humanist manner; and tales of chivalric adventure and fame. This combined history as entertainment and political tract, as Caxton urged a new crusade on Edward IV and his court. Other texts related to crusading translated into English and printed included Richard Pynson's 1520 edition of Prince Hayton's *Flowers of the History of the East* (1307).[38] There was also a market for new crusading texts, such as the Middle English romance poem *Capystranus*, a fictionalised description of the events surrounding the successful defence of Belgrade by crusaders in 1456, which survives in three printed fragments dating from 1515, 1517 and 1520.[39] Scholarly and ecclesiastical libraries retained numerous manuscripts of crusade texts, some of which were more widely disseminated among collectors and antiquarians after the Dissolution of the Monasteries. For example, at least three manuscripts of William of Tyre seem to have been in circulation by the end of the century. The antiquary William Camden (1551–1623) possessed a chronicle based on the *Gesta Francorum* which he lent to Bongars.[40] This was an international market. Most of the relevant books and editions were in Latin, still the universal western language of learning.

However, a local tinge was lent to crusade studies by force of circumstances. England, though concerned, was more detached from the Turkish menace than continental Europe, tending to see it in secular or cultural not faith terms. The establishment of state Protestantism under Elizabeth I consigned overt sympathy for the theology of crusading to Catholics, *ipso facto* enemies of the state for much of the later sixteenth century. The cult of national providential exceptionalism encouraged serious historical writing in the vernacular, which made such works unreadable outside England as very few foreigners learnt English, while equally relegating the crusades to a less prominent place in historical imagination than in France or parts of western Germany. Long periods of deliberate international neutrality, especially under the first two Stuarts (with the brief exception of the late 1620s), made crusading even less appealing as a model or a memory. Take the case of Richard I, with Edward I, the only plausible candidates for 'English' crusade heroes. Traditionally, Richard had been taken at his high medieval repute. However, in his *Collection of the History of England* (1612–18) Samuel Daniel (1562/63–1619), poet, courtier and historian, accused Richard of highhandedly impoverishing England to pursue a 'remote and consuming war' at a time when the English government was trying hard to avoid continental entanglements. 'During this businesse abroad in the East, the state of England suffered much at home.'[41] Such was the popularity and influence of Daniel's history that this disparaging judgement became standard. Even the bankrupt religious writer and historian Sir Richard Baker (c. 1568–1645), who composed his *Chronicle of the Kings of England* (1643) while incarcerated in the Fleet debtor's prison in London, tempered his praise for Richard ('valiant ... wise, liberal, merciful, just' etc.) with some slightly ambiguous asides about the raising of the required money: 'of taxations properly so called there were never fewer in any king's Raigne; but of ways to draw money from the subject, never more'.[42] The idea of the crusade's wastefulness of European domestic resources became a central ingredient of historical criticism.

Baker acknowledged that the crusades were an important feature on the medieval landscape: 'it may well passe, if not for a work of Devotion, at least worthy to be remembered'. In general, Baker, who had read widely if uncritically and advanced some strange notions (such as Henry I being a Cambridge man; Baker himself had been at Hart Hall, Oxford), adopted a neutral or rather admiring stance regarding the heroism of the crusaders, notably the future Edward I, an especial hero of his (as he was of Fuller's).[43] Daniel, by contrast, pursues a consistently hostile line in assessing the phenomenon as a whole. He dismisses the crusades as a 'humour' that persisted despite difficult journeys, defeats, illnesses brought on by the alien climate, and vast numerical odds cast against them. 'It consumed infinite Treasure and most of the bravest men of our west world, and especially France.' The Germans and Italians were preoccupied in the wars of popes against emperors. Above all, Daniel argued, the 'great effect' of the crusades lay in the Ottoman invasions of Europe by showing how even when combined the west was weak: 'the Christians who were out to seeke an enemy in Asia brought one thence'. Papal power corrupted whatever initial idealism there had been and, by encouraging rulers to depart on crusade, popes ruined them in order to extend their power. Daniel affected bewilderment but also admiration at how crusade enthusiasm caused people to ignore 'worldly respects', even commenting on crusaders' psychology: 'so powerful are the operations of the mind as they made men neglect the ease of their bodies'.[44]

However, both Daniel and Baker studied the crusades only as part of national history. More comprehensive, systematic and influential was Richard Knolles's massive *The Generall Historie of the Turkes* (first edition 1603 of over 1,150 folio pages). Knolles, a schoolmaster in Sandwich for most of his career, was chiefly concerned with Ottoman history, part information, part background briefing for a plea for Christian unity and a counter-attack against the Turks who, still immensely powerful, nonetheless appeared to be in decline. Although clearly influenced by the backwash of continental Turcophobia around the turn of the century, Knolles was almost entirely non-judgemental about the crusades. His detailed but lively and readable narrative of the Holy Land crusades that prefaces the account of the rise and triumphs of the Ottomans appears to take the holy wars more or less at the assessment of contemporary sources. Individual crusades are called the 'great and most sacred', 'most honourable', 'devout'. Crusaders were 'Christian champions', 'religious and venterous', the whole enterprise 'worthie eternal memorie'. While insisting that in Christendom 'questions of religion' are 'never by the sword to be determined', Knolles concluded with the hope that 'the Mahometane superstition, by the sword begun, and by the sword maintained, shall at length by the Christian sword also be dethroned'. No serious consideration let alone criticism of the theology of crusading or the role of church and papacy interrupts the narrative that in places can be genuinely and movingly empathetic, as in the description of the different ways the First Crusaders expressed their feelings on first espying the walls of Jerusalem in June 1099. As well as conveying a huge weight of information, Knolles sought literary impact, as in his highly dramatic rendering of the battle of Lepanto, which some allege provided Shakespeare with the basis for a description of a battle against the Turks in *Othello*. In two central interpretations, Knolles argues that divisions among the Christians on crusade and in Europe led to their failure and the rise of the Turks, and that the diversion of the Fourth Crusade weakened Christendom and advantaged 'the common enemies', drawing a direct implicit parallel between the hostilities between Roman and Greek Christians in the thirteenth century and the divided Christendom of his own day.[45]

Despite Knolles's elegance and erudition, the first full investigation in English on the causes, course and nature of the crusades that adopted the critical academic approach familiar from continental historians came from a friend of Baker, *The Historie of the Holy Warre* (1639), by the Cambridge career cleric and historian Thomas Fuller (1607/8–61). Fuller made his name as a vocal advocate of moderation in church and state, opposing extremism and radicalism whether from the crown or its opponents. Like many who cling to the middle of the road, he was swept aside. During the Civil War his espousal of a balanced monarchical constitution and a comprehensive not exclusive episcopal church found little favour, and none with the victors. However, if thwarted in the church, Fuller developed into an original and innovative historian, pioneering detached study of the English Reformation and of the years before 1640. His *History of the Worthies of England* (1662) was also the first English biographical dictionary.

Fuller's *Historie of the Holy Warre* was his first book and, like his later work, is marked by a cool, detached, judgemental style, studded with memorable aphorisms. Based on extensive reading in medieval chronicles, such as Matthew Paris, William of Tyre and Nicetas Choniates, Fuller's *Historie* approaches the crusades from two angles, looking at the possible theoretical justifications for the enterprise but also at its practical causes and consequences. His general position appears that of a moderate Calvinist, hostile to the theology of the crusade and the role played by the papacy. Fuller cast a critical eye on his sources; thus, on Nicetas Choniates's account of the Fourth Crusade, 'hitherto an historian, now a plaintiff'. For all his lively uninhibited censoriousness, he did not condescend towards the past: 'Let us not raise the opinion of our own pietie by trampling on our predecessors, as if this age had monopolized all goodnesse to itself.' Although he regarded the crusades as the product of 'horrible superstition' that 'not only tainted the rind, but rotted the core of the whole action', lamenting that 'most of the pottage of that age tasted of that wild gourd', he refused to deliver a universal condemnation: 'no doubt there was a mixture of much good metal in them which God the good refiner knoweth how to sever'. While lambasting papal ambition and clerical exploitation of the laity (they 'had the conscience to buy earth cheap and sell heaven dear') and denouncing the idea of seeking the physical Holy Land as 'in their nature … wholly superstitious' of pious crusaders, he remarked 'I could only wish that their zeal herein had either had more light or lesse heat.'[46]

Fuller helped secure an audience by his attention to the prospects for a modern crusade against the Turks (none, without church unity) and by weaving the medieval past into the story of contemporary religion. Thus the Albigensians, who, like Foxe, he equates with Waldensians, are depicted as crypto-Protestants who despite their persecution 'continued to the days of Luther when this morning-starre willingly surrendered his place to him a brighter sunne'.[47] For the wider educated readership at whom Fuller aimed the book, *The Historie* acted as a sort of correction to the pervasive romanticism of Tasso. Fuller himself was not immune to Tasso's influence, as suggested by his attention to alleged Amazon crusaders (although Tasso's tended to be Muslims).[48] One of Fuller's friends put it neatly in a commendatory verse that prefaced the book: 'Tasso, be silent, my friend speaks; his storie/Hath robb'd thy poem of its long-liv'd glory./So rich his vein, his lines of so high state,/Thou canst not feigne so well as he relate.' The point was proved: by 1651 *The Historie* had gone into four editions.

The themes Fuller examined embodied most of the debates on the crusades that characterized its study from the sixteenth to nineteenth centuries. He was hardly original, except perhaps in the clarity of organisation and lucidity of prose, possibly the most elegant history of the crusades in English before Steven Runciman. The emphasis on waste and the role of the crusades in provoking the Ottoman invasions was shared with, for example, Daniel, whose views on Richard I seemed to have left a mark as well ('farre-fetched, dear-bought honour').[49] His concluding remarks about the need for Christian unity before any counter-offensive against the Turks had become a commonplace, not least from Knolles's *Generall Historie*, which Fuller used extensively. In places the debt seems very close. Both in the frontispiece to the first edition and in the text, Fuller refers admiringly to the simplicity of Saladin's funeral, his corpse preceded by a simply black cloth, a story prominent in Knolles. In his praise of Saladin, Fuller's borrowing from Knolles becomes plagiarist: Saladin 'wanted nothing to his eternal happinesse but the knowledge of Christ' (Fuller); Saladin 'wanted nothing to his eternall commendation more than the true knowledge of his salvation in Christ Iesu' (Knolles).[50]

The scheme of Fuller's work is deliberately grandiose, beginning with the crucifixion and the capture of Jerusalem by Titus in AD 70, allowing Fuller to indulge in some anti-Jewish polemic. His account of Islam is brutal: 'the scumme of Judaisme and Paganisme sod together and here and there strewed over with a spice of Christianitie'. Among the Turks 'it is a sinne to be learned'.[51] Before embarking on his narrative, Fuller confronts the intellectual arguments for or against the crusades. In its favour, he adduces the secular just war concept that has a jarringly modern ring: 'a preventative warre grounded on a just fear of an invasion is lawfull'.[52] But Fuller demolishes the traditional supports of crusading by pointing out that there was no real legality in Christian claims to the geographic Holy Land as the Muslims possessed rights of long occupancy and any claims transferred from the Jewish covenant of the Old Testament had long since gone the same way as Jewish rule. More fundamentally, visiting terrestrial Jerusalem was to succumb to superstition by 'placing transcendent holinesse in the place and with a wooden devotion to the material Crosse'. More practically, the crusades did not work; they provoked Muslim aggression and were destructively wasteful; 'the warre was a quicksand to swallow treasure and a hot digestion to devoure valiant men'.[53] This idea of material and financial loss in a pointless cause found clear expression in the frontispiece to the first edition where the ravaged crusaders, victims of God, disease and the Turks, return, if at all, 'empty'. Fuller was too good a historian simply to assert his ideas; he presented them at length supported by evidence, as in his long concluding discourse (Book V) on the reasons why the crusades failed: superstitious purpose; bad behaviour of crusaders and other Christians; the intrigues of popes and Greek emperors; the clergy assuming command; divided leadership; the climate of the Near East; the vices of the crusaders; the treachery of the Templars; the small extent of the kingdom of Jerusalem; the size of armies; and heavy casualties. He accepts that the French were the primary movers, coining the phrase 'merchant-pilgrimes' for what he saw as the mercenary Italians.[54] A brief sketch of post-1291 crusade schemes and the Hospitallers on Rhodes introduces the discussion about the Ottomans in the seventeenth century, the book ending, as did Knolles's, with a description of current Ottoman power.

Fuller's *Historie* thus appears as a portmanteau of early modern scholarship; textual, presentist, judgemental, seeking secular explanations, a humanist mine of uplifting or admonitory stories laced with an apparently distancing objectivity sustained by a concern with the pathology of belief. Whether seen as quaint, a model of religious war to be embraced or rejected, a lesson in how not to fight the Turks or as a feature in the progress of western European civilisation, through the work of these scholars, editors and writers, the crusades were recognised as a common inheritance across political, geographic and confessional division in Europe, ensuring, as David Hume was imperishably to record a century after Fuller's death in one of crusade historiography's most attractive clichés, that the crusades that had 'engrossed the attention of Europe ... have ever since engaged the curiosity of man kind'.[55]

Notes

1 F. Bacon, *Advertisement Touching an Holy Warre, Works*, ed. J. Spedding *et al.*, vii (London, 1859), 24.

2 F. Braudel, *The Mediterranean and the Mediterranean World in the Age of Philip II* (Eng. trans. S. Reynolds. London, 1973), ii, 842–4.

3 C. Tyerman, 'Holy War, Roman Popes and Christian Soldiers: Some Early Modern Views on Medieval Christendom', in *The Medieval Church: Universities, Heresy and the Religious Life*, ed. P. Biller and B. Dobson (Woodbridge, 1999), esp. p. 293. In general, C. Tyerman, *The Invention of Crusades* (London, 1998), pp. 100–9; J. Burrow, *A History of Histories* (London, 2007), esp. pp. 299–305.

4 In general, R. Schwoebel, *The Shadow of the Crescent: The Renaissance Image of the Turk* (Nieuwkoop, 1967); J. W Bohnstedt, *The Infidel Scourge of God: The Turkish Menace as seen by German Pamphleteers of the Reformation Era* (Philadelphia PA, 1968); M. J. Heath, *Crusading Commonplaces: La Noue, Lucinge and Rhetoric* (Geneva, 1986); N. Housley, *Religious Warfare in Europe 1400–1536* (Oxford, 2002); C. Tyerman, *England and the Crusades 1095–1588* (Chicago IL, 1988), pp. 343–70; Tyerman, *Invention*, pp. 100–9.

5 J. Herold, *De Bello Sacro* (Basel, 1560), p. ii.

6 J. Muldoon, *Popes, Lawyers and Infidels* (Liverpool, 1979); Schwoebel, *Shadow*, p. 223.

7 E.g. Bohnstedt, *Infidel Scourge*, pp. 12, 14, 20, 32, 34–5, 41–51; Tyerman, 'Holy War', p. 295 note 4.

8 J. Foxe, *Acts and Monuments*, ed. S. R. Cattley (London, 1837–41), iv, 18–21, 27–8, 33–4, 38, 52–4, 69, 113, 120–1.

9 Jacques de Vitry, *Historia Orientalis*, ed. F. Moschus (Douai, 1597), Preface to Reader.

10 Reinerius Reineccus Steinhemius, *Chronicon Hierosolymitanum* (Helmstedt, 1584; part II [1585] contains Dresser's commentary), ii, fols 2v and 5v for quotations. In general, see O. Harding, 'Heinrich Meibon und Reiner Reineccus', *Westfaelische Forschungen*, 18 (1965), 3–22; A. Grafton, *What Was History? The Art of History in Early Modern Europe* (Cambridge, 2007), pp. 123–4, 142–65.

11 *Chronicon Hierosolymitanum*, i, Introduction, fols 1v–6v.

12 Tyerman, 'Holy War', pp. 293–4, 301–6; for Petau and his Albert of Aachen manuscripts, Albert of Aachen, *Historia Ierosolimitana*, ed. and trans. S. Edgington (Oxford, 2007), p. xl.

13 Most obviously, Sanudo's *Secreta* (e.g. facsimile reprint, Toronto, 1972) and correspondence; *The Library of Edward Gibbon*, ed. G. Keynes (London, 1980), p. 133.

14 MS letter of William Walter of 1608, at fol. 6 of Bodleian Library copy of *Gesta Dei Per Francos*, E.2.8.Art.Seld.; for the Petau loan, *Gesta Francorum*

et Aliorum Hierosolymitanorum, ed. R. Hill (London, 1962), pp. xxxix, xli.

15 For an English translation, Pierre Dubois, *The Recovery of the Holy Land*, trans. W. I. Brandt (New York NY, 1956).

16 Braudel, *Mediterranean*, ii, 842–4; Heath, *Crusading Commonplaces, passim*; Housley, *Religious Warfare*, pp. 195–8; cf. Moschus in 1597, note 9 above.

17 See Burrow's discussion, *History of Histories*, p. 311; for a contrasting view minimising national emphasis until the nineteenth century, J. Richard, 'National Feeling and the Legacy of the Crusades', in *Palgrave Advances in the Crusades*, ed. H. Nicholson (Basingstoke, 2005), pp. 204–22, esp. pp. 207–9.

18 E. Pasquier, *Les Recherches de la France*, ed. M.-M. Fragonard and F. Roudaut *et al.* (Paris, 1996), ii, 1279.

19 Pasquier, *Recherches*, i, 623–5; ii, 1272–80 (see p. 1277, note 416 for papal animus against Henry IV); i, 657 and ii, 1272 for the six crusades.

20 Pasquier, *Recherches*, ii, 1270.

21 Pasquier, *Recherches*, ii, 1277.

22 N. Edelman, *Attitudes of Seventeenth-Century France toward the Middle Ages* (New York NY, 1946), *passim*, but esp. pp. 8, 47–55, 64–96, 102–3, 240–4, 315, 395.

23 Edelman, *Attitudes*, pp. 202–3.

24 G. W. Leibniz, *Projet de conquete de l'Égypte présenté à Louis XIV, Oeuvres*, ed. A. Foucher de Careil, v (Paris, 1864), 1–28, for Leibniz's own summary, pp. 29–265 for the full project.

25 Leibniz, *Projet*, p. 57.

26 Leibniz, *Projet*, pp. 126–7, 178.

27 Leibniz, *Projet*, p. 27; cf. p. 29.

28 Leibniz, *Projet*, pp. 302, 304, 313, 359.

29 Tyerman, *Invention*, pp. 110–11; R. Ellenblum, *Crusader Castles and Modern Histories* (Cambridge, 2007), p. 8; for Jefferson's copy, H. E. Mayer, 'America and the Crusades', *Proceedings of the American Philosophical Society*, 125 (1981), 38.

30 *Library of Edward Gibbon*, p. 125; Fleury devotes his sixth discourse to the crusades, *Discours au l'histoire ecclésiastique* (1691, Paris, 1763 edn), pp. 234–74.

31 Fleury, *Discours*, p. 246.

32 Fleury, *Discours*, p. 266.

33 Fleury, *Discours*, p. 244.

34 Fleury, *Discours*, p. 267; for seventeenth-century French ideas of progress in literary views of the past, Edelman, *Attitudes*, pp. 18–19.

35 Fleury, *Discours*, pp. 267–8.

36 T. Fuller, *The Historie of the Holy Warre* (Cambridge, 1639), p. 242.

37 Bacon, *Advertisement*, pp. 1–36.

38 Tyerman, *England and the Crusades*, pp. 304–6, 346–7.

39 *Middle English Romances*, ed. S. H. A. Shepherd (New York NY and London, 1985), pp. 391–408.

40 William of Tyre, *Historia*, ed. R. B. C. Huygens as *Chronicon* (Turnhout, 1986), i, 19–22; *Gesta Francorum*, ed. Hill, p. xli.

41 S. Daniel, *The Collection of the History of England* (London, 1621), pp. 100,

141; the significance of Daniel's view of Richard I was demonstrated by J. Gillingham, *Richard I* (London, 1999), pp. 10–12.

42 Sir Richard Baker, *Chronicle of the Kings of England* (London, 1643), pp. 90, 92.

43 Baker, *Chronicle*, pp. 48, 51, 85–91, 127–8; Fuller, *Historie*, p. 221.

44 Daniel, *Collection*, pp. 49–50, 98–101, 107, 141, 155–7.

45 R. Knolles, *The Generall Historie of the Turkes* (London, 1603), esp. Introduction and Conclusion (unpaginated) and pp. 12–83, 88–95, 98–9, 101–6, 119–21, 132; pp. 878–85 for Lepanto (see Tyerman, *England and the Crusades*, pp. 347 and 439 note 16 refs for supposed *Othello* connection); p. 1153 for hope of military destruction of Islam.

46 Fuller, *Historie*, pp. 18, 137, 242, 243–4, 256 for quotations.

47 Fuller, *Historie*, p. 145.

48 Fuller, *Historie*, author's prefatory poem and p. 18.

49 Fuller, *Historie*, pp. 128–9.

50 Fuller, *Historie*, p. 133; Knolles, *Turkes*, p. 73.

51 Fuller, *Historie*, pp. 7, 133.

52 Fuller, *Historie*, p. 14.

53 Fuller, *Historie*, p. 15.

54 Fuller, *Historie*, p. 266.

55 D. Hume, *History of Great Britain* (London, 1761), i, 209; cf. p. 211.

3

Reason, faith and progress: a disputed Enlightenment

It served the didactic and rhetorical purposes of early nineteenth-century enthusiasts to characterise the previous century's attitudes to the crusades as uniformly hostile or ignorant, at least until William Robertson's reappraisal in his *History of the Reign of Charles V* (1769). Superficially, they had a point. Fashionable and influential eighteenth-century intellectuals, even more than their predecessors, tended to use the crusade not as a historical study in its own right but as a tool in conceptual arguments about religion and the progress of civilisation or manners (*moeurs*). However, most of what self-consciously philosophical historians such as Voltaire, Hume or Gibbon declaimed about the crusades was, in fact, old hat, rehashing earlier themes. Voltaire's 1751 essay on the crusades identified them as wasteful, pointless, ruined by excessive papal ambition for worldly power, an example of the corrosive fanaticism of the middle ages. Fuller would have felt at home, so much so that such disdain for the crusades was wrongly attributed by the great early nineteenth-century crusade promoter Joseph François Michaud to a specifically Protestant tradition of criticism.[1]

Yet the philosophical critics held no monopoly on eighteenth-century attitudes to crusading. Chivalry was not as universally condemned as its later champions would claim. There was no unified rationalist response to the crusades. The ideas of Fleury and of Leibniz that cast the crusades as a stage in the improvement of European civilisation continued to be developed alongside root and branch evisceration of the whole enterprise. There was no simple or single Enlightenment view of the crusades. Moreover, those who later criticised philosophical condescension were as guilty as those they decried in using the crusades as mirrors to their own partisanship. Each generation of crusade scholars has claimed objectivity for itself and castigated the bias of its elders; each has been deluded.

Widening scholarship

Since the Renaissance humanists and Reformation controversialists, one attraction of the crusades had lain in their scope: recruited from all western nations, motivated by apparently transcendent belief systems and fought across three continents. From the perspective of western Europe's engagement with the rest of the globe from the sixteenth century, the crusades provided the only post-classical example to hand of an ideological and military world war, providing a unique, distinctive parallel with the conquest of the Americas. This was not a new perception of the eighteenth century. However, the nationalism or localism that drove certain seventeenth-century scholarly examination of crusade sources, as in France, did give way to a wider conspectus, setting the crusades in a context of the secular history of the world, not least in the study of Asia and Arabic. Described by one modern scholar of the Enlightenment as part of a ' dechristianisation of history', this process allowed the crusades to be fitted into a history of human progress in manners not faith, a logical step from the materialism of post-Reformation Protestant and Catholic sceptics.[2]

Interest in Asiatic sources in part stemmed from changing political and commercial circumstances. After the Treaty of Karlowitz (1699), under which the Turks ceded large swathes of central, eastern and south-eastern Europe, the Ottomans seemed to western eyes to be in retreat. Already travellers' tales had reported the shabbiness and destitution to be found within the Turkish Empire, encouraging contrasts between supposed western dynamism and eastern stagnation. Although the Ottoman Empire proved much more resourceful, resilient and lively than its denigrators imagined, nonetheless the impression of Ottoman decadence allowed for less heated assessment of relations between Christendom and Islam. Apparent confirmation of a shift in the balance of advantage came from increasingly extensive trading links, with western merchants, especially the French Levant company, establishing themselves as a permanent presence in ports along the Levantine coast, in Egypt and Asia Minor. Increasingly privileged and protected trading rights, while essentially peripheral to the economy of the Ottoman Empire, added to the appearance of eastern dependency and weakness. It also encouraged a limited interest among western scholars in Turkish, Persian and Arabic art, literature and history. This opened the possibility of an alternative western vision of the crusades that recognised a more diverse historical landscape than had been available to earlier generations. In a backhanded compliment to this process, acknowledging the importance of newly available Arabic sources while noting their peripheral impact on interpretation, Gibbon remarked of the Ayyubid prince, geographer and historian Abu al-Fida (1273–1331): 'Had he not disdained the Latin language, how easily might the Syrian prince have found books and interpreters!' Gibbon himself possessed at least seven Latin translations of Abu al-Fida's historical and geographical work, most produced by the Dutch scholar Johann Jacob Reiske (1716–74), despite the Englishman's dislike of his 'petulant animadversions'.[3]

While the serious study of Arabic in Christian Europe was as yet idiosyncratic, patchy, incompetent or downright misleading, the importance of texts from the Islamic world was increasingly acknowledged. Bongars had planned a third volume to include Armenian and what he called 'Tartar' sources.[4] Louis XIV's finance minister Colbert collected Turkish and Arabic manuscripts and patronised orientalists and oriental studies, an adjunct to his schemes for French commercial domination in the Mediterranean. Among those encouraged were the scholars of the Benedictine congregation of St Maur, based at the abbey of St Germain des Prés in Paris. Maurist monks, who regarded historical scholarship as integral to their religious vocation, gathered an extraordinarily rich library and essayed a series of the grandest scholarly projects. This included an attempt, largely complete by 1739, to compile a comprehensive anthology of western texts on the crusades. In the event, the collection was editorially uncritical, derivative of earlier editions, lacked adequate manuscript research and was limited to French and Italian sources. So poor was it that the project was abandoned and disowned. However, a parallel scheme to collect Arab texts was initiated in 1740. The Maurists had a long tradition of interest in Arabic works, pursued by scholars such as Barthélémy d'Herbelot (1625–95), author of the encyclopaedic *Bibliothèque orientalé*; Eusèbe Renaudot (1646–1720), who wrote an unpublished life of Saladin; and Antoine Galland (1646–1715), first western translator of *The Thousand and One Arabian Nights*. In introducing Herbelot's posthumously published *Bibliothèque orientale* in 1697, Galland suggested that Arabic sources should be used in studying the crusades. He later wrote, but did not publish, a history of the Ayyubids, like most other early European works on Islamic history largely a pot-pourri drawn directly from the few extant translated primary sources.[5]

By the 1750s, some of the main Arabic texts relevant to the crusades were appearing in translation, such as Beha al-Din ibn Shaddad's life of Saladin (1732, with extracts from Imad al-Din's biography appended). This formed a basis for the *Histoire de Saladin* (1758) by the conservative lawyer and royal censor François-Louis Claude Marin (1721–1809). Following the well-established and almost universal admiration for Saladin, Marin adopted the familiar critical opinion of the crusades: 'more fanaticism than zeal', 'unfortunate enterprises that depopulated Europe, producing great deeds and even greater crimes', representing the 'barbarism and ignorance' of their time. Crusaders' motives were mixed. Nobles sought glory and possessions. The common people, the simpler driven by a sincere desire to liberate the Holy Land, wanted freedom and wealth. The secular clergy wished to gain respect and authority, while monks regarded the crusade vow as a means to evade their vows. In contrast to Saladin, Richard I received short shrift. One possible benefit of the crusade Marin unoriginally identified was the reduction of the power of lay lords to the advantage of the church.[6] Elevation of Saladin as a hero served a number of purposes. To Christian sympathisers, such as Marin, he could stand as a moral exemplar to shame corrupt believers and a corrupt society, medieval or contemporary. Alternatively, for the non-believers or *philosophes* like Voltaire, his career could act as a metaphor for modern enlightened rule, civilised, tolerant, moderate, not fanatical, in contrast, by implication, to the Bourbons.

That the crusades formed an important part of French history was not in doubt, as witnessed by J. D. Schoeplin's enthusiastic account *De Sacris Galliae Regum in Orientem Expeditionibus* (*Holy Wars of the Kings of France in the East* 1726). A similar assumption underlay the overt national pride in the meticulously researched *Esprit des croisades* begun in 1774 by Jean-Baptiste Mailly (1744–94).[7] The Maurists' historical researches enjoyed royal patronage and tended towards burnishing the fame of the kings of France. In 1740, Louis XV had granted permission for a Vatican librarian to assist the Maurists in translating Arab texts. However, only in 1770 was the Maurist project placed on a systematic footing under the direction of Georges François Berthereau (1732–94), who had to learn Arabic from scratch. Over the following quarter of a century, Berthereau collected and translated a mass of material from Arabic sources, leaving at his death 1,100 folio pages. However, almost nothing was published or arranged into coherent order. The Maurists were swept away by the French Revolution in 1792. However, almost as soon as the Institut de France was created (1795), the idea of a collection of the Latin, Greek and Arabic sources for the crusade was revived, if in less nationalistic terms. A few years later, a paper to the Institut in 1798, not coincidentally the year of Bonaparte's invasion of Egypt, spoke of the 'reciprocal influence' of Europe and 'l'Orient' on each other's people. In 1807, a committee was established, that included the greatest Arabist of his time, Silvestre de Sacy, to investigate the possibility of reviving the scheme based on Berthereau's surviving papers This, too, ran into the sands. The *Recueil des historiens des croisades* had to wait for the political will of Louis-Philippe's government in the 1830s.[8]

More immediately influential than the costive antiquarianism of the Maurists was the *Histoire générale des Huns, des Turcs, des Mongols et des autres Tartares occidentaux* (4 volumes in 5, 1756–58) by Joseph de Guignes (1721–1800). De Guignes, who read both Arabic and Chinese, saw the Eurasian past in homogeneous terms. Huns, Turks, Mongols and Tartars were successive names for one 'foule de barbares', their interaction with other peoples and cultures providing a central dynamic of historical development. Influenced by a unitary biblical model of human history, some of his ideas were distinctly eccentric, as with his insistence that the Chinese had been colonised by the Egyptians, while others, such as the interaction between different faith systems, pointed to a more sophisticated acceptance of cultural exchange. Although the crusades appear as 'un morceau' in the wider scheme, they hold especial interest for 'la Nation Française'. The account of the crusades, primarily in Books XI and XII, was innovative in relying more on eastern than western sources for tone, perspective and information, Arabic sources containing detail 'beaucoup plus exacte' than their western counterparts. In consequence of the slant of his eastern sources, de Guignes's version of events is presented in a more dispassionate manner than those of some of his contemporaries. The crusades formed a 'mélange bizarre de Religion et de Chevalerie', essentially barbaric in their violence. The even-handed approach distinguishes de Guignes's commentary from the standard tropes of crusade historiography. The Turks are considered as equally barbaric as the Franks. The Ayyubids are correctly branded as parvenus with a more recent title to rule in thirteenth-century Palestine even than the crusaders. However, the military leadership of Zengi receives high praise as does his son, Nur al-Din, 'si juste'. Perhaps of wider historiographical significance, cultural exchange is assumed: new western horizons of trade, manufacture and technology were opened while the Franks of Jerusalem were corrupted by 'les moeurs Asiatiques'. Not exclusively or chiefly concerned with the crusades, de Guignes included useful descriptions of the later medieval Mamluk regime in Egypt and a potted history of the Ottomans. Supported by marginal references and substantial bibliographies of primary sources, the *Histoire des Huns* challenged the customary Euro- even Francocentric stance of crusade history.[9]

While appealing to writers seeking a broad chronological and geographic vision of the past, such as Gibbon, de Guignes's universalism ran into fierce opposition from Voltaire who challenged his neo-biblical unified interpretation of world culture. However, de Guignes's insistence on the importance of his 'Huns' (i.e. invaders of sedentary cultures from the Eurasian steppes) in conquering China, parts of Europe, India, Persia and Syria and their role in the fall of the world empires of Rome and the caliphate, helped shift the terms of engagement in the academic controversy about the crusades. Beside old arguments about their religious, moral or practical efficacy, about cultural progress or retardation within Europe, de Guignes presented the crusades as an episode in secular world history devoid of a moral charge. He provided a refreshing – if somewhat fanciful and largely ignored – critique of Asiatic history, comparing the achievements and significance of the steppe peoples with those of Greece and Rome 'well able to humiliate our own *amour-propre*'.[10] De Guignes furnished more evidence in support of those who sought in the crusades signs of material change, for good or ill, most of it hard to contest by those ignorant of the sources he employed (although unsurprisingly this did not stop Voltaire). He also reduced the crusades to a side-show of Eurasian history, an invigorating inter-pretation that nonetheless failed to dampen contemporary interest.

The rebirth of chivalry?

Louis XV's permission to allow a Vatican librarian to assist the Maurist crusade project in 1740 had been advised by the courtier, medieval historian and philologist Jean-Baptiste de la Curne de Sainte-Palaye (1697–1781). An editor of texts for the Maurist Martin Bouquet's *Receuil des historiens des Gaules et de la France* (published from 1738), Sainte-Palaye sought to understand the middle ages on what he deemed their own terms, collecting historical and literary manuscripts and preparing an ency-clopaedic *Glossaire de la langue française* as well as, among other things, an edition of Froissart and a book on the French trouba-dours. He was an indefatigable researcher and copyist, providing, for instance, the Maurist crusade project with notices of relevant Italian manuscripts. His influence on crusade historiography rested on his *Mémoires sur l'ancienne chevalerie* (first edition 1759 – both Hume and Gibbon had copies).[11]

In seventeenth-century France, chivalry, defined as the code of behaviour of medieval nobles and gentlemen, was used both to entertain and to serve as a model against which to chart a perceived decline in nobility and noble habits. Du Cange laid out details of the institutions of chivalry in his Latin *Glossarium* (1678). Crusade heroes featured prominently in nostalgic accounts which lauded chivalry's supposed virtues of modesty, loyalty, generosity, humility and faith: 'the only contradiction between the devout man and the brave one is in language not substance'. Chivalry and its poets, the troubadours, were regarded as civilising forces in a barbaric landscape, an association Sainte-Palaye was to reinforce. Over all lay the romanticism of Tasso. However, the origins and impact of chivalry became a matter of controversy when handled by historians and social commentators trying to identify progress from post-classical barbarism to modern enlightenment. Was chivalry an intrinsic feature of barbaric society, an ameliorating force mitigating the more destructive forces of a militarist, feudal society, or an agent in moving western European culture towards renewal and enlightenment? These considerations were tightly bound to the crusades that seemed to embody and promote many of chivalry's most prominent characteristics: honour, faith, adventure, duty. As de Guignes remarked, the crusades combined religion and chivalry. Were the crusades therefore a consequence or a cause of the social order in warfare and manners attributed to the institutions of chivalry? Such arguments chimed in with interpretations of crusading as a product of human social, cultural and economic forces rather than as transcendent.

Sainte-Palaye traced the origins of chivalry to the Germanic world described by Tacitus, even though its formal ceremonies, such as oaths and dubbing, first appeared in the records of Charlemagne, and its full flowering only came with the eleventh and twelfth centuries. Building on the historico-philological work of du Cange, he saw the code of chivalry as a rigid set of rules, 'the most sacred and honourable laws of ancient chivalry', a formalism briskly dismissed by Voltaire as purely imaginary.[12] Sainte-Palaye derived his theory from chronicles but also from poems and romances (he had taught himself Provençal to appreciate troubadour verse). He summed up his historical approach as being less interested in 'the account of what happened than in the picture of how it was'. This led him to assign equal credibility to fiction as to histories, with bizarre effects, as in his discussion of knight errantry: 'These heroes ... resided principally in forests

... they lived wholly on venison; and on flat stones, placed expressly for the purpose of those knights errant in the forests.'[13] Such absurdities featured indiscriminately beside analysis of actual historical events such as John II of France's foundation of the Order of the Star. Sainte-Palaye's method was analytical not chronological, his *Mémoires sur l'ancienne chevalerie* being organised according to the institutions of chivalry – squires, dubbing, knight errantry etc. The importance of Sainte-Palaye's work lay in that it took the middle ages seriously (if fancifully), integrating chivalry into a thesis of social development and progress that suited the very different approaches of philosophical historians. Both Gibbon and Robertson based their commentaries on chivalry on Sainte-Palaye. Neo-medievalism was far from being the invention of post-French Revolution romanticism or reaction.

While acknowledging that it could produce 'monsters' and had led to abuses such as rashness, indiscipline and lack of unity on the battlefield, Sainte-Palaye saw in chivalry 'the work of an enlightened policy and the glory of those nations among whom it flourished'. Chivalry, born of friendship and brotherhood 'tended to promote order and good morals' and 'produced the most accomplished models of public valour', 'an institution founded solely for the public welfare, as in the most enlightened times have never been surpassed, and very rarely equalled'. Thus chivalry tempered the anarchic and violent tendencies inherent in feudalism. For the crusaders, the ceremonies of chivalry 'were the necessary spur to animate the knights, who would otherwise have been discouraged by the miseries of the crusades and the vast conquests of the Turks'. In the wider context of the origins of modern European nation-state politics that so occupied many Enlightenment thinkers, Sainte-Palaye noted that chivalry, with its emphasis on individual honour and the bonds of nobility, militated against loyalty to monarchs or nations, although kings later assumed prominent roles in chivalric orders and promoting chivalric values.[14]

The significance of Sainte-Palaye's *Mémoires sur l'ancienne chevalerie* in the historiography of the crusades rests on locating past manners in concrete external social rituals recoverable from original sources. Establishing the nature of chivalry in such clear terms allowed Sainte-Palaye, despite his social conservatism, to hold up past values in scarcely disguised criticism of later habits while avoiding both nostalgic sentimentality and the rhetoric of contemptuous superiority that fuelled the *philosophes*. Sainte-Palaye lent precision to contest vague libels about medieval barbarism and fanaticism. This, in turn, secured the crusades a more measured hearing. By taking chivalry as a social phenomenon of itself, born of a secular warlike culture allied to but not synonymous with medieval Christianity, Sainte-Palaye's views challenged writers across the ideological spectrum.

Voltaire was dismissive. Hume, although possessing a copy, tacitly but firmly rejected Sainte-Palaye's positive view of medieval noble mores.[15] By contrast, William Robertson's description of chivalry in the introduction to his book on Charles V, *The Progress of Society in Europe* (1769), echoes the theme of its refining influence on manners. Like Sainte-Palaye, Robertson accepted the reality of chivalry's literary claims to oppose oppressors, redress wrongs and succour the distressed, the imprisoned and the weak. Valour, humanity, courtesy, justice, honesty, honour and generosity tempered the anarchy and 'military fanaticism' of the feudal system. The clear implication is that chivalry formed one of the positive consequences of the crusade and the contact with the more sophisticated manners of the east and thus fitted Robertson's grand conception of social progress. Chivalry, through its tenets of humanity, gallantry and honour in war, directly influenced modern manners.[16] Gibbon, although less convinced of chivalry's beneficent or lasting quality, was heavily dependent on Sainte-Palaye for his somewhat mechanistic portrayal of the character of the knights of the First Crusade, not least because the Frenchman separated chivalry from religion. Associating the 'virtue of a perfect knight' improbably with Tancred of Lecce, Gibbon talked of 'the true spirit of chivalry which inspired the generous sentiments and social offices of man far better than the base philosophy, or the baser religion, of the times'. Gibbon remained firmly on the fence as regards the relationship of chivalry to crusading, 'at once an effect and a cause of this memorable institution'.[17] In his *View of Society in Europe* (1778), the Scottish journalist, historian and notorious alcoholic Gilbert Stuart (1743–86), eager to contradict Robertson's progressive interpretation of the crusades, insisted that chivalry gave rise to the crusades not as some (i.e. Robertson) imagined vice versa. Stuart embraced Sainte-Palaye's secularism to the extent of arguing that religion 'interfered' with chivalry. Thus, any progressive refinements to medieval barbarism were due to chivalry not crusading.[18] This conflict over the effect of the crusades within the progressive pattern imposed by Enlightenment historians provided a springboard for the very different attitudes adopted by writers after the French Revolution. Sainte-Palaye's work on chivalry was central to this controversy because it provided a pathology of knighthood and knightly society against which the role of religion could be assessed with greater nuance if not greater objectivity. Sainte-Palaye had shown, or had tried to show, that medieval knights were not simply barbaric thugs inflamed by greed and manipulated by false superstition or misplaced piety.

Manners and materialism: French *philosophes*

The greater emphasis on social structures, cultural attitudes and material development in assessing the medieval past scarcely reduced historians' massive condescension to the crusades. Yet because crusading could be placed in more or less any discussion of the development of European civilisation, it gained greater definition as a historical phenomenon and, consequentially, linguistically. In academic circles, from the early sixteenth century the phrase 'holy war' had tended to prevail, despite or because of its ideological baggage. More neutral terms entered the vernacular, the German term *Kreuzzug* (war of the cross) and the French *croisade* becoming well established. In English, it was only in the eighteenth century that the particular word 'crusade', a hybrid word derived from Spanish, French and Latin, became the accepted term. Samuel Johnson's *Dictionary* (1755) includes four variants: crusade, crusado, croisade and croisado (the word used by Francis Bacon). 'Crusade', perhaps first coined in 1706, certainly in vogue by 1753, when it was used in the English translation of Voltaire's essay (published as *History of the Crusades*; the following year as part of *The General History and State of Europe*), was popularised through its use by Hume (1761) and

Gibbon. Within a generation, 'crusade' had become so familiar as to be used as a synonym for a vigorous campaign in a good cause or issue of principle, thus the counter-Enlightenment 'Magus of the North' Johann Georg Hamann's *Die Kreuzzüge des Philologen* (*Crusades of the Philologian*, 1762); Voltaire's unexpectedly positive use of the *croisade* in describing combating smallpox (1767–68); or Thomas Jefferson's 'crusade against ignorance' (1786).[19] It was ironic that this recognition was born out of a sustained and far from unsuccessful campaign of vilification.

The classic statement of Enlightenment disdain for the crusades appeared in Denis Diderot's *Encyclopédie* (1751–72). Olympian condescension was underscored by rhetorical amazement at the quest for 'a piece of rock not worth a single drop of blood', a consequence of emotional and intellectual 'vertigo', its participants moved variously by 'imbecility and false zeal', political self-interest, intolerance, ignorance, violence and the church. The consequences of the crusades were unremittingly negative: the Inquisition; vast loss of life; the impoverishment of the nobility; a decline in agriculture; a dearth of bullion; the collapse of ecclesiastical discipline; and an ill-deserved increase in monastic wealth.[20] While few if any of these criticisms were original, their force derived from their political not historical purpose. Any positive gloss, such as the honour and glory that characterised many popular accounts, was rejected not because it was bad history but because it pandered to the values and self-image of the *ancien régime*, one of the immediate targets of the *Encyclopédie*. The potency of the root and branch condemnation of crusading lay in its contemporary resonance as a metaphor for a morally corrupt, intellectually decadent, religiously obscurantist and irrationally oppressive absolute monarchical system. However, the touchstone of reason Diderot and his collaborators insisted upon so loftily was no less partisan or more impartial than the mocked conservatism of their opponents.

The austerity of the *Encyclopédie* rested on rationalism not research, a precarious basis for the study of history. Voltaire's *Histoire*, although no less sceptically hostile, was more nuanced and more informed. From Anna Comnena, he drew a flattering portrait of Alexius I Comnenus, while Joinville provided the basis for his startling praise of Louis IX: despite ignoring the 'voice of reason' and misled by the 'madness of the crusades', 'it is not in the power of man to carry virtue to a greater height' than the sainted monarch. In detail, much of Voltaire's commentary was unoriginal. He plagiarised Pasquier's image of the Levant as a tomb for westerners and depended on Fleury for information. Depopulation; economic ruin; the abuse of papal power; the irresponsibility of crusade leaders and the barbaric irrationality of crusading (likened, in a casually racist aside, to the actions of 'Hottentots or Negroes') are all vigorously rehearsed. The crusaders boasted 'giddy, furious, debauched and cruel minds', their enterprise likened to an epidemic illness.

However, approval of certain protagonists pointed to a subtler message. While accepting the general theme of crusading fanaticism, Voltaire weaves into his disapproval a discussion of liberty as well as reason. Saladin, for long a western hero and moral exemplar, is depicted as 'at once a good man, a hero and a philosopher' who promoted the idea that 'all men are brethren' delivering charity for what they suffer not what they believe: liberty and reason. It was the lack of reason that misled Louis IX into an unjust attack on Egypt. Papal and ecclesiastical abuse of power 'must sooner or later have irritated the minds of mankind who are naturally fond of liberty'. Free from the thrall of superstition and reluctant to accept papal authority, the conduct of Frederick II, who had negotiated rather than fought for the restoration of Jerusalem to Christian rule in 1229, earned the accolade of 'a model of the most perfect policy'. The irrational pointlessness and lack of justification of the crusades is undimmed in Voltaire's critique: there was no more reason in attacking Egypt because it was inhabited by Muslims than it would have been to attack the Chinese for following Confucianism. The theme of liberty repeatedly intrudes, reminding readers that Voltaire's target was more eighteenth than thirteenth century. Thus the sole advantage produced by the crusades 'was the liberty which many boroughs purchased of the lords', impoverished by crusading. This resulted in municipal government growing 'out of the ruins of the possession of fiefs'. It was axiomatic for philosophical historians that towns were the cradles of civilised rational manners. Fleury had pointed to the growth of Italian cities nurturing the renewal of European civilisation. Voltaire's target was more parochial and political, the supposed beneficial result of the crusades of free boroughs supplying another barb directed at the creaking edifice of the *ancien régime*.[21]

Voltaire's general reputation assured his opinions on the crusade wider currency than the stature of his historical sketch by itself merited. The much read and translated *Histoire philosophique et politique des établissements et du commerce des Européens dans les deux Indes* (first edition, 1770) by G. T. F. Raynal, although derided by Voltaire as old hat and bombast, nevertheless employed the same idea of the crusades as an epidemic, while more empathetically than Voltaire noting the apocalyptic dimension and, in a nod to Fleury, acknowledging the effect of contact with the east on western tastes and manners.[22] Whether the crusades fitted the narrative of progress either as a spur or a hindrance, an issue skirted around by Diderot and Voltaire, became a central issue when addressed by their colleagues and correspondents further north whose conclusions were to set the study of the crusades into fresh channels.

Progress? Hume, Smith and Robertson: the Scottish debate

In a celebrated footnote to his discussion of the 'General consequences of the crusades' in the *Decline and Fall of the Roman Empire* (published in the final instalment 1788), Edward Gibbon commented:

> On the interesting subject, the progress of society in Europe, a strong ray of philosophic light has broke from Scotland in our own times; and it is with private, as well as public regard, that I repeat the names of Hume, Robertson, and Adam Smith.[23]

This was typically and doubly disingenuous. The remark in fact appended a flat rejection of Robertson's and Smith's idea that the crusades exerted a 'propitious influence' and concealed a fundamental interpretive division among these well-acquainted Scottish writers. The disagreement mattered because to a degree the opposing positions framed much subsequent debate on the effects of the crusade.

David Hume (1711–76), philosopher turned historian, was

not centrally concerned with the crusades, but was crushingly dismissive of them nonetheless as 'the most durable monument of human folly that has yet appeared in any age or nation'. In detail, his references to the crusades in his *History of England* (1761 for the medieval sections) suggest hack work, with a smattering of Voltaire (particularly obvious in the comments on Louis IX) and Diderot (with both of whom he subsequently corresponded). There are some errors of basic information, such as calling Urban II 'Martin'. In general, the middle ages are condemned as ignorant, violent, priest-ridden. The crusades, profligate of lives and treasure, manifested motives of 'effeminate superstition', 'heroic courage' and 'fiercest barbarity', testimony to the inconsistency of human nature. Hume stressed the superiority of the Muslims in 'science, moderation, humanity' not just as demonstrated by the paragon Saladin, but by Islam itself. In Hume's view, the Koran, while displaying some 'violent precepts', in its absence of bigotry and persecution compared well with Greek, let alone Latin, Christians of the time. Hume was clearly unmoved by the virtues of chivalry, as expounded by Sainte-Palaye, whose book on the subject he possessed, or the progressive theory of Fleury. Given his attitude to organised religion, Hume's stance on the crusades is unsurprising.[24] Perhaps more notable was the way his attitudes and phrases seeped into the common perception of crusading. His *History* was popular and contained instantly memorable aphorisms. Even William Robertson, whose views on the crusades differed markedly from Hume's, nonetheless quoted his views and plagiarised his language ('a singular monument of human folly'), as did the vociferous critic of Robertson, Gilbert Stuart.[25]

Hume's empiricism made him wary of historical determinism. He nevertheless subscribed to the humanist idea of cycles of cultural renewal. From the low points of civilisation (e.g., in his view, the middle ages), the only way forward was upwards towards more enlightenment. How this process was initiated elicited various arguments. Hume's successor as librarian to the Faculty of Advocates in Edinburgh, Adam Ferguson (1723–1816), in his widely consulted *Essay on the History of Civil Society* (1767), attempted to establish a non-determinist, non-legalistic 'natural' account of the creation and development of civil society and civilised manners. In his discussion of the 'History of Arts',

Ferguson proposed that improvement in manners came from emulation and exchange: 'Ages are generally supposed to have borrowed from those who went before and nations to have received their portion of learning and art from abroad.' This idea of cultural borrowing had clear implications for the crusades, as did Ferguson's insistence on wealth as the basic building block of polite as well as political society. One of Ferguson's earliest local readers took up both these themes in radically refashioning both the perception and reputation of the crusades.[26]

William Robertson (1721–93), sometime principal of Edinburgh University and Moderator of the General Assembly of the Church of Scotland, has been described as one of the first modern historians, despite Gibbon's rather belittling comparison of him with Hume in 1773 as 'another animal of *great*, though not perhaps of *equal* and certainly not of *similar* merit'.[27] Robertson's *Charles V* eschewed simple narrative and partisan polemic, trying to base its commentary on primary sources, despite its author's ignorance of German, while employing the intellectual scheme of philosophical writers and a grand literary style. It sought to explain a grand theme, the creation of the system of nation states, and took as its evidence material from across society, the arts and the economy as well as political history. Robertson sought to give a history of the progress of society founded not on theory but evidence, much of it contained in learned appendices to each chapter. Despite his own confessional allegiance, he avoided cheap shots at the papacy or Catholicism. Discussing the crusade in his introductory chapter, he placed it firmly in a secular frame and, despite recognising the 'superstition, frenzy and extravagance' of the enterprise, avoided the distracting condescension of his peers. To Robertson has been attributed the beginning of the positive reading of crusade history that places it within a narrative of progress, in particular expanding on the ideas of Fleury regarding the cultural consequences of the growth of trade and the rise of the Italian cities. In support of his interpretation, Robertson used Sainte-Palaye's arguments about the refinement brought by chivalry, which he saw as a result of the crusades, thus transforming them into agents of modernity. By placing this idea of progress in the context of commerce, manners, the arts and manufacture, rather than generalities about barbarism and superstition, Robertson established the subject on a new, apparently empirical and objective footing.[28]

Robertson did not come to his theories without assistance. The legacies of Fleury and Sainte-Palaye are clear, as is his acknowledgement of Hume, whom coincidentally he consistently defended against the religious bigots of the General Assembly. The footnotes relevant to the crusades in the analytical introductory conspectus of European history c. 400–1500, *The Progress of Society in Europe*, include references to du Cange's *Glossarium Latinitatis* and his edition of Villehardouin; Bongars's *Gesta Dei Per Francos*; Muratori's great collection of Italian evidence; as well as secondary works including Hume, Ferguson and Etienne Pasquier.[29] One influence not specified but possibly so pervasive that it has attracted scarce modern comment, was that of Adam Smith. This may appear at first sight unlikely. Smith's *Wealth of Nations* (1776) appeared seven years after *Charles V*. The passage in it on the beneficent if accidental effects of the crusades, appears simply to mimic Robertson in attributing the increase in the wealth of the Italian maritime cities to their role in transporting crusaders. After admitting that 'the cruzades ... must necessarily have retarded the progress of the greater part of Europe', Smith nonetheless concludes that 'the most destructive frenzy that ever befell the European nations was a source of opulence to these republics', thus providing the conditions for civility.[30] However, by 1766, Smith had already touched on the crusades in his *Lectures on Jurisprudence*, following Sainte-Palaye in attributing to the crusades the introduction of 'a greater degree of humanity' in the conduct of war.[31] Robertson had been associated with Smith in the mid-1750s as fellow members of an Edinburgh debating society and as a co-collaborator on the short-lived *Edinburgh Review* of 1755–56. The relationship between commerce, economic development, social progress and the refinement of manners, central to the thought of Smith, heavily influenced Robertson. According to someone who had heard Smith's lectures on Jurisprudence c.1750–51, 'Dr Robertson had borrowed the first volume of his History of Charles V from them as every student could testify.'[32] Whatever the precise intellectual gestation of Robertson's *Charles V*, the pivotal idea that civilisation benefited from the growth of commerce leading to the increase in the wealth of towns and cities and the fostering of civic values was shared and developed by members of his intellectual circle, including Smith and Ferguson. This went beyond Hume and was to incur the disapproval of Gibbon.

Robertson's *Progress of Society* traced the transformation 'from barbarism to refinement', to 'observe the first dawnings of returning light'. The crusades were 'the first event that roused Europe from its lethargy ... that tended to introduce any change in government or in manners'. The crusades provided a classic illustration of an unintended benefit from a malign cause, a favoured trope of philosophical historians anxious to square the circle of the progress of civilisation from barbarity: 'to these wild expeditions, the effect of superstition and folly, we owe the first gleams of light which tended to dispel barbarity and ignorance'. The agent of change lay in the crusaders' contacts with Byzantium and the Near East: 'their views enlarged, their prejudices wore off; new ideas crowded into their minds' through exposure to 'a more polished people'. Before the wider cultural exchange could take effect, the loss of noble property through the expense of crusading and the absence of nobles on crusade led to a shift of power towards monarchs, a point made by Pasquier two centuries earlier. The peace in western Europe imposed by the church during crusades also gave rise to a more even administration of justice, the beginning of regular government. Of far greater significance was the increase in commerce and the rise of the Italian cities which led directly to the growth of communes supported by civic liberty and independence, producing in these cities 'free and equal government as would render property secure and industry flourishing', almost a manifesto for the Hanoverian settlement and the Act of Union. (Appropriately, Robertson had joined the forces of the government against the Jacobite rebels in 1745.) While chivalry mitigated the barbarism of the rural aristocracy, so the communal movement spread from Italy to the rest of western Europe, undermining feudalism and noble privileges while improving public manners and the exercise of rule and law. The central benefit lay not in wealth alone but, as Ferguson argued, in the advance of civil society and public virtue through 'a general passion for liberty and independence', a theme that not only brought the argument back to the basic tenets of *philosophes* such as Voltaire, but foreshadowed what was to be one of the central concerns of Edward Gibbon's *Decline and Fall of the Roman Empire*.[33]

Gibbon

Edward Gibbon's sonorous judgements on the crusades have become something of a historical and literary cliché. 'At the voice of their pastor, the robber, the incendiary, the homicide, arose by their thousands to redeem their souls by repeating on the infidels the same deeds which they had exercised against their Christian brethren; and the terms of atonement were eagerly embraced by offenders of every rank and denomination. None were pure; none were exempt from the guilt and penalty of sin; and those who were the least amenable to the justice of God and the church were the best entitled to the temporal and eternal recompense of their pious courage.'[34] To rescue Gibbon from his own prose, his comments should be located both in the immediate intellectual context and in the longer perspective of earlier historians he had read.

Edward Gibbon (1737–94) was highly unusual; an Englishman with extended cosmopolitan experience not just tastes and a writer of European vision who wrote in English. His theme of the decline and fall of classical Rome was the grandest imaginable. Conceived on the largest canvas, and intended to display the author's massive, if self-satisfied erudition, his limpidly sonorous prose and his delight in combative intellectual polemics, *The Decline and Fall* examined some of the central pillars of western European history and culture. Gibbon set out to make a name for himself not only by the huge scale of the work but by challenging a host of accepted orthodoxies about the Roman Empire, the role of early Christianity and, most unusually, the middle ages, the long hiatus, as he saw it, before the new enlightenment began in the Renaissance. Gibbon's general approach to religion, like Fleury's, was institutional not confessional, marking him as one of the inventors of serious ecclesiastical history. His own brush with faith, an adolescent conversion to Roman Catholicism and a subsequent return to uninvolved Anglicanism, perhaps allowed him, in contrast to some *philosophe* contemporaries, more insight, if no greater enthusiasm, for the complications and contradictions of belief. However, subtlety hardly characterised his account of the crusades.

The chapters Gibbon devoted to the crusades, published in 1788, show a close dependence on previous writers in part to engage and frequently to refute their arguments. The organisation of his crusade material indicates a lack of interest in the crusades as a medieval phenomenon except in so far as they illustrated Gibbon's wider themes: the loss and rediscovery of civil liberty; the corrosively irrational and oppressive nature of organised religion; anti-clericalism; the transmission and continuity of classical culture. His treatment of the crusades to the Holy Land is presented in two unequal chapters.[35] The first dealt with the origins and nature of the enterprise coupled with an account of the First Crusade and a summary of the internal organisation of the kingdom of Jerusalem, which Gibbon significantly if rather eccentrically viewed as a model of constitutional liberties and a cradle of pioneering urban freedom. The second chapter takes the form of a brisk canter through a narrative of 1099 to 1291, the main emphasis being on the moral quality of crusade leaders. The content scarcely matches the rhetoric. The famous peroration on the loss of Acre to the Mamluks in 1291, 'a mournful and solitary silence prevailed along the coast which had so long resounded with the WORLD'S DEBATE', is hardly supported by the preceding analysis.[36] More central, perhaps, to Gibbon's interests was the Fourth Crusade and the relations between the Latins and Greeks, covered in two further chapters which lead to a brief final summary of the general consequences of the crusades.[37] Gibbon is keen to denigrate Byzantium as the preserver and conduit of classical reason, chiefly because of the lack of the 'free spirit' which Gibbon attributed to western Europeans. With Byzantium as with the crusaders, Gibbon appears determined to marginalise their role in the progress of civilisation, in so doing allying himself unequivocally with those opposed to the Fleury–Smith–Robertson revamping of the history of progress in the middle ages.

Gibbon acts as a guide to two centuries of discussion of the crusades. His primary sources included Bongars's collection of

Latin texts; du Cange's Villehardouin; Odo of Deuil; Jacques de Vitry; Joinville; the Jewish twelfth-century traveller Benjamin of Tudela; the national collections of source extracts by Muratori (Italian) and Bouquet (French); Mansi's series of documents from church councils and synods; the Assizes (i.e. laws) of Jerusalem; English chroniclers such as William of Malmesbury, Roger of Howden and Matthew Paris; the Greek writers Anna Comnena, Nicetas Choniates and John Kinnamos; and the Arabic texts Abu al-Fida and the biographies of Saladin by Imad al-Din ibn Shaddad and Beha al-Din. His secondary reading appeared comprehensive: Voltaire, Hume, de Guignes, Mailly's *Esprit des croisades*, Sainte-Palaye, Fleury's *Discours* ('an accurate and rational view of the causes and effects of the crusades'), Maimbourg, Robertson, and Vertot's 1762 history of Hospitallers. Directly or indirectly, Gibbon's comments share the legacy of Pasquier and Fuller. His disdain echoed that of the influential (if unoriginal) anti-Catholic barbs in the recently translated *Ecclesiastical History* (1726, Eng. trans. 1764) of the German Lutheran Johann Lorenz Mosheim (1693/94–1755).[38] Despite, or perhaps because of, this erudition, genuine and pretended, Gibbon's reflections on the crusades are best regarded as polemic not history as, with a highly selective use of his primary sources, the arguments of his fellow commentators were picked up or picked off.

Following Fuller, Gibbon began his discussion by considering the justice of crusading. He dismissed the idea that the crusades were legitimate defence and resistance because they were disproportionate to the threat. Palestine was only a proper military goal because of fanaticism and superstition, not reason. The whole concept of holy war – 'from Egypt to Livonia and from Peru to Hindostan' – was derided as hypocritical by a neat reversal of perspective; the secular conquests by the Germanic barbarians in the west were regarded by succeeding generations of Christians as legitimate whereas those of Islam were rejected by Christian subjects and neighbours alike. The religious motivation of the crusades was at once accepted but derided through a critique of the penitential system of indulgences which, Gibbon insisted, acted for many as a sop to baser motives, arguing that religion is 'feeble to stem' but 'strong and irresistible to impel' social manners, in this case superstitious, fanatical, violent and mercenary. Yet within this hostile critique, Gibbon allowed place for his view of the active energy inherent in the culture of western Europe: 'the love of freedom was a powerful incitement to the multitudes'. This underlying myth of pristine Germanic vigour was popular among northern European intellectuals who saw it revealed in crusading, from Gibbon's Scottish contemporary Gilbert Stuart to Friedrich Schiller (1759–1805).[39] Following writers at least since Pasquier, Gibbon concluded that the material consequences of this mass action – alienation of property by princes, nobles and even peasants at rock-bottom prices caused by the sudden glut of sales led to an increase in the power of both monarchs and the church, who bought up the cheap lands and goods.

This close awareness of the ideas of previous historians permeates Gibbon's subsequent detailed discussion of the First Crusade. Du Cange, Sainte-Palaye and the seventeenth-century English legal historian John Selden inform his account of chivalry; de Guignes provides the ballast of eastern sources while Mailly supplies a sometimes rejected commentary on the western texts. Hume and Voltaire are constant reference points, if only occasionally explicit. Whereas Gibbon shared their solid anticlericalism, he seeks to adjudicate their interpretations of miracles (preferring Hume) and crusaders' psychology when contemplating the blood-soaked victorious crusaders praying at the Church of the Holy Sepulchre on 15 July 1099. Hume, reflecting his unsentimental view of human nature, saw the mingling of 'the fiercest and most tender passions' in individual crusaders as easy and natural; Voltaire, more polemically superficial, insisted such emotional contradictions were absurd and incredible.[40] Gibbon sought to argue that different crusaders held different balances of motive, those most violent not being among those leading the way to the Holy Sepulchre. In fact, this may be seen as a rather feeble quibble, hardly worth the precisely noted disagreement with his two distinguished predecessors. However, it is typical of Gibbon's whole account of the crusades, a somewhat meretricious attempt at novelty and difference which amounts to very little of original interpretive substance. Thus, his account of the 'political liberty' inherent in institutions of the kingdom of Jerusalem, is framed by the increasingly common trope of condescension regarding the surrounding 'slaves of Asia'. His singling out of the rise of cities and corporations in Outremer as early evidence of the movement that would destroy feudalism derives from Fleury, Voltaire and Robertson, as does his general conclusion that almost the sole advantage derived from the crusades was, as Voltaire had argued, the rise in free boroughs in the west. Gibbon used Voltaire's very words in describing Louis IX, a victim of 'holy madness'. Even his unusual criticisms of Saladin ('a royal saint', 'in a fanatic age himself a fanatic') seem forced, designed simply to be different rather than offering a new judgement based on critical consideration of the sources; literary knock-about not measured argument.

However, in his summing up 'the General Consequences of the Crusades', Gibbon is compelled to take a clear position between what could be called a Humean and a Robertsonian position. If anything, he is even more negative than Hume, who at least accepted the crusades were part of a process as well as period in which civilisation began to recover. In rejecting Robertson, Gibbon may have been influenced by the sustained critique of Gilbert Stuart in his popular *View of Society in Europe* (1778; many editions thereafter – Gibbon certainly had the 1782 one – and translations into German 1779 and French 1789). Stuart rejected the idea that the crusades spawned the civilising force of chivalry and relegated their role in positive cultural exchange to neither the first nor 'very powerful cause of refinement in Europe'. Rather, 'they drained Europe of rulers, inhabitants and wealth thus [a direct dig at Robertson] discouraging trade and the arts', causing disorder, the rise of papal power and the promotion of 'every pious impertinence', advancing 'the most abject superstition'.[41] Gibbon hardly put it better.

The crusades, Gibbon argued, had little impact on Islam. In a characteristic reversal of accepted wisdom, the Greeks learnt from the Latins, not philosophy, industry or art, but western freedom of spirit and 'the rights of man'. However, any cultural benefit derived by the crusaders' presence in the Near East and Greece in trade or manufacture (e.g. windmills, silk, sugar) was wholly accidental and peripheral. Although some Arabic knowledge of medicine and mathematics may have been spread, the crusaders who settled in the east or transmitted ideas back to the west did not learn Arabic or Greek. Greek philosophy reached the west, Gibbon insisted, via the Arabs and Jews of Andalusia not Outremer. The most important effects of the crusades were 'analogous to the cause' which was 'a savage fanaticism'. Thus, 'from the baleful fountain of the holy war', flowed relics, legends, the Inquisition, friars, indulgences and 'the final progress of idolatry'. Here, the use of the word 'progress' was carefully calculated to presage a direct assault on the progressive interpretations of Smith and Robertson. 'If the ninth and tenth centuries were times of darkness, the thirteenth and fourteenth were the age of absurdity and fable.'[42] Although after the irruption of 'anarchy and barbarism' from Vikings, Saracens and Magyars, the 'tide of civilisation ... began to flow with a steady and accelerated course' from the eleventh century, this was not a conscious, direct or even, in the cherished philosophical model of the unintended consequences, accidental result of the crusades. Gibbon takes care not to be misunderstood either in thesis or target.

> Great was the increase and rapid progress, during the two hundred years of the crusades; and some philosophers have applauded the propitious influences of these holy wars, which appear to me to have checked rather than forwarded the maturity of Europe. The lives and labours of millions which were buried in the East could have been more profitably employed in the improvement of their native country; the accumulated stock of industry and wealth would have overflowed in navigation and trade; and the Latins would have been enriched and enlightened by a pure and friendly correspondence with the climates of the east.[43]

Thus, in a typically Gibbonian flourish, the economic determinism of Fleury, Smith and Robertson is embraced in the same instant as their application of it is denied, leaving us, essentially, with Fuller's theory of waste. Whether Gibbon came to this conclusion out of reason, competitive argumentativeness or aesthetic preference for the aphorisms of his seventeenth-century predecessor must remain a matter of conjecture. He rubbed in his disapproval of the Smith–Robertson line by proceeding to underline his traditionalist views while adopting a key conceptual element from the Smith–Robertson line. Admitting the 'accidental operation of the crusades', Gibbon adopts the Voltaire line that stretched back to Pasquier that the crusades undermined the stultifying oppression of feudalism through causing the poverty of the nobility that produced charters of freedom that liberated people, industry and communities. Yet even as he completed his assessment of the crusades, Gibbon failed to resolve the contradiction inherent in his lack of originality. He wished to say the crusades were a regressive not progressive force and yet he admitted they led, in some measure at least, to the growth of liberty which he regarded as the prerequisite for civilised manners, whether in the classical or modern age.

For all his elevated tergiversation, Gibbon's opinion was not to influence the greatest change in attitudes towards the crusade since the sixteenth century. Long before Gibbon pronounced, Robertson's *Charles V* had been translated into French (in 1771). It was read by, among others, Chateaubriand, the apostle of a sympathetic reading of the middle ages whose advocacy of respect for the crusades on their own terms helped fundamentally recast French attitudes towards them. Robertson's economic ideas became so widely accepted that in 1806 the Institut de France offered a prize for an essay on the subject of the influence of the crusades on European civil liberty, civilisation and the progress of learning, commerce and industry, the latter assumption hardly suggesting neutrality, let alone hostility.[44] As it transpired, far more influential to the subsequent transformation of the rational into an empathetic response to the medieval past and the crusades, was one of Robertson's own Edinburgh pupils: Walter Scott.[45]

Notes

1 On this Protestant angle, see now R. Ellenblum, *Crusader Castles and Modern Histories* (Cambridge, 2007), pp. 4–5.

2 J. G. A. Pocock, *Barbarism and Religion* (Cambridge, 1999–2005), ii, chap. 7 title and *passim* for transformations in the writing of history.

3 E. Gibbon, *The History of the Decline and Fall of the Roman Empire*, ed. W. Smith (London 1862), chap. LXI, note 63; *The Library of Edward Gibbon*, ed. G. Keynes (London, 1980), pp. 43–4; R. Irwin, *For Lust of Knowing: Orientalists and their Enemies* (London, 2006), p. 120 and generally pp. 109–40 for this and what follows.

4 Marino Sanudo Torsello, *Secreta Fidelium Crucis*, ed. J. Bongars, *Gesta Dei*

Per Francos (Hanau, 1611), i, fol. 28v.

5 Comte Riant, 'Inventaire des matérieux rassemblés par les Bénédictines au XVIIIe siècles pour la publication des *Historiens des croisades*', *Archives de l'Orient Latin*, ii (Paris, 1884), 105–30; H. Dehéran, 'Les origines du *Recueil des historiens des croisades*', *Journal des Savants*, n.s. 17 (1919), 260–6.

6 F.-L. C. Marin, *Histoire de Saladin, sulthan d'Egypte et de Syrie* (2 vols. Paris, 1758), esp. i, ix, 43–4, 48, 63; ii, 11–12, 262–3.

7 J. Richard, 'Jean-Baptiste Mailly et l'*Esprit des croisades*', *Mémoires de l'Académie des sciences, arts et belles lettres de Dijon*, 136 (1997–98), 349–59.

8 Dehéran, 'Origines', pp. 261–5; A. Beugnot, 'Rapport sur la publication du *Recueil des historiens des croisades*', *RHC Occ.*, i–i, i–xv.

9 J. de Guignes, *Histoire générale des Huns, des Turcs, des Mongols et des autres Tartares occidentaux* (Paris, 1756–58, 4 vols in 5), esp. i, vi-vii, xv, xvi; ii, 14, 220 and Books XI and XII *passim*; iv, 337–8 and 363–75 for bibliography; cf. Pocock, *Barbarism and Religion*, ii, 114.

10 De Guignes, *Huns*, i, vi–vii.

11 Dehéran, 'Origines', p. 261; Riant, 'Inventaire', p. 118; D. F and M. J. Norton, *The David Hume Library* (Edinburgh, 1996), p. 127; *Library of Gibbon*, p. 170; in general, L. Gossman, *Medievalism and the Ideologies of the Enlightenment* (Baltimore MD, 1968).

12 Translation by Mrs S. Dobson from English edition, *Memoirs of Ancient Chivalry* (London, 1784), p. 336.

13 Gossman, *Medievalism*, p. 169; *Memoirs of Ancient Chivalry*, p. 317.

14 *Memoirs of Ancient Chivalry*, esp. pp. 1–2, 69, 78, 165, 305–7, 310, 312–17, 336, 339.

15 Gossman, *Medievalism*, pp. 291–3, 327 *et seq.*

16 W. Robertson, *The Progress of Society in Europe: A Historical Outline from the Subversion of the Roman Empire to the Beginning of the Sixteenth Century*. [The introduction to *The History of the Reign of Charles V* (1st edn Edinburgh, 1769)], ed. F. Gilbert (Chicago IL, 1972), pp. 26, 57–9; despite not citing Sainte-Palaye in his footnotes, the debt is direct, Pocock, *Barbarism and Religion*, p. 281, note 72.

17 Gibbon, *Decline and Fall*, vii, 199–201 and note 58.

18 Gilbert Stuart, *A View of Society in Europe in its Progress from Rudeness to Refinement or Inquiries concerning the History of Laws, Government and Manners* (Edinburgh, 1778), esp. pp. 46, 50, 57, 64, 70–1, 306–7.

19 *Oxford English Dictionary* (2nd edn, ed. J. A. Simpson and E. S. C. Weiner), iv (Oxford, 1989), 85; S. Johnson, *A Dictionary of the English Language* (London, 1755; facsimile edn Harlow, 1990), i, *sub* croisade, croisade, crusade; C. Tyerman, *The Invention of the Crusades*, (London, 1998) pp. 112, 155; , G. Dickson, *The Children's Crusade* (London, 2008), pp. 171, 234, note 52.

20 D. Diderot, *Dictionnaire encyclopédique, Oeuvres complètes* (Paris, 1821), xiv, 496–511.

21 Voltaire, *History of the Crusades* (trans. London, 1753), pp. 49, 52, 54, 57, 59, 66, 74, 76, 84–5, 88, 91–2, 95, 108–10, 114, 119, 127; *idem, The General History and State of Europe* (Eng. trans. London, 1754), *Of the East*

and the Crusades, pp. 189, 258–307, 315, 322; L. Albina, 'Voltaire et ses sources historiques', *Dix-Huitième Siècle*, 13 (1981), 349–59; J. M. Brumfitt, *Voltaire: Historian* (Oxford, 1970), esp. pp. 4, 6, 37, 45, 68, 72, 82–4.

22 G. T. F. Raynal, *Histoire philosophique et politique des établissements et du commerce des Européens dans les deux Indes* (Geneva, 1780 [1st edn Amsterdam, 1770]), vol. 10, esp. 334, 415–16, 458–9; the work was heavily influenced by Diderot, who collaborated in some of the text.

23 Gibbon, *Decline and Fall*, vii, 349, note 69 (cf. p. 188 and the teasing comment on the empathetic limits of 'the cold philosophy of modern times').

24 David Hume, *History of England from the Invasion of Julius Caesar to the Revolution of 1688* (1st published London, 1754–61, medieval vol. 1761; edition used London, 1796), esp. pp. 186–90, 197–9, 291–2, 301–14, 442–3. For Hume's books touching on the crusades, *Hume Library*, pp. 35, 41, 91, 112, 125, 127, 131, 135.

25 Robertson, *Progress*, p. 25; Stuart, *View of Society*, p. 64.

26 Adam Ferguson, *An Essay on the History of Civil Society* (Edinburgh, 1767), Part III, section VII ('On the History of Arts'); Part V, 'On the Decline of Nations', section II, 'Of the temporary efforts and relaxations of the National Spirit' and section V; for Robertson using Ferguson by 1769, *Progress*, p. 170.

27 *Letters of Edward Gibbon*, ed. J. E. North (London, 1956), Gibbon to J. B. Holroyd, 7 August 1773; J. Burrow, *A History of Histories* (London, 2007), p. 339.

28 Robertson, *Progress*, pp. 21–8.

29 Robertson, *Progress*, p. 170.

30 Adam Smith, *An Inquiry into the Nature and Causes of the Wealth of Nations*, ed. R. H. Campbell *et al.* (Oxford, 1976), i, 406.

31 Adam Smith, *Lectures in Jurisprudence*, ed. R. L. Meek *et al.* (Oxford, 1978), p. 549.

32 John Callander of Craigforth, *The Correspondence of Adam Smith*, ed. E. C. Mossner and I. S. Ross (Oxford, 1987), p. 191, note 2; he also alleged that Smith had said that Robertson 'was able to form a good outline but he wanted industry to fill up the plan'.

33 Robertson, *Progress*, pp. 21–31, 64.

34 Gibbon, *Decline and Fall*, vii, 188.

35 Gibbon, *Decline and Fall*, vii, chaps LVIII and LIX, 178–277.

36 Gibbon, *Decline and Fall*, vii, 277.

37 Gibbon, *Decline and Fall*, vii, chaps LX and LXI, 278–357.

38 For the assessment of Fleury, *Decline and Fall*, vii, 186, note 21 and in general Gibbon's notes to chapters LVIII–LXI; cf. *Library of Gibbon*, pp. 43–4, 63, 67, 77, 85, 125, 133, 141, 144, 147, 156, 158, 162, 169, 170, 179, 189, 200, 202, 203, 239, 252–3, 259, 262, 275, 279.

39 F. Schiller, *Über Volkwänderung, Kreuzzüge und Mittelalter, Werke*, ed. R. Roxberger (Berlin and Stuttgart, 1886).

40 Gibbon, *Decline and Fall*, vii, 228.

41 Stuart, *View of Society*, pp. 306–7; *Library of Gibbon*, p. 259.

42 Gibbon, *Decline and Fall*, vii, 348.

43 Gibbon, *Decline and Fall*, vii, 349 (cf. the echo of Smith, note 30 above); see David Womersley's edition of *Decline and Fall* (London, 1994), introduction, pp. xcviii–ci for a relevant discussion.
44 Below, Chapter 4.
45 Burrow, *History of Histories*, p. 349.

4

Empathy and materialism: keeping the crusades up to date

During a course of lectures delivered in Munich in 1855, Heinrich von Sybel (1817–95) reflected on writers on the crusades. He had made his name a decade and a half earlier demolishing the reputation of William of Tyre and Albert of Aachen as reliable sources for the First Crusade and now suggested that 'every new commentator must find fresh subject for interest and instruction according to his own requirements and inclinations'.[1] The legacy of the Enlightenment had established the crusades as a reference point for cultural commentary as much on contemporary as on medieval society. Writers responded in broadly two ways, complementing or contradicting the judgementalism of the *philosophes*. The essentially materialist analysis, that decried religious fanaticism while observing the crusades' positive or negative contribution to the progress of civilisation, was challenged by a new eagerness to empathise with medieval attitudes, an emotional or political reaction to rational orderliness and disdain, even to the point of sentimental approval. This conflict was rarely neat, either between authors or within one writer's own work. New, romantic enthusiasm for knightly piety and bravery could be tempered by dislike of violence and disappointment with arcane systems of belief and observance. Religious enthusiasm could play in favour of or against the crusaders' reputation. Some keen to avoid anachronistic modern condemnation nevertheless drew parallels with contemporary developments in relations between Christian and Muslim powers in the Mediterranean. Materialism and empathy were thus not necessarily discrete interpretations but could combine together in new syntheses.

Nonetheless, the most striking feature of post-Enlightenment investigation of the crusades was, as von Sybel had hinted, a willingness to marry the crusades to contemporary obsessions and experience. Just as the Reformation had done, so the French and Industrial Revolutions fundamentally recast debates and understanding of crusading's nature and significance. The crusades could be regarded as the antithesis of modernism, whether that was considered good or bad, matching an astonishing range of political and cultural developments: the idea, consequences and desirability of material progress; the place of religion in secular society; the tensions of nationalism and international community; extra-European conquest and colonialism; the dominance of western European culture; Christian missionaries; the aesthetics of romanticism and medievalism and the politics of reaction; the rise of popular mass movements; the emergence of critical scholarship and the academic professsion. Changes in education provided a large readership encouraging both fiction and popular and academic history. Small wonder novelists, painters, dramatists and musicians were attracted to the subject. More significantly, again as von Sybel, a Rhenish liberal later committed to a Prussian unification of Germany, observed, the crusades could be regarded as 'one of the greatest revolutions that has ever taken place in the history of the human race', a view essentially shared by Joseph-François Michaud, a conservative Roman Catholic romantic French nationalist whose uncritical history von Sybel nevertheless deplored.[2] In nineteenth-century Europe, revolution was neither neutral in word nor deed. To it or from it historians were attracted or repelled, their responses to Jacobinism, anti-clericalism, atheism, Bonapartism, legitimism, counter-revolution or the Rights of Man colouring their attitude to the crusade. Dismissive disdain was replaced by protean identification with, in the words of a recent observer, 'Crusading itself as a re-enactment of the past and a metaphor of the future'.[3]

Revolution and reaction: Bonaparte, Chateaubriand and crusade revival

While of very different stamp to von Sybel, François-René Chateaubriand (1768–1848) was more influential. Where von Sybel stands at the head of a tradition of critical textual scholarship, Chateaubriand inspired a new positive empathy with the beliefs and emotions of the crusaders that avoided the condescension of most commentators since the Reformation. His insights came from a complicated, some might argue confused set of responses to the events of his life: a rejection of the aridity of the *philosophes* that had produced the Jacobin Terror; a belief in the virtues and genuine uplifting power of religion for individuals and societies alike; an abhorrence of tyranny; respect for hierarchy and tradition; and a belief in liberty. These possibly divergent positions echoed the accommodations and rhetorical flexibility of the Bonapartist regime with which Chateaubriand had an equivocal and changing relationship, from exile, to protégé, to critic. However unwittingly, Chateaubriand and Bonaparte initiated two of the most influential nineteenth-century developments in nineteenth-century crusade studies: interest in the crusades as a Christian-cultural mission and a precursor of new direct western European political engagement with the Muslim world and the Near East.

Bonaparte's Egyptian and Syrian campaign of 1798–99 was the first western invasion of the Levant since Louis IX's in 1248–50. Although bizarrely portrayed as a war of liberation, an attempt to create a new brotherhood of man on the Nile, the French foray stimulated new fascination not only with the suitably distant and hence apolitical Ancient Egypt, but also in the scenes of the crusades, not least as Bonaparte led his troops to besiege Acre, and in colonisation. While Bonaparte expressly repudiated the legacy of crusading as morally decadent, the eastern opportunities his expedition revealed inevitably stimulated the search for historical parallels. Chateaubriand reported, provocatively, that during his visit to Jerusalem in 1806, the Armenian patriarch told him over coffee that 'all Asia awaited the arrival of the French' and that the reappearance of just a single French soldier would provoke a general uprising against the Turkish authorities.[4] Although Bonaparte's campaign incidentally ended the last crusader order-state, when the Knights of St John on Malta surrendered to the passing French armada, it encouraged observers to place the crusades in what some fondly believed was the inexorable ascent of civil society to liberty, equality and fraternity. Such attitudes were fuelled by the almost contemporaneous, and apparently fortuitous, rediscovery of Leibniz's 1672 proposal for a French conquest of Egypt. This first resurfaced c. 1795 and was circulated among the French military top brass. Although it was forwarded to Bonaparte in August 1798, he does not seem to have read the abridged version until after his return from the east. It reached a wider audience through an English summary published as part of anti-Bonaparte agitation in 1803. Although not, as the English edition implied, part of a long-standing plan for French Mediterranean domination, the Leibniz rediscovery was timely. Reassessment of the crusades, reflecting the meeting of politics and history, now appeared under the guise of academic enquiry. One commentator, with an ear for contemporary resonance, summed up the results of the crusades in 1808 as the creation of a Third Estate, 'le foyer de la vraie civilisation', a conceit of more significance in Napoleon's Europe than St Louis's.[5]

In 1806, the French Institut in Paris offered a prize for a monograph on 'the influence of the crusades on the civil liberty of the people of Europe, on their civilisation, on the progress of learning [*lumières*, literally 'enlightenment'], commerce and industry'. While directly reflecting Enlightenment concerns, the issues also spoke to the self-proclaimed progressive political and cultural agenda of post-Revolutionary Napoleonic France. The influence of Robertson was implicit in the title and his work was mined by a number of entrants. However, this was not an isolated or uniquely French interest; other academies had offered similar or related prizes. In 1798 at Göttingen, the liberal university founded in 1734 by the elector of Hanover, King George II of England, a prize on the age of the crusades had been won by a precocious twenty-one-year-old German orientalist Friedrich Wilken with a thesis on Abu al-Fida's account of the crusades. This later formed the kernel of his massive seven-volume history. One of the winners of the Paris 1806 prize, announced in 1808, Arnold Hermann Ludwig Heeren, was a Göttingen professor. Another candidate, whose entry got lost in the post, was a Dutchman and future professor of Theology at Leiden, Jan Hendrik Regenbogen, who, in search of regional colour, emphasised the role of Frisians in the enterprise. Given the state of general warfare at the time, it is perhaps surprising that only one entry got mislaid; Heeren's reached Paris via Copenhagen and running the English blockade. The key to success, however, was not national affiliation, but the level of enthusiasm for the positive material effects of the crusades, a stance that united Heeren and his French co-winner, Maxime de Choiseul Daillecourt. Jacques-Joseph Lemoine's more Gibbonian criticism may explain why he was only a runner-up. The entrants reflected the international appeal of the subject, Heeren's orginal German having to be translated into French before submission, while the luckless Regenbogen wrote in Latin.[6]

Most of the entries subsequently published (1808–9) reveal the absorption of Robertson's instrumental interpretation of the crusades evident in the prize's title. Essentially they were continental versions of what became known in English historiography as 'Whig' history, a judgemental approach characterised by a teleological use of the past to illustrate or even vindicate the present, founded on an assumption of inexorable, usually material progress towards a better state than had previously existed. The value of events and people were gauged according to how far they served or hindered this ineluctable process. Choiseul Daillecourt, an aristocrat in his twenties who later served as a prefect under Louis Philippe and became a member of the Institut/Academy, was to write a highly Whiggish book (in 1844) comparing the English 'revolution of 1688' with that of 1830 in France. His 1806 essay was similarly Whiggish, avoiding debates on the morality of the crusades and confident in their utilitarian role in furthering the progress of western civilisation in commerce, culture and social change. However, he also noted their achievements of heroic belief, in a tradition that stretched back at least to Louis Maimbourg, thus combining two dominant motifs in future crusade histories: materialism and romanticism.

This cocktail of apparent scholarly objectivity spiked with somewhat formal doses of empathy was the formula pursued by other entrants. They regarded study of the crusades as part of a wider project aimed at charting the progress of European civilisation which had assumed a very different aspect after 1789. The lofty intellectual advocacy of abstract liberty by the *philosophes* was replaced with an analysis of the concrete social, political and economic bases for liberty in practice, an unavoidable commentary on the contemporary scene. The crusades were placed beside other moments or movements generating change, such as the Reformation. In this project the writers of 1806 were generally dependent less on their own original researches (of which there is almost no evidence in any of the prize essays) but on reorienting the information and conclusions of the historians of the previous centuries, authorities cited including Pasquier, Bongars, Fleury, Voltaire, Mailly, Sainte-Palaye, de Guignes and Gibbon as well as Robertson. There was almost unanimous agreement on the centrality of the crusades to the growth of trade; the development of urban life; the decline in feudal hierarchies; the end of serfdom; the rise, in France at least, of royal power; western access to eastern learning as well as goods; a new interest in and knowledge of Asia and an awareness of wide global geography that led to the impetus towards the discoveries of sea routes to southern Africa, the Far East and the New World. The crusades were regarded as helping transform western society, its manners as well as institutions, stimulating a greater civility. So much, so Robertson. In this account, the crusades inevitably possessed 'a great practical interest' for contemporaries (Heeren) and, in humanist vein, taught lessons for the both present and future (Lemoine).[7] Even the one obviously dissenting voice, Lemoine, acknowledged the positive and broad influences of the crusades, although, in clear imitation of Gibbon, concluding that the balance sheet was negative, the crusades 'an evil', 'without sufficient compensation for humanity'. However, the judges of the 1806 prize appeared to have been preconditioned by the newly fashionable Robertsonian view. Lemoine's entry was not obviously less well written or well researched than the others. He was clearer than the others in his description of the historiographical traditions: medieval writers seeing the crusades in religious terms as legitimate and salutary; later writers regarding them as 'pious follies'; and, latterly, others, such as Robertson, accepting them as 'necessary' and positive in result if not action. That his ultimately hostile assessment received only an 'honourable mention' is unsurprising as the 1806 competition was run against a backdrop of official academic concern to promote the history of the crusades.[8]

Although the Maurists had been swept away by the

Revolution, their scheme for a collection of crusade texts was refloated at one of the earliest meetings of the post-Revolution Institut de France in 1796. Two years later, its proposer, the national archivist Armand Gaston Camus, returned to the idea, arguing that interest in the crusading period lay especially in the mutual influence between east and west, a hot topic in the year of Bonaparte's invasion of Egypt. This was to be no parade of the crusades as a French national trophy. Arabic and Greek texts formed an integral part of Camus's plan. The emphasis on eastern texts lay behind a resurrection of Camus's proposal in 1807, at the very time the Institut was considering the crusade prize entries, when the orientalist Silvestre de Sacy reported on the state of Dom Berthereau's surviving papers. However, despite a committee being established to consider a new crusade collection, nothing was done due to the hard bargaining over the price of Berthereau's papers by his family; the labour of effecting new translations from the very few remotely competent Arabists available; and Napoleon's indifference. By the time the plan was revived in the early 1830s not only was the political climate much altered, so too were attitudes towards the crusades, by then regarded as the especial preserve of France.[9]

The shift from regarding the crusades as a staging post in the development of European civilisation in general to an enterprise intrinsically and predominantly a glorious episode in French history represented an apparent break with the Enlightenment debates of Gibbon and Robertson. The new approach was characterised by three elements. It sought to understand the crusades on their own terms though an exercise in often imaginative, speculative or downright fanciful empathy, typical of the new romanticism of the period. Informed by an unembarrassed embrace of religion, it fundamentally rejected Enlightenment dismissal of faith as scarcely explicable superstition encouraging fanaticism. Finally, Islam in general and Turkish rule in particular were denigrated, even demonised as violent, corrupt, decadent and antithetical to freedom, progress and civilisation, a view by no means novel but which took on new force as western, especially French, rulers began to turn their political ambitions towards the lands of the Muslim Mediterranean.

Pivotal to this realignment of perspective was Chateaubriand.

A royalist and reconvert to Roman Catholicism, Chateaubriand's highly influential *Génie de christianisme* (published 1802) sought to refute and overturn Enlightenment analysis by arguing that Christianity was not only true and excellent in itself but essential to the progress of arts and learning. The Christian middle ages preserved and nurtured civilisation after the fall of Rome. The crusades and the military orders were exemplary manifestations of the strength and virtue of faith in defiance of ignorance and barbarism. Chateaubriand developed this argument in his account of his travels in Greece and the Near East in 1806, *Itinéraire de Paris à Jérusalem*, published in 1811. Chateaubriand imagines himself as a medieval pilgrim reborn. His responses to people, places and events are emotional, sentimental and empathetic. His virulent, rancid contempt for Islam and its destructive influence is rampant throughout. To underline his insistence that Islam preaches only hate and tyranny (Christianity, by contrast, apparently espousing only peace and tolerance), he compares Muslim despotism and greed to that of French republican soldiers and proconsuls. Turks are portrayed as savages ('sauvages') devastating the landscape; even the olive groves he found in Palestine he attributed to the crusaders of Godfrey de Bouillon. Cultural superiority of the western Christian is assumed and illustrated at every turn.[10]

Chateaubriand begins his account of the crusades themselves in typical style, reflecting on the tombs of the twelfth-century kings of Jerusalem in the Church of the Holy Sepulchre: 'these ashes are French ashes and the only ones buried in the shadow of the Tomb of Jesus Christ. What a title of honour for my homeland!' Observing the so-called footprint of the ascending Jesus displayed to tourists in the Chapel of the Ascension on the Mount of Olives, he imagined that Christ turned his face northwards as if in summons of the northerners who would in the future cleanse the Holy City of 'temples of false gods ... and plant that standard of the cross on the walls of Jerusalem'. Warming to his theme, he directly attacked Hume: 'the crusades were not folly neither in principle nor result'. The crusaders were not the aggressors, merely responding (a few centuries late) to the Arab conquests of the seventh century. They were fighting not just for the Holy Land but against 'a system of ignorance, despotism and slavery', a defensive war to save the world from 'an invasion of new barbarians'. 'Who will dare to say that the cause of these holy wars was unjust?' Not only did the crusaders take the fight to the Muslim heartlands of Asia but in so doing relieved the west of Malthusian population pressure and helped end internal conflict in Europe. They also, and here the debt to Robertson is explicitly acknowledged, promoted progress in learning and civilisation.[11]

Chateaubriand's thesis was not simply nostalgic and retrospective. His sentimental empathy drew him to the present and even the future. He recalled his installation ceremony as a Knight of the Holy Sepulchre, during which initiates were dubbed with the alleged sword of Godfrey de Bouillon; a touristic charade drained of all but snobbish value, more pretentious but no more serious than being photographed with a Beefeater at the Tower of London. 'I was French; Godfrey de Bouillon was French; his own sword, in touching me, filled me with a new love for the glory and honour of my homeland.' Observing the current state of Palestine, he asserted that the land was ripe for a new French invasion. Locals, leaderless and vulnerable, expected it. Bonaparte could have taken Jerusalem 'as easily as a camel in a field of millet'. The grounds for conquest and colonisation were explicit: the tyranny, neglect, corruption and decadence of Turkish rule; the devastation they had wrought on the region; the cultural and moral superiority of western Christians; the depressed and enervated state of eastern Christians infected by the habits of 'these stupid Musulmans' who could not even manage to emulate the Ancient Egyptians in making the Nile valley prosper. Later, describing his visit to Tunis on his return journey, he drew a direct colonial parallel with the crusades and the memory of St Louis who had died there: 'lucky the people who are able to glory in saying ... he was the king of my fathers!' Contemporary colonial experience was evoked, if playfully: 'our sailors say that in new colonies the Spanish begin by building a church, the English a pub and the French a fort – to which I add a ballroom'. Despite this playfulness, the message was clear and echoed that of Leibniz's recently rediscovered project: the crusades stood as a model for future western conquest of Muslim lands in the eastern Mediterranean, an enterprise at once beneficial, necessary and praiseworthy.[12]

Chateaubriand's refashioning of the crusades was not entirely the product of his own sensibilities, prejudices or literary and religious fancies. His published pilgrimage account owed much to earlier or contemporary descriptions, studies and travelogues of the Near East, even if he did not always acknowledge his debt. In places, he deliberately falsified his originality, claiming that in 1806 Jerusalem had almost been forgotten, almost in an echo of Burke's comment on the demise of Marie Antoinette: 'as there are no more knights, it seems there is no more Palestine'. In fact, the eighteenth century produced over 300 published works on the Holy Land, fifty or so in French.[13] Chateaubriand's primary sources included both Robert of Rheims and, no less suited to his approach, Tasso, used indiscriminately as a historical document. Of more modern writers, he cited Maimbourg, a fellow patriot in matters crusading, and clearly had read the main Enlightenment texts. He may have read Robertson's *Progress*, available in French since 1771, but certainly used the Scotsman's later *Historical Disquisition concerning the Knowledge which the Ancients had of India* (first published Edinburgh, 1791) which summarised his theory of the crusades, commerce and the advance of civilisation.[14] It is possible that he became acquainted with the range of Anglophone Enlightenment commentary whilst in exile in England in the 1790s, at precisely the time that he was being drawn back to Roman Catholicism.

Not all were convinced by Chateaubriand's sentimental empathy, glorification of past French heroics, assertion of western cultural superiority, bigoted dismissal of Islam and racist condemnation of the Turks. One reviewer took him to task for his insulting depiction of Islam, his selective scouring of the Koran for texts advocating violence and his crude attribution of bad government to religion rather than politics.[15] Chateaubriand's views were never universally accepted. The poet and politician Alphonse de Lamartine, who visited the eastern Mediterranean in 1832–33, rejected his predecessor's combination of 'Gospel and Crusades' and became very impressed by the simplicity of Islamic theology, a sort of purified Christianity ('un christianisme purifié'), and by the achievements of Muhammed.[16] However, Chateaubriand's central tenets of French glory, respect for the crusaders' faith and the beneficence of their legacy convinced one journalist friend, literary entrepreneur and political ally who became, perhaps somewhat improbably, the most influential, although not universally admired, crusade authority of his time whose legacy still casts a not entirely benign shade on attitudes to the wars of the cross.

Michaud: romance, nation and empire

In 1805, the fashionable novelist, the genteel widow Sophie Cottin (1773–1807), published her fourth romantic novel, *Mathilde ou Mémoires tirés de l'histoire des croisades*, a laborious but very popular fiction set during the Third Crusade, a Tasso-esque exotic tale of royal lovers across enemy lines and of faith-conquering love conquering all. One of the publishers, Joseph François Michaud (1767–1839), who had previously advised the author to consult Tasso, provided a substantial historical preface tracing the story of the crusades from the First to the Third Crusades. From this early sketch he developed a plan for a major new narrative of the crusades to the Holy Land, based on primary materials, shorn of Protestant or Enlightenment condescension and disdain. This grew into his monumental *Histoire des croisades* (1811–22 but under constant revision until his death and the definitive posthumous edition of 1841), a literary and academic achievement that led to his election to the French Academy. Parallel to his construction of an epic narrative, Michaud also presided over the production of four volumes of translated western and eastern sources, *Bibliothèque des croisades* (1829), including western texts largely derived uncritically from Bongars and others, and a fourth volume of Arabic translations by Joseph-Toussaint Reinaud (1795–1867). By the time he died, Michaud felt confident enough to proclaim that 'more honest scholarship and the experience of great revolutions' had exposed the ideas of the Enlightenment as ignorant and wrong. Now, he declared, 'everybody agrees what the crusades were and what they produced', that is, they agreed with him.[17] While untrue, nonetheless Michaud transformed attitudes to the crusades, rendering them as fashionably acceptable to nineteenth-century audiences as they had been equally fashionably unacceptable the century before.

Michaud had enjoyed a chequered career as a royalist pamphleteer and journalist in the 1790s, twice condemned to death by the Republic and frequently imprisoned for his strongly legitimist Bourbon views, the last occasion as late as 1800. He had previously tried his hand at history with a book on India which included an account of the 1798–99 French invasion of Egypt, a pointer to his later interest in medieval colonialism. For Michaud, the crusades offered a familiar but apparently apolitical and safely distant subject with which to capture a lucrative audience while promoting his far from neutral ideas about western religion, culture, civilisation and France. Whilst by no means as uncritically enthusiastic as Chateaubriand, Michaud combined admiration for the crusaders' idealism and condemnation of Islam with a novelist's eye for empathetic romance and fictional narrative. His ideas developed over time. Experience of the east during a tour in 1830–31 sharpened the focus of his assertion of Christian European supremacy and his identification of the crusades as precedents, even justifications, for colonialism and cultural imperialism. Michaud's *Histoire* attracted great popularity, going into four editions by 1830, a sixth by 1841, a ninth in 1856 and a total of nineteen by the end of the century, as well as translations into English, German, Italian and Russian.

Crusade writing of this period has been described as 'une historiographie engagée'.[18] Michaud's project was immensely assisted by the use made of the medieval past by successive French regimes. Michaud, having received the Légion d'Honneur from Napoleon in 1812 and becoming a member of the Academy in 1814, served as a deputy after the Bourbon restoration. His vision of past French greatness under the benevolent leadership of a sainted Christian monarchy chimed precisely with Bourbon efforts to refashion a French past to obscure the trauma of Revolution and febrile glory of the empire. Louis XVIII revived the Order of St Louis. Charles X evoked the saintly crusaders in his propaganda before the Algerian invasion of 1830. Under the Orleanist government after 1830, the crusades, now seen in Michaud-esque terms as a particularly French achievement, were employed as an image binding together the different strands of French society and politics. Louis-Philippe's government sought to promote a glorious common past that embraced rich and poor, merchants and knights, clergy and laity in a unique show of French spirit and potential. This received tangible visual form in the decoration and paintings in the elaborate *Salles des croisades* (from 1837) at Versailles. Michaud profitably exploited this fashion, enjoying royal patronage, even if his support for freedom of speech made him an awkward client for the increasingly repressive Bourbons in the late 1820s. By the time he came to the final revision of his *Histoire* in the 1830s, Michaud's history and events of his own time seemed to have converged. At the start of his journey to the Near East in 1830, a trip subsidised by Charles X's government, he saw the French Algerian invasion fleet at Toulon, later described by his travelling companion, along with the subsequent campaigns there, as 'nothing other than crusades'.[19] For Michaud, it can reasonably be claimed, with Benedetto Croce, that all history was contemporary history.

The crusades in early nineteenth-century France were politics. Michaud's success cannot be understood without this context. Current debates repeatedly forced their way into his history: the Revolution, Bonaparte, the virtues of monarchy, the destiny of France. However, the crusades were not just hijacked by conservatives, reactionaries, royalists and those, like Michaud, on the Right. There existed a wider set of ideas inherited from the Enlightenment that Michaud also mined, one that operated beyond local political conflict and embraced more extensive cultural warfare. The medieval past could be appreciated both by conservatives as a model of an ordered Christian hierarchic community (the view attacked by the *philosophes*) and, by liberals, as a period of dynamism and progressive change, as in the 1806 prize. Michaud tried to resolve the tension inherent between these apparently contradictory views. Partly, this was achieved by falling back on a reshaped version of the old Enlightenment paradox of unintended good results from evil or malign causes. Michaud argued that calamitous events, such as revolutions, could, by providential design (i.e. God's), 'enlighten mankind to ensure the future prosperity of empires'.[20] Thus the French Revolution and its consequences resulted in a strengthening of the French monarchy (not least by exposing the alternatives) and thus the crusades – seen by Michaud as revolutionary – although military failures, enhanced civilisation. While appreciative of faith, Michaud rejected slavish Roman Catholic devotion to superstitious practices, was sceptical of miracles and even-handedly critical of crusader atrocities. He preferred to draw attention to wider admiration of such intangible (or impenetrable) obscurities such as 'l'esprit des croisés' and, following Robertson, to stress consequences as much as causes. The action of the crusades encouraged empathy through a powerful narrative constructed on an uncritical and manipulative use of contemporary primary sources, reinforced by imaginative flights of invention and fancy.

However, when noting the results of the crusades, the account was elevated from the battlefield to a conceptual plane where moral value was assessed far above any crude balance sheet of victory or defeat. Here, the march of civilisation supplied its own positive verdict. The friction between the crusades as exemplars either of hierarchy or progress was removed by using the infinite elasticity of a central assertion. The enemy of civilisation was not Christian religion or institutions, moribund tradition, or, alternatively, revolutionary progress, but moral weakness producing social servility, despotism, decadence and a 'politics of violence'.[21] The enemy, Michaud relentlessly insisted, was Islam, no longer a metaphor for the *ancien régime*, but a past and present danger: stagnant, unchanging, menacing and barbaric. Against this enemy, the polemical quibbles of earlier historians melted away. The crusades were no longer either hindrances or encouragements to the progress of civilisation; they *were* the battle for civilisation itself. Nevertheless, few alert readers would miss the additional modern parallel between Muslims and republicans. The crusades were a time of revolution, the consequence of a time of 'confusion and decadence that favoured the invasion of new ideas, especially when those ideas appear supported by the sword'.[22] Although a description of the epoch of Arab conquests, this could just as easily be applied to the period of the Revolution and Napoleon. Thus crusaders were also good monarchists, heroic champions of the virtues of the *ancien régime*. Michaud's casting of the crusades simultaneously as a battle against the barbarism of Islam, a demonstration of the superiority of western culture and a vindication of conservative religious and political values, placed crusade studies on a new footing, not entirely to their advantage. The idea of the crusades as a witness to western supremacy reflected and informed the creation of the colonial mentality in France. The portrait of crusading as mortal combat with a degraded almost demonised Islam, was one that when, literally, translated into Arabic produced ideological and rhetorical consequences still being played out in modern political conflicts. Michaud was never and is not neutral. Perhaps uniquely among crusade historians, his ideas, work and their transmission in Europe, America and the Muslim Near East over the following two centuries repay the serious attention of students of modern international affairs. A recent website commentary dedicated to crusader historians could not have been more wrong to say that 'given Michaud's 'romantic' approach to the subject, his works are now mostly of value to modern scholars of medievalism'.[23] The author could, as easily, have added 'and to students of al-Qaeda'.

Michaud may have transformed the reception of the crusades as glorious and exciting episodes of western, especially French, history, establishing them firmly in the popular literary imaginations (as well as sales). Yet he was tapping into existing interest and employing, even where condemning, previous scholarship and commentary. Shortly before his death, he claimed that he had studied 'all the chronicles, all the documents'.[24] This may be the case, and his appendices of documents are full and interesting. However, his narrative is founded on uncritical acceptance of the obvious chronicles, such as William of Tyre who looms large in the early volumes. The primary sources are largely those in Bongars, plus Tasso and some documentary material such as the Jersualem *Assises*. Even so, as von Sybel unkindly pointed out in 1841, Michaud lifted part of his account of the council of Clermont from a secondary, sixteenth-century text.[25] Indeed, Michaud's method was as much that of a novelist as of a historian, somewhere between the historical narrative of Thomas Macaulay and the evocative fiction of Walter Scott, as in dramatic episodes such as the scaling of the walls of Antioch. Here the primary sources are merely a starting point to construct an almost cinematic visual tableau: clouds scudding across the night sky, a howling wind deafening the sentries, a comet illuminating the sky, all inventions of Michaud.[26] This willingness to embroider (such as placing Peter the Hermit at Clermont) makes Michaud readable but misleading. In his general analysis of the consequences of the crusades, he stays firmly wedded to the Robertsonian orthodoxy, hardly straying from the detailed schema established by the 1806 prize entrants in claiming the crusades' centrality in the progress of European society from barbarism to manners, from violent anarchy to civil liberty. His general reading was similarly predictable: Maimbourg, Sainte-Palaye (whose corps of eternal knight errants make another appearance), 'judicious' Robertson, but also Francis Bacon and Leibniz's Egyptian treatise, as well as contemporary authors, such as Henry Hallam's *A View of the State of Europe during the Middle Ages* (1818). Michaud's erudition, such as it was, was conventional, antiquarian, designed to appeal to and appease the tastes of his customers. For Michaud the crusades constituted nothing less than 'a vast and mysterious enterprise which had as its goal the conquest and civilisation of Asia'.[27] However, beyond an exhaustive, vivid, coherent and compelling story well told, two features marked out his *Histoire* and secured its lasting significance: a contemporary agenda wrapped up in the concept of 'la France en Orient'; and throughout a unifying concern with what he called 'le monde moral'.[28]

In the final version of the *Histoire*, published in 1841 but largely complete by the time of Michaud's death two years earlier, these elements reached mature refinement. In a neat inversion of previous historiography, Michaud presented himself as the rationalist in contrast to the ignorant prejudices of the *philosophes*. He traced his own intellectual journey to uncover what he claimed had been twenty-five years earlier a hidden and obscure historical episode. Instead of focusing on the nature of the crusades, Michaud, somewhat misleadingly, claimed to be more interested in events and consequences. Hence his eagerness to complement his researches with a physical journey to the scenes of the Holy Land crusades in 1830–31, an experience that informed his descriptions of past events, especially the establishment of western colonies. Not only did Michaud's tour lead to changes in his accounts of the main military expeditions, it also confirmed his view of an unchanging east – 'the same people, the same customs, the same languages as at the time of the crusades' – ripe for present as for past colonisation.[29]

The frame of a clash of religions and civilisations was quickly established at the beginning of Book One, an account of the history of Palestine from New Testament times, through the Arab invasions, with its consequent 'symptoms of decadence', Byzantine wars and on to the western Holy Land pilgrims of the eleventh century. Location became a key literary device to lend clarity and force to the narrative. However, the conceptual drive was no less insistent. Comparing western Europeans to Byzantines and Near Eastern Muslims on the eve of the crusades, Michaud set out his theory of western supremacy: 'the barbarism of western peoples in no way resembled that of the Turks, whose religion and customs denied all hope of civilisation or learning, nor that of the Greeks, who were nothing more than a corrupted people'.[30] Westerners possessed honour and chivalry which encouraged justice and virtue; religious enthusiasm produced saints and heroes; western Christianity inspired good customs and laws and a fierce desire to defend the faith, especially in France, 'une nation belliqueuse'.[31] In a literary tradition that went back through writers such as Pasquier to contemporary commentators on the First Crusade itself, crusading was depicted as particularly the preserve of the French who provided the example followed by other nations. Equally, it was in France that most benefits from the crusades accrued. The crusades encouraged material progress of civilisation, perfected chivalry, civil liberties, the beneficent influence of the church and the power of the monarchy, significantly branded as 'the only hope of peoples' against the power of social and institutional elites, the essential focus of national identity. France, Michaud confidently asserted, became the 'model and centre of European civilisation', a 'happy revolution' (presumably in contrast to the unhappy one of 1789 or even 1830) to which, since their very start, the holy wars had contributed much. Thus the crusades were secured as determinant features of the ascent of Europe and the greatness of France.[32]

Michaud's message transcended the Eurocentric navel-gazing of the *philosophes*, who, for all their self-conscious internationalism, globalism even, in fact were obsessively constrained by the history and culture of their own civilisation. Not only were Michaud's crusades affairs not of Man but of God, and therefore not comparable to ordinary human events, they possessed an inescapable aggressive and acquisitive dimension. Wars between Christianity and Islam were wars 'of extermination'. As well as being most bloody, the character of religious wars made the acquisition and maintenance of conquests more difficult. The material element in crusading was implicit from the start, the promise of earthly wealth and power matching the spiritual rewards. While defending Christianity wherever it was threatened 'against those who rejected its laws and beneficence', piety was always mingled with commerce and conquest. Specifically, the 'Christian colonies' of Outremer 'were for the Franks like a new homeland ... another France, dear to all Christians, which one might call *La France en Orient*'.[33] Moreover, the 'astonishing triumphs' of the crusaders caused Muslims to believe what at times it seems Michaud himself did, that 'the Franks were a race superior to the rest of mankind'. In an almost mystical trope, Michaud repeatedly referred to the design of providence in bringing together east and west, a direct nod at nineteenth- as much as twelfth- and thirteenth-century colonisation, Outremer becoming 'the Christian empire in Asia'. By the end of his life, Michaud was explicit: 'What has occurred at the time of writing has proved to us that the vows of St Louis were a form of prophetic revelation of the designs of providence which has thrust Christian Europe into this now worm-eaten Muslim East.' Musing that crusading seemed to be beginning again, Michaud described the ultimate goal of this providence of which the crusades formed one part as holding 'always the same moral aim: the civilisation of barbaric peoples and the reunion of West and East' in a sort of resurrected version of the Roman Empire, speaking French not Latin and run by Frenchmen. 'The attention of Christian Europe is now fixed on most of the eastern countries where the Frankish warriors planted the cross of Jesus Christ.'[34]

Faith, progress, nation, monarchy and empire were all evoked by Michaud. The upheavals of his own revolutionary era had helped him 'paint with greater truth ('avec plus de verité') the troubles and passions of another period'. The verb is revealing: vivid, imaginative, empathetic. If in an Academician's not Impressionist's style, there is something very visual in Michaud's prose, a dimension wonderfully captured by Gustave Doré's illustrations to the 1877 edition. While new opinions tried to destroy the old France of heroism and religion, Michaud drew the contrast between their goal of an unknown future and the crusaders' marching to conquer the east for Jesus Christ. The parallels were irresistible and Michaud is frank about drawing on the lessons of the evils he had witnessed the better to comprehend the past he wrote about because they revealed to him 'the human heart always the same'.[35] From this Michaud argued that, despite the long years of crusading failure, defeat and retreat, the moral force and superiority of western Christianity and civilisation ensured ultimate success. Religion held the key. In an aside that looked forward to many critical later nineteenth-century assessments of the crusades, Michaud even conceded that the medieval Christian missionary foundations among the 'pagans' and 'savages' proved more lasting that the crusader colonies.[36] However, for Michaud, in contrast to his friend Chateaubriand, religion was important as much as a signifier of an ordered civilised society as for its transcendent claims. It was this superior, ordered, monarchical society that would advance now that the politics of Eurasia had turned, with the east offering fresh colonial opportunities for a restored Christian Europe.

Beside nostalgia for the *ancien régime*, Michaud's vision was intellectually rooted in the past. His identification of the positive consequences of the crusades was almost wholly unoriginal, parroting the ideas and detail of Robertson, Heeren and Daillecourt Choiseul, as he did in his assumption of the almost ubiquitous influence the crusades exerted on the development of western society. His depiction of Islam could have been penned by his friend Chateaubriand. None of them, however, combined Michaud's literary skills as a journalist and publisher of novels with his penchant for research, a writer who could weave source evidence and imaginative invention into a convincing and vivid whole. No little part of Michaud's success was that, like Macaulay and Scott in Britain, or Jules Michelet in France, he could write. However, just as he fed on the preoccupations of his own times, he never escaped his own past or the legacy of the *philosophes*. The latter provided useful Aunt Sallys; through constant belabouring, they showed Michaud's freshness of approach to advantage. Not the least of his achievements was to wrest from the *philosophes* the championing of progress and reason. They, not their anti-revolutionary, Christian opponents, were the real purveyors of bigotry, bias and ignorance. Michaud, by contrast, saw himself as standing for the rationality of source criticism, the objectivity of academic probity and the empirical observation of progress as the undeniable fruits of reasoned faith. This was a very neat reversal.

Michaud and the continuing debate

It was also very effective. Michaud set the tone for a modification, reversal even, of the universal condemnation of the crusades that Robertson's materialist apologia had scarcely contradicted. After all, Robertson thought the crusades malign even if accidentally producing beneficial consequences. Michaud's crusades, for all their horrors, follies and blunders, were in essence events to be wondered at, central to the development of the global supremacy of western European civilisation. An obvious academic challenge, this altered the terms of engagement. The crusades became politicised in an immediate partisan and national fashion inconceivable a century before. Concurrently, riding and encouraging the tide of popular medievalism, Michaud's *Histoire* asked its readers to share the crusaders' hopes, aspirations and fears, to enter their world. One of his cleverest tricks was to pretend that he was writing from an objective, carefully researched, contemporary medieval perspective; that his empathy stemmed from understanding not prejudice. In fact, purple passages of invented imaginative narrative and sculpted analysis according with early nineteenth-century sensibilities and politics drew readers in. Few western European writers on the crusades after the 1830s could entirely be free from a popular backdrop that owed something to Michaud, because his vision of holy war mirrored much of the prevailing self-image of western society. Even the austere young von Sybel had to spend time excoriating Michaud.[37]

This is not say that Michaud was universally accepted, but rather that his ideas became standard interpretations for or against which later writers responded. In particular, his themes of nationalism and colonialism redefined popular as well as academic debate on the crusades. Crusade heroes – St Louis in France, Frederick Barbarossa in Germany, Richard I in England, even Godfrey de Bouillon in newly created (1830) Belgium – were dragooned into the service of national identity. Previously, including in Michaud's own early work, regarded as quintessentially international expressions of Catholic Christendom as a whole, crusading became increasingly nationalised. The new nationalisms of the nineteenth century invented appropriate characteristics derived from a freshly minted past, whether as part of movements for unification, as in Germany and Italy, or in recasting existing nationalities, as in France and Britain in the wake of revolution and industrialisation. Crusade leaders were recruited to symbolise these fresh aspirations. Thus von Sybel, by the 1850s a powerful advocate of strong Prussian leadership of a united Germany, could portray Frederick Barbarossa as a strong Hegelian ruler of vision with 'ideas ... beyond his time', while in the 1870s Bismarck was persuaded to sponsor vain attempts to unearth Barbarossa's grave at Tyre. In this case it was the medieval emperor's heroic and charismatic leadership rather than specifically his crusading that appealed. But such was the prominence now afforded these paladins of holy war that Godfrey de Bouillon, now a 'Belgian', found himself on a plinth in Brussels, and Richard I, most incongruously, rode with raised sword outside the mock-Gothic Mother of Parliaments at Westminster. The virtues these crusaders represented were of generalised national spirit not precise political arrangements. Nonetheless, such reimagining securely incorporated the crusades into national histories and public consciousness.[38]

No less contemporary was Michaud's other central thesis. The notion of European states planted in Asia and Africa reflected contemporary reality. French nineteenth-century colonialism, from Algeria to south-east Asia, under successive regimes from the Bourbon and Orleanist kings to the Second Empire and Third Republic, was consistently decorated with crusading rhetoric and the parallels of crusade history.[39] The German philosopher Georg Friedrich Hegel, lecturing on the philosophy of history in 1822–23, suggested that 'it is the necessary fate of Asiatic Empires to be subjected to the Europeans'.[40] So ubiquitous was the assumption of crusader colonialism that it came to be accepted even in circles that hardly shared Michaud's enthusiasm. Thus, at the end of the century, the English military engineer and first great surveyor of Palestine, Claude Conder, compared Frankish rule in the kingdom of Jerusalem to British rule in India 'under somewhat similar conditions'.[41] Michaud's phrases entered the academic lexicon. Joseph Delaville le Roulx's pioneering study of crusading in the fourteenth century was titled *La France en Orient au quatorzième siècle* (Paris, 1885–86). In France, Michaud's vision framed the approach of a new school of historians investigating what one of them, Emmanuel Rey, called 'this distant national enterprise'. With one eye on promoting current French colonies around the Mediterranean, from the mid-1860s Rey presented a roseate view of Outremer as a 'société franco-syrienne' that embraced both settlers and locals. The new inhabitants 'remained always French', but they adopted some eastern customs and lived under the same legal system ('même droit') as the Syrians. While the Franks/French of Outremer retained an inherent cultural superiority, their rule was marked by paternalism, cooperation, accommodation, tolerance, cohabitation and the sharing of geographic, commercial, social and even religious space in 'a blending of the two societies'. This picture of mutually beneficial colonial harmony was developed further over the next seventy years by other French scholars, notably Gaston Dodu, Louis Madelin and finally René Grousset. Rooted in a more or less uniquely French historiography, Rey's theory nonetheless proved potent through the twentieth century, not least in providing a model to be criticised and dismantled once colonialism and empire ceased to attract intellectual approval. However, its essence derived directly from Michaud.[42]

Michaud's ideas carried less weight outside France, despite the easy export of his nationalist interpretation and the attraction of Robertsonian progress. The German orientalist Friedrich Wilken's massive *Geschichte der Kreuzzüge* (seven volumes, 1807–32) adopted a parallel but entirely different approach in assessing the crusades on their own terms. Basing his account firmly on medieval sources, he gave prominence to Arabic texts and avoided any implied or stated presentist polemic. Elsewhere, the hostile assessment of the Enlightenment persisted, even if in less austere guise, particularly in Protestant and Gibbonian Britain. An influential assessment in the *North British Review* of 1844 of the sixth edition of Michaud's *Histoire* condemned his Roman Catholic 'bigotry', his Bourbon monarchism and his nationalist bias. Yet the debates were rarely as clear-cut as the reviewer imagined, between total 'reprobation' and complete admiration, Michaud versus Gibbon, or Robertson against Voltaire.[43] For example, new Christian evangelical missionary expansionism produced a fresh critical reception both to the positive Robertsonian material gloss and to Enlightenment condemnation. Thus a Church of Ireland clergyman, Charles Foster, in his *Mahometanism Unveiled* (London, 1829), while accepting the fashionable anti-Islamic rhetoric as well as the conclusions of Robertson, Heeren and Daillecourt Choiseul for the importance of the crusades, argued for the agency of providence (i.e. the Christian God) not man. Yet he saw in the crusaders' religious motives not fanaticism but 'political expediency' in resisting the tide of Islam, a 'signal monument', nodding to Hume's famous phrase, of 'divine wisdom' as well as human folly.[44] Conversion was Foster's ideal, which he saw as a beneficial consequence of colonialism, such as British rule in India. Seeing this as based on commercial exploitation, he drew a tenuous link with the crusades not, like Conder, through a parallel with the kingdom of Jerusalem, but as a consequence of the crusades opening western geographic and economic horizons to Africa and Asia. The missionary context, both in Britain and on the continent, fuelled many later assessments. The reviewer in *North Britain Review* cast missionaries as the true modern crusaders, neither ruffians nor fanatics, prone neither to 'sentimental sigh' nor 'romantic dream'.[45] In his *Sketches of the Crusades* (1849), George Etell Sargent, a prolific writer of improving pamphlets, contrasted the depraved character of the medieval crusades with the new 'crusading spirit' of Christian missionaries, 'Gospel crusaders'.[46] The sense among Christian writers or students of the Christian church that the crusades were in some senses a distortion of the New Testament has a long pedigree, and formed and forms one antithetical constant in opposition to the empathetic relativism of the continuing Michaud tradition.

Nevertheless, the main early nineteenth-century battleground remained the competing interpretations represented by Robertson, Michaud and Gibbon, even in Britain, where intellectuals' interest in the crusades was less intense than in France or Germany. Joseph Berington, an unorthodox Roman Catholic priest educated on the continent, was content to paraphrase Fuller, Hume and Gibbon in his *Literary History of the Middle Ages* (1814).The crusades, which 'Europe had long reason to deplore' were 'utterly sterile', their benefits marginal, in no way compensating for the waste of men and treasure. Only in the tangential conquest of Byzantium did the crusades contribute to the development of western culture.[47] The Gibbonian anti-Michaud interpretation received its popular and possibly subtlest advocacy in this period in *The History of the Crusades for the Recovery and Possession of the Holy Land* by Charles Mills (1788–1826), first published in 1820, into a fourth edition by 1828. Mills was an erudite autodidact who wrote one of the key texts for the medieval revival of the early nineteenth century, *The History of Chivalry, or Knighthood and its Times* (1825). Earlier, he had published a widely circulated and translated *History of Muhammedanism* (first edition, 1817) regarded by its non-Islamic readers as comprehensive and definitive, despite its title indicating a fundamental misunderstanding of its subject and its author being apparently unable to read Arabic. The context for Mills's *History of the Crusades* was popular interest in crusading generated for example by Walter Scott's *Ivanhoe* (1819), later pursued in his *Talisman* (1825). Mills skilfully negotiates a path between Gibbonian condemnation and evocative sympathy or, to put it another way, he tries to have his cake and eat it. On the one hand, 'the fair face of religion was besmirched', the crusades 'encouraging the most horrible violence of fanaticism', 'a frightful calamity on the world'. The crusades' relationship to chivalry was a constant theme, crusaders being seen as 'armed devotees' (of a religious cause) not 'gentle knights', lacking the polish of knight errants (again the shadow of Sainte-Palaye). The 'mixture of the apostle and the soldier was a union which reason abhors', the ideal of relieving the Holy Sepulchre 'a romantic superstition'. Yet, on the other hand, participants – 'noble adventurers in arms' – were merely 'deluded'. Despite the enterprise being 'the extremist idea of madness', 'the crusades were not a greater reproach to virtue and wisdom than most of those contests which in every age of the world pride and ambition have given rise to'.[48]

Sitting comfortably in an English tradition of crusade historiography, Gibbon and 'honest Fuller', Mills had read widely if unsystematically in primary sources, including Bongars, Muratori and Duchesne, the main, chiefly English chronicles, some in manuscript, but also translations of Beha al-Din's biography of Saladin and Matthew of Edessa and more esoteric material such as the thirteenth-century French vernacular poet Rutebeuf. The obvious secondary works were also mastered, such as de Guignes.[49] One of Mills's targets was Michaud's recently completed *Histoire*. He announces this at the very start by arguing that, while they may have formed a 'theatre of English chivalry', the crusader states in the Levant 'were colonies of all the states of the west and not of any one in particular; a detail of the *World's Debate* does not naturally form a portion of any single nation', thus dismissing both of Michaud's central insights. Whilst agreeing with Michaud's identification of a holy cause – 'the redemption of the Holy Land' – he insisted that 'no dangers hung over Christendom' in the 1090s.[50] He wholly rejected the Robertsonian thesis. Blood and treasure were wasted for no benefit. Advances in learning were chronologically coincidental. Mills even argued against the prevalent cherished idea that the crusades advanced urban civil liberties, thus going further even than Gibbon. The progress of Italian cities was dismissed as 'insignificant' when compared with the opening of the sea route to India. Confronting Michaud directly, Mills accepted that the crusades were inspired 'for holy objects, not for civil or national ends' but followed Gibbon in final condemnation:

> The crusades retarded the march of civilisation, thickened the clouds of ignorance and superstition, and encouraged intolerance, cruelty and fierceness. Religion lost its mildness and charity, and war its mitigating qualities of honour and courtesy ... We feel no sorrow at the final doom of the Crusades, because in its origin the war was iniquitous and unjust.[51]

Mills's *History* occupied a prominent place in an increasingly extensive discussion of the crusades in Britain, some supposedly academic, others obviously romantic. Although his careful distinction between the virtues of chivalry and the vices of crusaders chimed in with the views of Walter Scott, other medievalist enthusiasts were far less convinced. Some, like the very popular hack writer G. P. R. James in his works on chivalry

(1830) and Richard I (1842–49), accused Mills of ignoring the spirit of the medieval age and of judging the past in terms of modern sensibilities, a very Michaud-type call for empathy. Few took as wholly positive a view of the crusades as Kenelm Digby's *Broad Sword of Honour* (1828–29).[52] Some were content to see the crusades in Michaud's context of cultural conflict and widespread hostility to Islam. Robert Southey, radical turned reactionary, declared that, but for the crusades, 'Mahommedanism would have barbarized the world'.[53] Much impetus to study the crusades in Britain stemmed from the desire to see in medieval chivalry a set of distinctive aristocratic values and behaviour to challenge the utilitarian ethos of industrialisation, the rise of the commercial classes and the emergence of popular politics, although in some ways the extreme violence and alien religiosity of the crusades confused this vision, the 'grand but erring spirit' as Henry Stebbing described it in his *History of Chivalry and the Crusades* (1830).[54]

The crusades' role in the progress of civilisation remained of abiding interest. Frederick Oakeley won the Chancellor's Essay prize in Oxford in 1827 with a meditation on this theme, *The Influence of the Crusades upon the Arts and Literature of Europe*, in focus very similar to the 1806 French prize entries. As late as 1854, *The History of the Crusades* by Major R. E. Proctor (RMA, Sandhurst) is largely a rehash of Mills and Robertson, the crusades at once being 'thoroughly misguided and iniquitous' yet, perhaps confusingly, ultimately and fortuitously, 'very salutary to mankind'.[55] In lectures in the late 1870s and early 1880s, the verdict of one of the most influential English medievalists of the nineteenth century, William Stubbs, Regius Professor of History at Oxford (1866–84) and editor of key English chronicles covering crusading, was far more positive. While admitting material motives of some, which he memorably dubbed 'a sanctified experiment of vikingism', he argued, in terms very similar to Michaud, that others were engaged in 'a war of idea'. Elsewhere, again like Michaud, he drew contemporary parallels, in his case the Crimean War, and, with his French predecessor, assumed that 'the state of Palestine' in the 1860s differed little from the 1090s. For Stubbs, the crusades 'with all their drawbacks were a trial feat of a new world ... striving after a better ideal than that of piracy and fraternal bloodshed'. 'That in the end they were a benefit to the world no one who reads can doubt.'[56]

Tension between material, sentimental, religious and political interpretations ensured intellectual and popular debate, while current affairs suggested a spurious continuing relevance. Academic and pseudo-academic commentators, novelists, polemicists, religious homilists and politicians all derived useful material. Remarkably, the patterns of analysis of the late eighteenth and early nineteenth century have scarcely gone away: empathy; disapproval; relevance; the role of religion; materialist reductionism. Despite the explosion of literary attention, behind the empathetic romanticism of Michaud or the criticism of Mills and Scott, the themes identified by Fuller, Fleury, Hume, Gibbon and Robertson persisted. While the crusades' manifestations in popular culture are beyond the immediate scope of this study, the connection with profound historical trends in the nineteenth century and beyond is not. The tradition of the crusades being of especial interest to conservative, even right-wing scholars and writers was born in the era of Michaud, precisely the period when such political characterisations were first emerging in European public life. The idea of the crusades as explicit precursors to modern events, either as features of teleological historical progress or as parallels to modern actions remains potent. The combination of ideology, action, change, European conquest and religious fanaticism acted as a contrast or a comparison with the tone of revolutionary and reactionary politics. Wars fought for ideas were far from alien concepts in nineteenth-century Europe; still less in the century and more thereafter. While much focus in nineteenth-century crusade historiography settled on nobles, knights and leaders, the involvement of people's armies indicated to some 'a new phase in social history', a 'new mass possibility in human affairs', similar to contemporary democratisation.[57] At the very least, as the issue of past, present and future social, political and economic change lay at the centre of much intellectual and historical debate in the nineteenth century, from Hegel to Macaulay to Marx, the crusades could not fail to attract attention not just of writers of *belles lettres* but also of their more self-consciously academic scholarly colleagues.

Notes

1 Trans. Lady Duff Gordon, *The History and Literature of the Crusades* (London, 1861), pp. 1–2.

2 Duff Gordon, *History and Literature*, p. 1; cf. J. F. Michaud, *Histoire des croisades* (4 vols in 2, Paris, 1857 reprint of the author's final revision, the 6th edn published posthumously in 1841), iv, 199.

3 M. Brett, reviewing E. Siberry, *The New Crusaders* (Aldershot, 2000), www.history.ac.uk/reviews/paper/brettMichael.html, May 2001.

4 F.-R. Chateaubriand, *Itinéraire de Paris à Jérusalem*, ed. E. Malaki (Baltimore MD, Oxford and Paris, 1946), ii, 146; for 1798–99, see, e.g., H. Laurens, *L'expédition d'Egypte, 1798–1801* (Paris, 1997).

5 C. Villers's introduction to A. H. L. Heeren, *Essai sur l'influence des croisades* (Paris, 1808), p. x. For Leibniz, above pp. xxxx and R. Ellenblum, *Crusader Castles and Modern Histories* (Cambridge, 2007), pp. 11–12.

6 Gary Dickson seems to have been the first modern scholar to draw especial attention to this episode, in 1999, see J. Richard, 'National Feeling and the Legacy of the Crusades', in *Palgrave Advances in the Crusades*, ed. H. Nicholson (Basingstoke, 2005), pp. 209–10; more information in Heeren, *Essai*, pp. vii–xix; Choiseul Daillecourt's essay was published in 1809, Lemoine's *Discours* in 1808, both in Paris; Regenbogen's *Commentatio* in Latin, in Amsterdam in 1809; cf. Ellenblum, *Castles*, pp. 3–4.

7 Heeren, *Essai*, p. 69; J. L. Lemoine, *Discours sur cette question proposée par ('Institut de France* (Paris, 1808), p. 3.

8 Lemoine, *Discours*, pp. 32–4, 36–77; pp. 146–65, esp. pp. 164–5.

9 H. Dehéran, 'Les origines de *Recueil des historiens des croisades*', *Journal des Savants*, n.s. 17 (1919), pp. 260, 262–5.

10 *Itinéraire*, i, 146, 329, 335, 336; ii, 35, 53, 130.

11 *Itinéraire*, ii, 103, 118, 129–30, 131.

12 *Itinéraire*, ii, 146, 199–200, 219, 247, 299.

13 *Itinéraire*, i, 1 and note 3.

14 *Itinéraire*, ii, 131.

15 *Itinéraire*, ii, 459, 463–5, 470.

16 *The French Romantics*, ed. D. G. Charlton (Cambridge, 1984), p. 52; Siberry, *New Crusaders*, p. 69.

17 *Histoire*, i, iii–iv. For Michaud's Arabic sources, R. Irwin, 'Orientalism and the Development of Crusader Studies', in *The Experience of Crusading*, ii, *Defining the Crusader Kingdom*, ed. P. Edbury and J. Phillips (Cambridge, 2003), pp. 221–3. Cf. J. Richard, 'De Jean-Baptiste Mailly à Joseph-François Michaud', *Crusades*, 1 (2002), 1–12.

18 D. Denby, 'Les croisades aux XVIIIe et XIXe siècle: une historiographie engagée', in *Les champenois et la croisade*, ed. Y. Bellenger and D. Quéruel (Paris, 1989), pp. 163–70.

19 *Histoire*, i, iv–vi; ii, 173; iv, 343–4; K. Munholland, 'Michaud's *History of the Crusades* and the French Crusade in Algeria under Louis Philippe', in *The Popularization of Images: Visual Culture under the July Monarchy*, ed. P. Ten-Doesschate Chu and G. P. Weisburg (Princeton NJ, 1994), p. 154 and generally pp. 144–65; cf. M. Marrinan, 'Historical Vision and the Writing of History at Louis Philippe's Versailles', in *Popularization of Images*, pp.

113–43; W. C. Jordan, 'Saint Louis in French Epic and Drama', in *Studies in Medievalism*, viii, ed. L. J. Workman and K. Verduin (Cambridge, 1996), 174–94; A. Knobler, 'Saint Louis and French Political Culture', in *Studies in Medievalism*, viii, 156–73; M. Glencross, 'The Cradle and the Crucible: Envisioning the Middle Ages in French Romanticism', in *Studies in Medievalism*, viii, 100–24; J. R. Dakyns, *The Middle Ages in French Literature 1851–1900* (Oxford, 1973), pp. xiii, 13, 32–3, 43; Siberry, *New Crusaders*, esp. pp. 5–8, 18–20; Ellenblum, *Castles*, esp. pp. 18–23.

20 Quoted by Siberry, *New Crusaders*, p. 8.

21 *Histoire*, i, 8, 18, 41; ii, 2–3, 85; iv, 201–3.

22 *Histoire*, i, 7.

23 W. Purkis, 'Joseph François Michaud', in *Resources for studying the Crusades* at www.crusaderstudies.org.uk/resources/historians/profiles/michaud; and below, pp. xxxx.

24 *Histoire*, i, ii.

25 *Histoire*, i, 49–56; Duff Gordon, *History and Literature*, pp. 347, 350.

26 *Histoire*, i, 171.

27 *Histoire*, iv, 344.

28 *Histoire*, i, 374; ii, 172; iii, 297; iv, 202–3; 206.

29 *Histoire*, i, 5.

30 *Histoire*, i, 18, 41.

31 *Histoire*, i, 49.

32 *Histoire*, i, 57, 86, 273–6, 374; ii, 206; iii, 28, 51, 297, 352; iv, 206. Cf. the rejection of Michaud as a nationalist, Richard, 'National Feeling', pp. 209–11, 214.

33 *Histoire*, i, 59, 85, 270, 302, 331, 374, 412.

34 *Histoire*, ii, 206, 297, 338; iv, 200–1, 203, 344.

35 *Histoire*, ii, 173.

36 *Histoire*, iv, 266.

37 Duff Gordon, *History and Literature*, pp. 345–53.

38 In general, Ellenblum, *Castles*, pp. 23–37; Siberry, *New Crusaders*, *passim* but esp. chaps 1 and 2.

39 See note 19 above.

40 G. F. Hegel, *The Philosophy of History*, trans. J. Sibree (New York NY, 1956 edn), pp. 142–3; quoted in A. Pagden, *Worlds at War* (Oxford, 2008), p. 309.

41 C. R. Conder, *The Latin Kingdom of Jerusalem 1099–1291* (London, 1897), p. 428.

42 E. Rey, *Les colonies franques de Syrie au XIIme et XIIIme siècles* (Paris, 1883), pp. i, vi, 3, 60, 78; cf. Ellenblum, *Castles*, pp. 44–9.

43 *North British Review*, i, 115; Siberry, *New Crusaders*, p. 19.

44 C. Foster, *Mahometanism Unveiled* (London, 1829), esp. pp. 145, 149–50.

45 Siberry, *New Crusaders*, p. 19.

46 G. E. Sargent, *Sketches of the Crusades* (London, 1849), pp. 1, 203.

47 J. Berington, *A Literary History of the Middle Ages* (London, 1814), pp. 268, 269, 607–8.

48 C. Mills, *The History of the Crusades for the Recovery and Possession of the Holy Land* (2 vols. London, 1820), i, iv, vi, 33; ii, 218, 341, 342, 348–51, 371, 373–5.

49 Mills, *History*, i, 459–63; ii, 377–408 (pp. 399–402 for Rutebeuf).
50 Mills, *History*, i, iv; ii, 337.
51 Mills, *History*, ii, 351, 355, 368, 371, 373, 375–6.
52 See on this, K. L. Morris, *The Image of the Middle Ages in Romantic and Victorian Literature* (London, 1984), p. 105 and, generally, chap. IV.
53 R. Southey, *The Life of Wesley and the Rise and Progress of Methodism* (2 vols. London, 1820), i, 310.
54 Quoted in C. Tyerman, *The Invention of the Crusades* (London, 1998), p. 115.
55 Major Proctor, R. E., *The History of the Crusades* (London and Glasgow, 1854), p. 200.
56 W. Stubbs, *Seventeen Lectures on the Study of Medieval and Modern History and Kindred Subjects* (Oxford, 1886), pp. 157, 222; *Chronicles and Memorials of the Reign of Richard I*, i, *Itinerarium Peregrinorum et Gesta Ricardi Regis*, ed. W. Stubbs, Rolls Series (London, 1864), p. cxxxix.
57 H. G. Wells, *The Outline of History* (5th revision, London, 1930), pp. 667, 958.

5

Scholarship, politics and the 'golden age' of research

A generation after Michaud's death, the creation of an academic society devoted to crusade studies, La Société de l'Orient Latin, bore witness to a transformation of the subject. Founded by the wealthy gentleman scholar Paul Riant (1835–88), the Society produced two initial volumes of research materials, the *Archives de l'Orient Latin*, in 1881 and 1884 as well as later sponsoring publication of texts and producing a regular if short-lived *Revue de l'Orient Latin* (12 volumes, 1893–1911). Contributors to the *Archives* included historians from across Europe, including some of the most innovative and influential figures from what has been described as 'the golden age of crusade studies'.[1] These included pioneers such as the numismatist and sigillographer of the Latin East, the right-wing anti-semitic Alsatian medical doctor Gustav Schlumberger (1844–1929); the French nationalist professor of diplomatic and historian of Latin Cyprus, Louis de la Mas Latrie (1815–97), like Riant a papal count; and the innovative historian of Italian trade in the Levant, Wilhelm Heyd (1823–1906). French crusade studies were prominently on display. Alongside Riant himself were the colonial historian Emmanuel Rey (d. 1916), editors of literary texts such as Charles Schefer, Paul Meyer and Paul Viollet, and younger scholars such as Joseph Marie Delaville Le Roulx (1855–1911), historian of the military order of the Hospital of St John. True to Riant's personal internationalist credo, other contributors came from across Europe (although significantly none from Great Britain). Notably, only a decade after the Franco-Prussian War, a powerful contingent came from Germany, including editors such as S. Löwenfeld and

W. Wattenbach and the major crusade scholars Heinrich Hagenmeyer (1834–1915), 'the first serious historian' of the First Crusade,[2] and the Prussian schoolmaster, indefatigable antiquarian and excavator of crusade references, Reinhard Röhricht (1842–1905). Such scholars represented the new range of historical study, based on fresh standards of textual criticism, serious interest in archival research, and the beginnings of the creation of an academic community of professional historians, sustained by feelings of national pride and supported by universities, private money and public funds.

However, this scholarly galaxy did not chart wholly fresh directions in the understanding of the nature or significance of the crusades, even if they transformed knowledge of the events and historical context. The dominant themes established earlier in the century persisted: the crusades as colonialism, commercial expansion, cultural exchange, enterprises of national endeavour or triumphs of the human (specifically white, Christian and European) spirit; admirable even if shocking in extreme physical religiosity, violence and futility. In the contest between Christianity and Islam, between 'East' and 'West' the crusades were assumed to be asserting as well as, in the Levant at least, defending western civilisation. Despite a methodological and scholarly revolution heralding myriad fresh nuances of interpretation and detail, the conceptual context remained remarkably static. Reviewing the historiography of the previous two centuries and more in 1935, the influential American crusade historian Dana C. Munro, while modifying emphases, concluded by essentially parroting the materialist functionalism of Heeren and Robertson. Similarly, twenty years later Steven Runciman revived a very traditional romantic disdain in a potent cocktail of Gibbon and Walter Scott.[3] In a sense, the familiarity of the intellectual tropes allowed scholars to transform the substance of the subject without changing its apparent shape.

One feature of this transformation in the mid-nineteenth century was the cosmopolitan reach of the intellectual energy devoted to the crusades. Riant's manifesto for the Société de l'Orient Latin in 1881 was explicitly international in tone. Given the increasingly proprietorial nationalist attitude towards the crusades exhibited by collaborators such as Mas Latrie, who eccentrically criticised Michaud for insufficient appreciation of the French nature of the crusader states, or the marquis de Vogüé, who as early as 1860 had defined crusader architectural remains in the Levant as 'French', Riant's remarks appear delicately pointed. He noted that, although based in France, most of the Society's subscribers and purchasers of its publications were foreigners. He roundly declared that 'the history of the crusades is not national', the French who went east were accompanied by other nationalities. The Holy Land was sacred to all Christians. To restrict the Society's research to the French contribution would render its work 'mediocre, sterile and incomplete'. Consequently, Riant had assembled an international team of collaborators. He also compared the Society's ambitions and methods with national editorial projects elsewhere, such as the Rolls Series in England and, in particular, the *Monumenta Germaniae Historica* series, edited by Georg Heinrich Pertz, himself a former pupil of Heeren; a number of *MGH* editors regularly contributed to the Society's publications.[4] Riant's nod to German textual scholarship was both appropriate and an acknowledgement that even if the frame for much crusade study was that bequeathed by Michaud, not least interest in the Latin East, much of the impetus for new critical studies came not from France but from Germany.

Wilken, von Sybel and the Rankean tradition

German crusade scholarship precisely mirrored the contrast between methodological innovation and conceptual conservatism. Friedrich Wilken (1777–1840) established a narrative that exerted a similar influence in Germany as Michaud's had in France. Ranke's pupil von Sybel challenged traditional approaches to reading texts, even if he replaced them with his own somewhat illusory romantic vision of the genesis of narrative sources. In the following generation, focus on the discovery, appraisal and editing of primary evidence by professional textual scholars placed crusade history on a new, intellectually more secure footing, culminating in the harvesting of references and texts by Röhricht and a shoal of critical monographs, such as those on the sources for the First Crusade by Heinrich

Hagenmeyer or the work of Bernhard Kugler (1837–98) on the Second Crusade and on Albert of Aachen, in which he effectively challenged much of von Sybel's critique.[5] With concurrent French scholarship, these works provided the basis for the serious academic study and discussion of crusading.

They also reflected contemporary and often competing political and cultural developments. Post-Enlightenment liberal traditions emphasised material, economic and political interpretations in the manner of Heeren of Göttingen. The Rankean search for an almost scientific historical truth moved debate away from narrow (or broad) confessional or anti-confessional diatribe. By contrast, the growth and assertion of German nationalism lent especial interest to relics, such as cathedrals and archaeological remains, and narratives of a supposedly 'German' medieval past of the first Reich of Frederick I and Frederick II. The influential *Volk* nationalism of Herder, while deploring the oppressive force of organised Christianity, nonetheless regarded the crusades as revealing 'the spirit of northern knightly honour' in the struggle for human progress.[6] To avoid the matter of German identity amongst intellectuals in the German-speaking world of the nineteenth century was almost impossible. In this, medievalism, including the crusades, played its part as a seemingly neutral witness to a German spirit that attracted nationalists of all persuasions: conservatives, liberals, Catholics, Protestants, politicians, propagandists, romantics and intellectuals. One fruit of this concern was the establishment of the *Monumenta Germaniae Historica* founded by the Prussian politician, reformer and German nationalist Baron Karl von Stein in 1818–19 devoted to the editing and publication of medieval texts specifically on German history down to 1500. Within crusade studies, it was no coincidence that much academic impetus came from the study of those episodes that involved 'Germans', from the First Crusade stories of Albert of Aachen to the Hohenstaufen involvement in thirteenth-century Outremer to the Germanisation of the southern and eastern Baltic by the Teutonic Knights.

An early centre for German crusader scholarship was the liberal university of Göttingen. Stein studied there, as did his first *MGH* chief editor, G. H. Pertz, where he had been taught by A. H. L. Heeren (1760–1842). There Wilken produced his 1798 prize thesis on the chronicle of Abu al-Fida and began to plan his great *Geschichte der Kreuzzüge nach morgenländischen und abendländischen Berichten* (*A History of the Crusade from Eastern and Western Sources*, 7 volumes, Leipzig, 1807–32). Both Heeren's economic and institutional interpretation of the middle ages and Wilken's non-judgemental narrative, derived as much from non-Christian and non-European as from more familiar western sources, were directed at combating emotional responses to the past, especially those rooted in present prejudice. Wilken's empathy lay in attempting to convey how medieval contemporaries viewed the crusades, a supposedly passive observation far removed from the heightened engaged empathy of Michaud. Although Wilken's great work was less internationally influential even than Heeren's technical study because of its length and being in German not French, it nonetheless formed the starting point for the great nineteenth-century German assault and conquest of crusade scholarship.

Wilken was perhaps the first major scholar of the crusades to earn his money from being a historian, in the modern sense the first professional. Robertson's academic role as Principal of Edinburgh University was of a different order while Heeren was primarily an ancient historian, his interest in the crusades part of a wider focus on the economic and structural bases for the creation of states, development of civilisation and historical change. Wilken occupied a chair of History at Heidelberg (1805–17) before going to Berlin as professor and, more influentially, Librarian of the Prussian Royal Library. His professional rise can be traced on the title pages of succeeding volumes of his *History*, the work that secured his reputation. Alongside the Heidelberg professorship noted in Volume One (1807), by Volume Two (1813) he had become an associate of elite academic societies in France and Prussia. The publication of Volume Three (1817) coincided with his move to Berlin, appropriately perhaps as this volume introduced the Baltic crusades.[7] By 1826, and Volume Four, Wilken had added the title of Prussian State Historiographer to that of Royal Librarian. By the time Volume Seven appeared in 1832, Wilken was very grand and internationally recognised by his fellow scholars. His eminence did not rest simply on honorific titles but on his research, writing and administrative skill in building up the Berlin collection. The years after the Napoleonic Wars were a golden age for bibliophiles and collectors as many private and institutional libraries, either looted or unsustainable by their displaced, ruined or impoverished owners, came onto the market. Wilken also used his position as Royal Librarian to gain access to foreign archives for his own work on the crusades, in 1829, for instance, visiting London, Oxford and Paris to consult oriental manuscripts as well as printed works. Wilken was especially impressed by the collection held in the King's Library in the British Museum.[8]

Two features distinguish Wilken's *magnum opus*: his eastern perspective and his attempt to allow the sources to speak for themselves. Both are reflected in the range and depth of the texts consulted, the more remarkable as the standard collections and editions of many of them still lay in the future. Unlike Michaud, Wilken eschewed flights of literary fancy. His method revolved around the comparison of sources to achieve the greatest accuracy; thus he tried to correct and make sense of William of Tyre's often opaque chronology by reference to Arabic texts. Although hardly the sort of close internal textual criticism advocated by Ranke and his pupils, this represented an advance on the more capricious selection criteria of earlier writers or of Michaud, whose work appeared almost simultaneously (1811–22). Not only are the main, familiar Latin, French, Greek and Arabic chronicles and collections of documents paraded, but Wilken's net catches less obvious morsels such as the poems of Theobald IV of Navarre and some works of theorists c. 1300. The whole apparatus is sustained by detailed academic footnotes, a weighty bibliography and an annexe of documents. Wilken's coverage stretches beyond the Holy Land (and therefore Michaud's), to include, for instance, the Baltic crusades from which the state he worked for ultimately derived. His inclusive use of sources permitted him to reconstruct coherent – often too coherent – accounts of previously obscure episodes, such as the Children's Crusade of 1212.[9] This could result in invention no less egregious than Michaud's, but considerably less obvious as it rested on selection of sources served up in dry academic phrases rather than literary drama in purple prose. As a detailed narrative and a mine of references, Wilken's *History* held a pre-eminent place for much of the rest of the nineteenth century. While Wilken's method precluded flashy polemics, his approach confirmed, at least to readers such as von Sybel, the positive appreciation of the crusades shared by his old professor Heeren. His orientalist perspective prevented crude analysis of cultural wars or western supremacism. While sympathetic to the middle ages, he avoided grandstanding moralising, content to let conclusions emerge implicitly from the narrative. Yet his scholarship, as well as his gallery of German crusaders, allowed the crusade to be regarded as a subject worth continuing national interest.

Not that national interest ostensibly provided the initial spur to Heinrich von Sybel (1817–95) whose use of critical techniques helped reshape the study of the crusades. Von Sybel's *Geschichte des ersten Kreuzzüges* (*History of the First Crusade*, Düsseldorf, 1841) loftily dismissed crusade histories 'of a purely national or patriotic tendency'.[10] At his seminar in Berlin in 1837, von Sybel's mentor Leopold von Ranke (who was to succeed Wilken as Prussian royal historiographer in 1841) had suggested that William of Tyre was not an original source for the First Crusade as his account was clearly dependent on Albert of Aachen, Raymond of Aguilers and the *Gesta Francorum*. Given the historiographical primacy of William of Tyre since the thirteenth century, this was a radical insight which Ranke's pupil, von Sybel, set about demonstrating in his book. This involved a reorienting of critical reading away from simply cobbling together the testimony of the different surviving sources to achieve some sort of coherent narrative, more or less as Wilken had done. Proper understanding only came from the scrutiny of the individual narrative sources in themselves to uncover the process whereby each one transmitted the memories of actual events through contemporary stories and later legends. No text, therefore, could be taken at face value. Although von Sybel's own account of the First Crusade is no more accurate than those he attacked, his approach to the problem of assessing the respective value of the chronicles allowed for a wholly new level of subtlety in the use of evidence, based on critical editing and analysis rather than simple transcription and descriptive choice. The contrast with Michaud is apparent. The interpretive impact of von Sybel's early work was plain, applying to the crusades the sort of textual rigour being employed by Pertz and the *MGH*. Subsequent serious accounts of the First Crusade derive in some way from von Sybel, even where they wholly reject his conclusions. At the very least, the dethroning of William of Tyre changed the landscape forever.

This is not to say that von Sybel's method was unimpeachable. It was one thing to demonstrate the derivative content or flawed structure of a chronicle; quite another to explain the reason for this and its significance. Von Sybel, like Ranke, seemed wedded to the idea that acceptance of a chronicler's testimony depended on his being 'one certain and known person, whose character and position enable us to recognise the value of his work', that is, presumably being an eyewitness of unimpeachably unbiased credentials.[11] While establishing that the chroniclers of the First Crusade enshrined in varying degrees traditions and mentalities rather than objective facts, he wholly misses the significance of his own insight by unimaginatively denigrating the importance of such evidence. In fact his assessments of chroniclers appear at odds with Rankean obeisance to objectivity, at times appearing to rest on idiosyncratic caprice. While he carefully established the independence of the *Gesta Francorum*, 'the most important authority for the true [sic?] history of the First Crusade', he excoriates Fulcher of Chartres's account as 'in no way important'. He doubts the miraculous in Raymond of Aguilers as facts, but accepts 'the truth of the impression they make on him'.[12] The famous attack on Albert of Aachen and William of Tyre acknowledges that they both bear witness to different stages of living traditions, but this appears to render them useless as evidence. Thus the central role of Peter the Hermit cannot be entertained, an opinion cemented by Hagenmeyer's *Peter the Hermit* (Leipzig, 1879) which thereafter went more or less unchallenged until the 1980s. While von Sybel's methods may have lent a narrow and occasionally spurious critical austerity to handling evidence, they did produce one important historiographic consequence. By rejecting the witness of Albert of Aachen, von Sybel promoted the accuracy of the circle of French observers which came to dominate interpretations of the First Crusade for the next century and a half. This was doubly ironic. The young liberal von Sybel was fiercely anti-Roman Catholic, attributing to 'religious excitement' the failure of the crusades. The French chronicle tradition tended to place the papacy at the centre of their approving narrative. These chroniclers also privileged the role of the western Franks, Michaud's Frenchmen, perhaps not entirely comfortable for the older von Sybel who became an increasingly outspoken advocate of German nationalism and of a powerful German nation state as a guarantor of secular liberal values.

Von Sybel's book also offered an intriguing critique of post-medieval crusade historiography, a pendant to his demolition of William of Tyre, as historian after historian are judged on their use of the discredited text. Fuller was noted as being the first 'to discuss the righteousness of the crusade'. Maimbourg is dismissed as a vain snob, with 'a good opinion of himself ... writing for great people and the best company', although his moderation 'between religious excitement and scepticism' is commended. Voltaire, 'very weak in point of research', is compared unfavourably with de Guignes, while Mailly receives a more positive critique, 'far better on all points', despite his adherence to the baneful William of Tyre. Particular contempt is heaped on Friedrich Wilhelm Heller's three-volume *Geschichte der Kreuzzügge nach dem Heiligen Lande* (1784) as representative of ill-informed hostility and bogus extravagant rhetoric. Characteristic of a confident young tyro, von Sybel was equally cutting about contemporary crusader writers. Mills and the popular French conservative historical hack Jean-Baptiste Capefigue (1802–72) are similarly branded as lacking critical method, the latter additionally corrupted by religiosity. Although accepting the crusades' positive aspects, von Sybel was no admirer of the romantic school of enthusiasts. By contrast, Wilken is afforded considerable respect, 'the first place in this province of history', as he narrates 'the history of those times in a spirit in accordance with their own' based on admirably extensive learning. But even Wilken cannot entirely escape censure for his uncritical attempts to reconcile sources instead of distinguishing between them and separating fact from legend within them.[13]

Michaud, on the other hand, is savaged, his pretentions to scholarship thoroughly derided. His research on primary sources, even the collection *Bibliothèque des croisades*, although useful in quantity is contrasted unfavourably – 'very inferior' – with

Wilken's. With deft specific examples, Michaud is accused of sloppiness and trickery with evidence, failing to differentiate between primary and secondary sources and concealing his use of anachronistic, even unhistorical material, including Tasso. The usual complaints about reliance on Albert of Aachen and William of Tyre are repeated. Equally damning – and entirely fair – Michaud is accused of repeatedly embroidering his narrative with dramatic invention. Listing a few of the more obvious instances from the story of the First Crusade, von Sybel comments drily that 'none of these interesting particulars are to be found in the original authorities'. Michaud is eviscerated with faint praise. 'Great diligence', 'activity of thought', 'power of expression' and 'an active and enquiring spirit' are undermined by 'a lack of careful investigation and ... of the sense of conscientious research in small matters' in an unholy combination of Tasso and William of Tyre.[14]

Von Sybel's self-confident methodological austerity, for all its novelty in crusader studies, formed just one part of the development of new critical techniques in assessing medieval texts. Perhaps of more immediate significance for general interpretations of the crusades was his acceptance of the positive nature and effects of aspects of the enterprises and a growing desire, as he moved into nationalist liberal politics, to associate the medieval past with issues relevant to nineteenth-century society and public affairs. His Munich lectures of 1855 on the crusades reflect this new dimension. While rehearsing his academic analysis of the parallel medieval histories of crusade events and crusade legends, he deliberately set his remarks in a wider, more publicly accessible context of world history. In ways he might not have consciously welcomed, von Sybel began to ape the once deplored cosmic generalisations of the previous century. This, too, can also be seen as following the lead of Ranke who, for all his concentration on forensic detail, promoted an overarching vision of world history, united by a providential or divine purpose that had seen successive cultures rise and fall to culminate in the conspicuous triumph of western civilisation, based on monotheism, classical learning and military power. Following this determinist line, the crusades were seen by von Sybel as 'one of the greatest revolutions' in human history, matching those of the Persian Wars of

Antiquity, the Germanic invasions that brought down the Roman Empire, the Reformation and the French Revolution. They formed 'one great portion' of the contest between Christianity and Islam but, at the same time, provided 'an agitation favourable to liberty and progress'. The very legends that von Sybel had identified as corrupting the witness of twelfth-century chroniclers were now seen as 'the first stir of a vigorous new life, the first pulsation of renewed mental activity ... a direction ... never again lost by Europe [that] gradually carried along the whole hemisphere in its course'. Along with many nineteenth-century historians, von Sybel was attracted to the concept of transformational great men. Saladin was a 'born ruler'. Pope Gregory VII possessed 'a universal genius for ruling' only matched since by 'the two greatest self-made men of modern history – Cromwell and Bonaparte'. What the two post-medieval heroes possessed in common was their creation of new national political societies. The modern implications of this were revealed in von Sybel's description of Frederick Barbarossa, a leader whose 'ideas were beyond his time'. Opposed by troublesome independent-minded subjects and an over-mighty international church, Frederick 'conceived the idea of a state complete within itself, and strong in the name of the common weal'. In short, Frederick, like von Sybel, was a nineteenth-century liberal anti-clerical German nationalist with a belief in the benefits of a powerful state under a strong leader. In painting a slightly chilling portrait of Frederick's ruthless and unwavering pursuit of imperial right, the modern connection was plain as Frederick was depicted as 'foreshadowing modern thoughts deep in the middle ages'.[15] Whatever else, von Sybel asserted the relevance of the crusades.

Both academic and popular strands of scholarship flowed from such work. The process of editing texts to satisfy the highest demands of *Quellenkritik* (source criticism) vastly extended the range and accuracy of the textual basis of crusade scholarship. For the first time the layers of composition, derivation, originality and transmission could be observed, putting the nature of the texts themselves and the status of what they described into sharper focus. The stimulus to revisit familiar sources and to discover new ones allowed genuinely new histories of the crusades to be written. Whilst it is true that Michaud or Wilken had produced more evidence than their predecessors, nonetheless the basic narrative texts tended to be those on which Fuller and Maimbourg had relied. Now, German philologists and historians, along with similarly inclined scholars in France, provided a more secure basis for research and writing. Critical assessment of sources now drove the composition of history, not vice versa. The conceptual path from von Sybel's 1841 book to, for example, Heinrich Hagenmeyer was unmistakable. It was also distinct from the previous three centuries of literary tradition. In a sense this new scholarship created almost an anti-literary genre. Thus Hagenmeyer rewrote and reshaped the history of the First Crusade through close scrutiny of the central texts and documents rather than fresh sweeping narratives or general theorising. He published new editions of the *Gesta Francorum* (1890; in which he agreed with von Sybel that the anonymous author was probably a southern Italian Norman knight), Fulcher of Chartres (1913), Ekkehard of Aura's *Hierosolymita* (1877) and Walter the Chancellor's *Bella Antiocha* (*Antioch Wars*, 1896). His edition of surviving contemporary letters concerning the First Crusade (1901) and meticulous reconstruction of its chronology (1898–1902) remain in scholarly use. His definitive examination (and demolition) of the role played by Peter the Hermit (*Peter der Eremite: ein kritischer Beitrag zur Geschichte des ersten Kreuzzuges*, Leipzig, 1879) developed the suggestions of Ranke and von Sybel and held sway for a century.

History through objective, passionless, themeless critical studies of the technical details of primary texts accelerated a notable feature of nineteenth-century and later debates on the crusades. No monographs of *Quellenkritik* could exert the same public, popular influence as had previous milestones in serious crusade literature, such as Michaud or even Wilken. The disconnection between the academic and the popular, or even between the academic and the reasonably well-informed and interested, became almost total, a position that has persisted to the present day. The classic example of this was to be found in one of the most generally erudite crusader historians of his or any generation, Reinhold Röhricht. A Berlin schoolmaster by profession, Röhricht managed to find time to amass a vast array of information, details and references chiefly on the crusades to the Holy

Land and Outremer. Much of his earlier published work lay in editing texts, some still in use. His *magna opera* dealt with the Latin kingdom of Jerusalem, the *Geschichte des Königsreich Jerusalem* (1898) and his until very recently indispensable collection of references to surviving charters and official documents, the *Regesta Regni Hierosolymitani 1097–1291* (1893 and 1904). Röhricht's contribution was his 'incredible and inexhaustible accumulation of references', providing a foundation for all subsequent research in these subjects.[16] Yet he was chiefly an antiquarian, a collector of detail without thesis or even much analysis. As history, despite or perhaps partly because of the dense scholarly precision of his footnotes, his book on the kingdom of Jerusalem is mediocre and dreary, narrowly political, stultifyingly bland, the relentless, day-to-day chronological form managing to obscure rather than illumine the pattern of events. One reviewer, otherwise sympathetic, was forced to notice the deliberate removal of authorial personality, judgements or conclusions beyond the textual. The concentration was on politics alone. Religion, the economy, law or culture were excluded. So too, the reviewer silkenly added, was 'all literary ambition'.[17] Even his obituarist in the *Revue de l'Orient Latin* in 1905, who tried very hard to be polite to one of its most industrious contributors, admitted that Röhricht pushed objectivity to 'extreme limits', divorcing facts from causes or long-term consequences. A bibliographer, impartial annalist, a 'veritable encyclopaedia', 'he always rebelled at the complicated work (*travail complexe*) of the historian'.[18] Sadly his scholarship failed to endear him to his employers. In 1898, the Prussian Ministry of Education advised against an imperial proposal to subsidise Röhricht for a visit to Palestine after the patriotic writer had presented a copy of his newly published *Geschichte* to the Kaiser who was about to embark on his notoriously showy grand tour of the Levant. Six years later, when Röhricht was forced to retire early through ill-health (he was sixty-two), the Prussian Ministry of Education skimped on his modest pension entitlement.

Unfair and mean though the Berlin bureaucrats may have been, Röhricht's brush with the eastern policies and fantasies of Wilhelm II pointed to the parallel consequence of the pioneering work of Wilken and von Sybel. If not in the form of Röhricht's austere erudite pedantry, nonetheless German academic attention to the history of the crusades could reach out to popular and political interest. Frederick Barbarossa became a figurehead for competing visions of German nationalism, from the strong independent self-reliant secular state of von Sybel to visions, centred more on Catholic southern Germany, for a restored Christian empire. As elsewhere in Europe, there was a revival in aristocratic pilgrimages to the Holy Places in Palestine. The cult of Barbarossa was taken up by Prussian propagandists, seeking pan-German legitimacy even in spurious legends of some sort of mystical reincarnation, as well as by historians, notably at Berlin university. One of them, Hans Prutz (1843–1929), after producing a massive biography of Frederick Barbarossa (l871–74), was hired to lend academic credibility to a scheme Bismarck himself had been persuaded to fund. This sought to excavate a site in Tyre hoping to discover the medieval emperor's remains. While dismissing fanciful claims that such relics had actually been unearthed, Prutz still promoted a Barbarossa connection with the Holy Land.[19]

Prutz's other, less exotic academic studies on the crusades similarly exemplified the special status the crusades could achieve in nationalist interpretations of the middle ages. That the crusades acted as a central medium of cultural development and progress was axiomatic to the insistence on their contemporary relevance, an argument given weighty support in Prutz's substantial *Kulturgeschichte der Kreuzzüge* (*Cultural History of the Crusades*, 1883). By adopting a maximalist line, exaggerating the familiar instrumental view of the Robertson–Heeren tradition, Prutz was tacitly accepting that the crusades required absorption into a narrative of German destiny and unification. Such an important catalyst of change could not be left without a national element. Although the dedication to Crown Prince Frederick might be regarded as conventional, Prutz's position by this time as professor at the University of Königsberg, itself a symbol of the role of crusading in the expansion of German power and culture, may have lent an added dimension to his emphasis on the wider ranging effects of the crusades. The great historian of Prussia and the Teutonic Knights, Johannes Voigt (1786–1863), had also been a professor there. Prutz acknowledged a specifically German dimension to crusade history. However, he also placed the cultural impact of the crusades in a Rankean context, in which all cultures and religions formed part of a single historical process. As if in support of this still fundamentally supremacist inclusive approach, as an appendix to the *Kulturgeschichte* Prutz published an edition of the Dominican William of Tripoli's *Tractatus de Statu Sarracenorum* (*Treatise on the Situation of the Saracens*, c. 1270). In it the Dominican friar had avoided cheap polemics and demonisation in noting the similarities between Islam and Christianity while expressing the hope and expectation that Muslims would in the end peacefully accept 'the baptism of Christ', not through philosophical disputation or force of arms but by the simple word of God. It should not be forgotten that parallel to these studies of crusading, Germany led the way in Arabic scholarship, much of which dealt with similar and related issues of religion, culture and the progress of civilisation. Prutz himself was keen to note examples of direct east/west cultural exchange, while, in contrast with many of his French contemporaries, disapproving of aspects of the Franks' behaviour in the Holy Land.[20]

Prutz's approach encouraged the temptation to regard all developments in the middle ages as consequent on the crusades if they occurred at about the same time, the *post hoc ergo propter hoc* view of history and 'the fallacy of the single cause'.[21] Prutz was guilty of this, but less crudely than some subsequent popularisers, such as the Swiss journalist and cultural historian Otto Henne am Rhyn (1828–1914). Unsurprisingly, Henne am Rhyn's *Kulturgeschichte der Kreuzzügge* (Leipzig, 1900) proved much more popular than Prutz's dense tome. It was illustrated and avoided either footnotes or bibliography. Clearly arranged, adopting a broad brush and seemingly based on the latest German scholarship, it aimed at a large readership and evidently proved sufficiently successful to attract the particular disapproval of the English academic Ernest Barker thirty years later. However, the resonance of the crusades, and the Rankean reconciliation of such events with a unified narrative of power and progress found perhaps unexpected non-literary manifestations. Even if Röhricht was excluded from the Imperial cavalcade to the Levant in 1898, on his tour the Kaiser – unflatteringly nicknamed in England 'Cook's Crusader' after the London travel agent through whom the travel arrangements were made – demonstrated the availability of the crusades for German political exploitation. At Jerusalem he postured as a pilgrim and patron of Christian ecumenism in the Holy Land while parading into the city on his white horse as some latter-day holy warrior. At Damascus, by contrast, he laid a bronze wreath on the tomb of Saladin, von Sybel's 'born ruler', bearing the legend 'from one great emperor to another'.[22] It is hard to see that any of these roles endeared him to his Turkish hosts. Whatever the diplomatic effect, such showy gestures projected certain public perceptions of the crusades: glamorous, exciting, significant for the development of western culture and German history, providing lessons for state-building and geopolitics.

If the learning of Wilken, the critical methods of von Sybel, the super-antiquarianism of Röhricht and the editorial precision of Hagenmeyer sired bizarre progeny, in places their efforts were still-born. For all the forensic erudition of the German school of crusade historians, critical method was often no match against entrenched assumptions, current prejudice, ignorance or lazy thought. Fifteen years after Hagenmeyer's *Peter the Hermit* there appeared an English history of the Latin kingdom of Jerusalem, *The Crusades* (1894) by T. A. Archer, whose works apart from a collection of translated texts on the Third Crusade included titles such as *A Book of Pussy Cats* and *The Frog's Parish Clerk*, and completed by C. L. Kingsford, who became a highly reputable later medievalist. This rather insouciantly reaffirmed the truth of Albert of Aachen's account of Peter the Hermit as the 'primus auctor' of the First Crusade not through any fresh critical insight into the nature or extent of the admitted 'taint of legend' in Albert's version but because 'the story as it stands is more plausible than if we had to assume that tradition [a clear dig at the Germans] had transformed the credit of the First Crusade from a pope to a simple hermit'.[23] Although tricked out with the trappings of scholarship with familiar source references and illustrations of seals and crusader artefacts, the text is a stew of sophistry, spurious invention and special pleading, laced with romantic sentiment and, as here, a piquant dash of snobbery. Not an unusual concoction among crusade historians, the fault lay in the lack of serious learning on the part of the authors. This confirmed the insignificant British contribution to the new crusade studies. More widely, the pursuit of research and the settled beliefs of its audience pulled in ever increasingly and awkwardly different directions.

Crusade and nation: Michaud's legacy

Nowhere was this tension potentially more acute than in France. Yet nowhere did popular, academic and political enthusiasm combine so productively. The influence of Michaud was hard to avoid: the crusades were essentially French enterprises, demonstrating the vigour and spirit of western Christian society as revealed in their pioneering colonialism in the eastern Mediterranean, leading to a French version of Manifest Destiny. For a society that experienced two invasions (1814–15; 1870–71) and six different political regimes in less than sixty years (Empire, Bourbon Restoration, Orleanist Monarchy, Second Republic; Second Empire; Third Republic), the medieval past adorned with French heroes strutting the international stage offered a relatively neutral focus for national pride and identity, one eagerly exploited by successive governments and the academic community alike. To this essentially passive reception of convenient historical myth was added a dynamic reimagining of medieval French colonialism as a model not just for European conquest but for the creation of distinct, new colonial societies. These were presented as active fusions between the cultures of occupiers and occupied, a demonstration at once of western superiority and the beneficial leavening effects of western culture. Not all agreed. The arguments between those called by one observer in 1844 as 'les fils des croisés et les fils de Voltaire' persisted.[24] The great historian of France and anti-clericalist Jules Michelet (1798–1874), amongst whose voluminous output were two volumes of edited documents on the trial of the Templars (1841 and 1851), regarded the crusades as violent and driven by fanaticism. Some crusade historians, such as Riant himself, were unpersuaded by nationalist appropriation. Yet fewer voices were raised against the increasing focus on the crusaders' activities in the east which marked French crusade studies after Michaud. Even Michelet argued that the true result of the crusade lay in the rapprochement between Europe and Asia, invisible, intangible, but no less real.[25]

Concentration on campaigns and conquests deflected traditional philosophical or religious controversy over the nature of the crusades. Left and right, legitimists and republicans, believers and secularists could unite in being impressed by the material actions of their ancestors in foreign fields, whether they admired their motives or saw them as religious dupes. The wide academic as well as popular acceptance of this consensus, gaining ground as the century progressed, can be explained in part by the close relationship between power and learning. Crusade studies in Germany depended on a network of separate universities; in France on individual private funds and government patronage. While German crusade studies were recruited to help create a national identity, their French counterparts were employed to confirm one. The creation of the *Recueil des historiens des croisades* (1844–1906) provides one prime example of this process; Louis-Philippe's *Salles des croisades* at Versailles (from 1837) another.

Attempts under the First Republic and First Empire to revive the Maurist plan for a collection of crusade sources failed. A suggestion from the ministry of Justice under the Restoration for an edition of the *Assises de Jérusalem* bore no immediate fruit. However, in 1833 the Académie des Inscriptions et Belles-Lettres revived the Maurist idea, soon including the *Assises* project as well. The compelling reason advanced by Count Arthur Beugnot, spokesman of the advisory committee established to prepare the new venture and himself a legal historian and editor of the Jerusalem *Assises*, was both clear and not narrowly scholarly. 'France has played such a glorious part in the wars of the crusades that the historical documents that contain the accounts of these memorable expeditions seem to enter her domain.' The proposed collection would stand as a 'monument', accurately preserving the memory of the 'greatest upheaval (*ébranlement*)' of the Middle Ages. The popularity of accounts of the wars to recover and defend the Holy Land, the abundance of primary sources available and the 'voice of *Europe savante*' committed 'France not to leave to others to clear the debt she has contracted'. Beugnot sketched the history of the project from the seventeenth century when the availability of more texts rendered Bongars's *Gesta Dei Per Francos* inadequate. Now that the Académie des Inscriptions had undertaken the enterprise, it was conceived on the grandest scale to include all the important Latin, French, Greek, Arabic, Syriac and Armenian sources, mainly chronicles but also pilgrimage accounts; letters; and, taking it over from the government, the *Assises*. The resulting *Recueil des historiens des croisades* comprised the laws in two volumes, 1841 and 1843; six volumes of western historians, 1844–95; five of eastern texts with French translations, 1872–1906; two volumes of Greek sources, 1875 and 1881, and two of Armenian sources and other related matters, 1869 and 1906. It thus fulfilled much of Beugnot's prospectus before the project ran out of steam in the early twentieth century, not coincidentally just as the generation of pioneering scholars was fading away. Many of the great names of French crusade scholarship were involved in some capacity, including Michaud, who gave early advice, and Riant. The quality of the editions was patchy, lacking the forensic intensity of the *MGH*, often too reliant on conveniently accessible rather than the best manuscripts. Nonetheless, as a research tool, the *Recueil* became indispensable. In conception, it had been more. As Beugnot described it at the end of his prospectus, the *Recueil* would not only give encouragement to historical research, it would stand as a 'national monument' and bear witness to the Académie des Inscriptions' labours to encourage serious studies which contributed so much 'to the glory and intellectual improvement of France'.[26]

Beside the general national agenda, the *Recueil* confirmed the focus on the 'colonies chrétiens en Palestine'. There were no texts about crusades in Spain or the Baltic or on the Albigensian Crusade (a clearly less than irenic French historical memory). The perceived medieval French diaspora received official and popular approval. In 1856, the Committee for the Language, History and Arts of France announced a plan to publish its own *Recueil des documents originaux sur la domination française en Orient pendant le moyen âge*. A decade later a modern French version of Joinville's *Vie* of Louis IX proved a publishing success.[27] The well-attested habit of commentators on French foreign adventures in the Mediterranean, the Crimea, North Africa and the Far

East to employ the language or even the historical parallel of the crusades indicated how ubiquitous this particular image had become in public discourse, one encouraged by political leaders from Charles X to Napoleon III. Under Louis-Philippe, almost overtly the crusades became government policy. The need to secure support for a monarchic regime that sat uneasily between royalist legitimacy and republican populism recruited the crusades both as a symbol of a shared history and as a mythic model for current action.

During the 1830s, the Orleanist government vigorously pursued the conquest of Algeria under the guise of a civilising Christian mission. All five of Louis-Philippe's sons fought there. The wars were commemorated in the museum of French history established by the king in the palace of Versailles. There too, in deliberate association, were the five rooms of the *Salles des croisades* in which were displayed about 120 paintings depicting crusade and related subjects from the Norman conquests in southern Italy and Sicily in the early eleventh century to the siege of Malta in 1565. The rooms were decorated with cod medieval fittings (and a genuine door from the Hospitaller convent at Rhodes given to Louis-Philippe by the Ottoman sultan Mahmud II) and the coats of arms of known crusaders, a badge of honour that led to a thriving Parisian black market in forged documents bought by aspirant nobles eager to prove their ancient ancestry among the status-challenged parvenu nobility of the Orleanist monarchy.[28] The message of the crusade gallery was carefully constructed, imposing a certain vision of the past on viewers in what has been described as a sort of history machine in which 'spellbound visitors, enmeshed in the mechanics of narration deployed in the galleries, were systematically tranquillized by the unfolding spectacle of their historical selves'.[29] That these supposed selves were a calculated invention scarcely detracted from the effect, as the aristocratic rush to find crusade ancestry indicated. Apart from prominent crusade leaders and heroes the emphasis was consistent – the battles of the French against other cultures: Saracens in southern Italy and Sicily; the Turks of Asia Minor and the Holy Land; the Ottomans of the later middle ages; and the decadent Byzantines of Constantinople, imagined for the gallery in Delacroix's famous painting of the city's fall in 1204 as enfeebled supplicants at the feet of their French conquerors. Heroism, conflict and a taste for the exoticism of an imaginary Orient were matched in the artistic scheme of the paintings by an insistence on religious inspiration, as in scenes of preaching and taking the cross as well as in certain battle pictures. In essence, the *Salles des croisades* were Michaud in pictures, as faithful to the writer as the great cycle of illustrations provided for the 1877 edition of his work by Gustave Doré. By sharing excitement and pride in the past, the gallery and its guide books sought a form of reconciliation in the present on at least two levels. The common inheritance of the crusades could help unite a bitterly divided society whilst at the same time pointing a current political parallel with the conquest and colonisation of Algeria.

Such an approach was not confined to government propaganda, but seeped into the very fabric of the French academic establishment's attitude to the crusades: nationalist; colonial; an early litmus test of western cultural supremacy. François Guizot (1787–1874), writer, orator and politician, the leading liberal intellectual apologist for the Orleanist regime, as Minister of Public Instruction in the 1830s had enthusiastically promoted the crusades as part of a specifically French heritage. A decade earlier he had included a number of crusade texts in his vast collection of translated sources for medieval French history. One prominent advocate of the 'Frenchness' of the medieval western settlements in the Levant, Charles Jean Melchior, marquis de Vogüé (1829–1916), was so intent on claiming national ownership of the crusades that he recruited Riant to the flag – posthumously. Vogüé, an early member of the Société de l'Orient Latin, combined his academic interests and patronage with a public career that included becoming French ambassador at Constantinople and Vienna. In his obituary of Riant in the first volume of the *Revue de l'Orient Latin* in 1893, de Vogüé gave Riant's work a nationalist tweak that the dead historian had rejected in life. De Vogüé insisted on the value of Riant's work for those wishing to conserve 'the cult (*culte*) of national traditions' and the 'memory of the great place France occupied in the history of the Latin East'.[30] Riant's 1881 internationalist manifesto was thus brushed aside by a colleague who devoted much of his time to arguing that the style of architecture in the crusader states was specifically French and, in slightly awkward conjunction, that the pointed arch of Gothic architecture was derived from France not the Arab world, as had become romantically fashionable to believe. What, in the 1830s, had been a particular, tendentious view of crusade history had become, by the end of the century, axiomatic.

In many ways, de Vogüé sketched the pattern of the French imperialists who went beyond the simple national categories of Michaud. As more and more work was conducted on the physical remains of crusader Syria and Palestine, and as more and more parts of the Mediterranean Islamic world and beyond fell under the sway of French rule or influence, the colonial question became more pressing. If medieval Outremer (or nineteenth-century Algeria) were French by occupation, how French were they in politics, culture and society? Clearly there existed a difference. To this question a succession of French scholars provided similar and increasingly elaborate and settled answers. Fired by his visits to the Levant, Emmanuel Rey created a vision of a Franco-Syrian society, dominated by wise and tolerant French rulers, virtuous colonisers who forged an efficient *modus vivendi* with indigenous people, in implicit contrast with the stories of mid-nineteenth-century Ottoman imperial excesses from Syria to Bulgaria. Rey noted examples of shared pilgrimage sites and suggested that Jacques de Vitry failed to appreciate Outremer culture because of his hostility to Islam.[31] This idea was extended by younger generations of scholars. Gaston Dodu (b. 1863), while never forgetting the innate superiority of the westerners, argued that apart from the installation of a feudalised French elite that imposed certain systems for necessary fiscal and military exploitation, Frankish Outremer created a new civilisation based on religious tolerance and the blending of the societies of conquerors and conquered. While his picture of an ideal limited feudal monarchy was hopelessly flawed, a rehash of the legal fictions of thirteenth-century Jerusalemite lawyers, Dodu trawled the sources for illustrations of contact, cooperation and cultural exchange, such as washing, education, eating, clothing, ornaments as well as apparent evidence of mixed marriages and friendly social, religious and commercial relations. In part this account of religious co-existence, a harmony contrasted with the vicious religious persecution in sixteenth-century Spain or the New World, contained a coded anti-clericalism at odds with much French crusade historiography of the period. Yet, like his contemporaries, Dodu happily dressed up a fantasy of beneficent French colonialism in medieval crusading costumes. The anachronism and special pleading seemed largely to escape local notice, although at least one austere and later highly influential transatlantic critic, the young D. C. Munro (1866–1933), took sharp exception to Dodu's historical method.[32]

This implicit politicisation of the crusades in support of a united French national identity and of the policy of colonial expansion received continuing succour from public events as well as academic agreement and complicity. French intervention in the Lebanon to assist Maronite Christians in the 1860s attracted explicit crusade rhetoric. Expansion in Africa was lent the language of crusading Christian liberation by Roman Catholic apologists, especially where it could be associated with combating the slave trade. Such a set of category confusions persuaded one energetic anti-slavery, anti-Muslim colonial cardinal, Archbishop Lavigerie of Algiers, to describe Leopold I of Belgium's annexation and exploitation of tracts of central Africa as a crusade (as, indeed, did Leopold himself). The conquest of Tunisia in 1880–81 by the Third Republic demonstrated that imperialism, even if promoted by a political minority, could remain a national calling transcending politics or religion.[33] This apparent consensus was reflected in the contributors to the *Archives* and the *Revue de l'Orient Latin*. The positions of de Vogüé, Mas Latrie or the anti-Dreyfusard Schlumberger were plain. Archaeologists as well as art historians and textual scholars also subscribed to versions of the national colonial myth. In the second volume of the *Archives de l'Orient Latin* (1884), Charles Clermont-Ganneau (1846–1923) talked of an inscription at Acre as of 'rare interest both for the history of the crusades and for our national history', as well as enjoying himself at German expense in describing the 'French' inscription unearthed at Tyre by the recent excavations there designed to promote 'the greater glory of Germanism'.[34] One of de Vogüé's protégés was Camille Enlart (1862–1927), an expert on French medieval architecture who had studied French style in southern Italy, Greece and Cyprus before, in the last years of his life, being asked by the French Mandate government in Syria to survey crusader monuments in the Levant. Some of his views on style were revealing. He judged French Gothic in Cyprus with enthusiasm, the physical dimension to Mas Latrie's nationalist take on Lusignan rule. By contrast, French-inspired architecture in Greece proved 'feeble'. In an early piece on a church at Barletta in northern Apulia, he remarked that 'the beauty of the sculpture reveals a French hand'.[35]

Another who acknowledged his debt to de Vogüé was Louis Madelin (1871–1956). A professor, historian (mainly of the Revolution and Napoleon) and far right-wing politician and activist, Madelin came from the Vosges region of Lorraine in eastern France. Like many from national peripheries, he possessed a heightened almost mystical sense of nation. While serving in the First World War, he wrote articles designed to demonstrate how French colonial rule flowed from some sort of racial ability or even destiny. In the tradition of Rey, he applied this to describe the benevolent rule of the Franks in Syria and Palestine, forcefully arguing for the existence of a Franco-Syrian society ('La Syria franque', *Revue des deux mondes* 38, 1916, and *L'Expansion française de la Syrie au Rhin* of 1918). Madelin combined a rehearsal of the now standard national and colonial academic orthodoxy with unmistakable present parallels. Recruits from the colonies fought alongside their French masters in the trenches, as he claimed local Syrians had in the Holy Land, and in the French crusaders themselves those fighting the Germans possessed a model. When a decade later, accepting election to the Académie Française, Madelin portrayed himself as de Vogüé's heir, the concept of the crusades as French and crusader Outremer as prefiguring French colonialism had received seeming confirmation of events.[36]

The creation of French mandates in Syria and the Lebanon after the Treaty of Versailles produced a rush to draw comparisons with the medieval past. Whether or not General Henri Gouraud, first High Commissioner of the French mandate territories, declared on entering Damascus in 1920: 'Behold, Saladin, we have returned,' as was later believed by resentful Arab nationalists, he certainly invited Camille Enlart to record the crusader monuments in Syria. As Enlart's pupil, successor and scholar of crusader castles Paul Deschamps (1888–1974) remarked, the First World War 'brought our troops to those shores where so many good Frenchmen had previously fought'.[37] The English scholar Ernest Barker, who had written a brilliantly compressed yet informed, intelligent and vivid essay on the crusades for the eleventh edition of the *Encyclopaedia Britannica* (1910–11), commented in 1931 that 'even today we may count the French mandate in Syria among the legacies of the Crusades'. The wishful association of past and present suffused works of apparent scholarship. One writer on Outremer laws in 1925, describing himself as 'Lebanese and Christian', looked for the day when all of Syria and its peoples would once more come under French law.[38]

The culmination of such attitudes can be found in the once influential, although now largely ignored, three volumes of René Grousset's *Histoire des croisades et du royaume français de Jérusalem* (1934–36), described by one hostile critic on its publication as largely derived from Röhricht's *Geschichte* but 'longer, less accurate, more prejudiced, more contradictory' although easier to read.[39] Grousset, an orientalist, sought to place the crusades in an eastern context and tried to incorporate recent research by Arabic scholars such as Gaston Weit and by Jean Longnon and Louis Bréhier into the Latin and Greek eastern Mediterranean. Unlike *The Crusaders in the East* (Cambridge, 1907) by the biblical scholar and semitic philologist W. B. Stevenson, who also based his narrative account on eastern sources as well as providing a very neat but full conspectus of western motives, Grousset's sympathies rested with the westerner settlers, even if his grasp of western texts appeared limited (chiefly to the thirteenth-century French version of William of Tyre). He developed further Madelin's idea of the creation of a Franco-Syrian society. Indeed, taking his cue from the overused and usually misunderstood twelfth-century memoirs of Usamah ibn Munqidh of Shaizar, Grousset contrasted the enlightened attitudes of tolerance and rapprochement of the settlers with the boorish insensitivity of visiting crusaders, the colonial challenged by the crusading. It has been suggested that Grousset had in mind the tensions between French colonists in Algeria and the interference from metropolitan France, the medieval *pullani* standing in for the *pieds-noirs* of the 1930s. More generally, and like many before him, he compared the crusades' mix of idealism and violence with that of the French Revolution. Whatever its historical merit, the ideological inheritance of Grousset's work was plain. He talks of 'New France' and 'La France du Levant'. The medieval Latin county of Tripoli is associated with Maronite appeals for French aid in 1860 and 1919. The peroration can stand for a century of French solipsism: 'The Templars held on only to the islet of Ruad (until 1303) south of Tortosa through which one day – in 1914 – the Franks were to set foot once again (*reprendre pied*) in Syria.' The '*reprendre*' undermines the academic credibility of the rhetoric. Despite the horrors of nationalist wars and the collapse of empires of the following decades, Grousset's pupil and apologist, Jean Richard, himself a towering figure of later twentieth-century crusade studies, still wrote in 1953 of Outremer and of the 'Frankish, perhaps even French, state in the East'.[40]

Such views were not simply romantic musings or clever academic *aperçus*. French negotiators at Versailles had referred in their claim to Syrian and Lebanese mandates to their historic role in the region, despite it being pointed out by T. E. Lawrence and the Hashemite delegation that the westerners had actually lost the Levant crusades.[41] Politics, scholarship and wishful thinking can form a toxic combination. Yet the French interpretation operated as the most comprehensive, flexible and dynamic interpretation of the crusades in the period between Napoleon and the Second World War. Its supposed relevance, while historically suspect, ensured attention and hence research. It came to be seen as the only way of regarding the phenomena, a dress rehearsal for the conquest of the Americas and the colonisation of Asia. It was the nineteenth-century French vision of the crusades as proto-colonising expeditions that penetrated the western Islamic world through later nineteenth-century translations, adaptations and criticisms, forming the basis for a local counter-rhetoric of anti-colonialism.[42] Other European national traditions modified detail and perspective, but mostly tended to stay within the same conceptual terms. Thus research followed national enthusiasms everywhere. The earliest editions of the fullest eyewitness account of the capture of Lisbon by an Anglo-Flemish fleet during the

Second Crusade were Portuguese and English (in 1861 and 1864). Johannes Voigt (1786–1863) pioneered not only the history of Prussia but also of the Teutonic Knights who, unsurprisingly, became symbols of German expansionism and state-building. The chief contribution of the English Rolls Series comprised editions of texts relating to the Third Crusade, seen through the prism of the deeds of Richard I. It has even been suggested that US academic engagement was encouraged by a shared interest in the processes of colonisation and the experience of frontiers. Even for those who for ideological or political reasons regarded the crusades with disgust, from the Polish anti-quarian critic of the Teutonic Knights Joachim Lelewel (1786–1861) to the likes of Prebendary George Perry of Lincoln, whose 'popular' *History of the Crusades* (1910) repeated a Gibbonian disdain for medieval religiosity and suspicion at 'what ever may be alleged in its excuse', their starting point was a version of the positive reading exemplified by the French or perhaps Franco-German school.[43]

One effect of the politicisation of crusade studies was, perhaps paradoxically, the draining of ideological and confessional concern. This in itself permitted more generally positive responses. For German nationalists of whatever persuasion – secular, romantic, religious – or Frenchmen attempting to construct an inclusive national narrative and a model of benevolent imperialism, this drew the divisive sting of religion. Christian apologists still were able to point to the crusades' defensive nature and the crusaders' religious sincerity. However, acknowledgement of the civilising elements of cultural exchange or colonial interaction could operate apart from any insistence on religious superiority, although many did so insist. Islam could be presented as the enemy because it presented a secular political menace. Muslims could be conquered because of inherent virtues of western culture which could, but equally need not, include religion. If not entirely secularised, this interpretation of the crusades as expressions of western social developments, eastern politics and a movement to colonise emphasised the material above other constituent elements. In this, both French and German schools found common ground. The crusades became a matter of investigation into the material causes and consequences; the course of the expeditions and eastern wars as political narratives; and the nature and structure of the colonial conquests. To suggest, as has been recently, that in 'neo-imperialist and materialistic' interpretations 'specialists have played no part' is at best misleading.[44] Rather it is against this consensus of materialism, racial supremacy, colonialism and progress that specialists in the twentieth and twenty-first centuries launched some of their sternest attacks. These, in their turn, have on occasion owed more than a little to contemporary and personal circumstance.

Notes

1 E.g. by J. Riley-Smith, *The Oxford Illustrated History of the Crusades* (Oxford, 1995), pp. 4–5.

2 N. Housley, *Contesting the Crusades* (Oxford, 2006), p. 38.

3 D. C. Munro, *The Kingdom of the Crusaders* (New York NY, 1935), esp. pp. 174–203; S. Runciman, *A History of the Crusades* (Cambridge, 1951–54).

4 P. Riant, *Archives de l'Orient Latin*, i (Paris, 1881), v–x. For the *MGH* and Rolls Series, D. Knowles, *Great Historical Enterprises* (London, 1963), pp. 64–97 and 101–34 is a place to start.

5 For Hagenmeyer and Röhricht, above pp. 136–8; B. Kugler, *Studien zur Geschichte des zweiten Kreuzzugs* (Stuttgart, 1866); idem, *Analecten zur Geschichte des zweiten Kreuzzugs* (Tübingen, 1877); idem, *Albert von Aachen* (Stuttgart, 1885).

6 J. G. Herder, *Philosophical Writings*, ed. M. N. Foster (Cambridge, 2002), p. 306; quoted in A. Pagden, *Worlds at War* (Oxford, 2008), p. 200.

7 F. Wilken, *Geschichte der Kreuzzüge nach morgenländischen und abendländischen Berichte* (Leipzig, 1807–32), iii, 88–90

8 F. Krause, 'The Royal Library, Berlin, and its Contacts with Great Britain in the Nineteenth Century', *The Library*, 6th ser., 7 (1985), 211–17.

9 Wilken, *Geschichte*, vi, 71–83 (discussed by G. Dickson, *The Children's Crusade* (London, 2008), pp. 176–7); for the poems, *Geschichte*, vi, 579, note 58; for the range of sources see the bibliography, *Geschichte*, vii, 55–74.

10 Trans. Lady Duff Gordon, *The History and Literature of the Crusades* (London, 1861), p. 312; pp. 131–356 for von Sybel's historiographical excursus; p. iii for Ranke; cf. C. Tyerman, *The Invention of the Crusades* (London, 1998), pp. 119–20 and note 63.

11 From his 1855 Munich lectures, trans. Duff Gordon, *History and Literature*, p. 237.

12 Trans. Duff Gordon, *History and Literature*, pp. 143, 148 *et seq.*, 159, 186 and chaps 2 and 3 for Albert and William.

13 Trans. Duff Gordon, *History and Literature*, pp. 332–45, 353–6.

14 Trans. Duff Gordon, *History and Literature*, pp. 345–53.

15 Trans. Duff Gordon, *History and Literature*, pp. 1–127 for the lectures, esp. pp. 1–4, 13, 45, 62, 104–5; cf. the discussion by R. Ellenblum, *Crusader*

Castles and Modern Histories (Cambridge, 2007), pp. 23–6.

16 H. E. Mayer, 'America and the Crusades', *Proceedings of the American Philosophical Society*, 125 (1981), 41, note 21; more generally *idem*, 'Der Prophet und sein Vaterland. Leben und Nachleben von Reinhold Röhricht', in *In Laudem Hierosolymitani*, ed. I. Shagrir, R. Ellenblum and J. Riley-Smith (Aldershot, 2007), pp. 233–41.

17 A. Lamarche, *Revue de l'Orient Latin*, 6 (1898), 294–9.

18 A. Lamarche, 'Reinhold Röhricht', *Revue de l'Orient Latin*, 10 (1903–4), 543–8.

19 H. Prutz, *Kaiser Friedrich I* (Danzig, 1871–74); T. S. R. Boase, 'Recent Developments in Crusading Historiography', *History*, 22 (1937), 110–25; Ellenblum, *Castles*, pp. 35–6 and generally pp. 32–6.

20 H. Prutz, *Kulturgeschichte der Kreuzzüge* (Berlin, 1883), esp. pp. v, 397–495, 575–98; on German Arabists, R. Irwin, *For Lust of Knowing: Orientalists and their Enemies* (London, 2006), esp. pp. 150–7, 185–8, 191–201.

21 E. Barker, 'The Crusades', in *The Legacy of Islam*, ed. T. Arnold and A. Guillaume (Oxford, 1931), pp. 50–1.

22 See, e.g., E. Siberry, *The New Crusaders* (Aldershot, 2000), pp. 67–8 and refs and fig. 8; Duff Gordon, *History and Literature*, p. 88.

23 Quoted, Tyerman, *Invention*, p. 120.

24 J. R. Dakyns, *The Middle Ages in French Literature 1851–1900* (Oxford, 1973), p. 43; in general see refs in Chapter 4 note 19 above; J. Richard, 'National Feeling and the Legacy of the Crusades', in *Palgrave Advances in the Crusades*, ed. H. Nicholson (Basingstoke, 2005), pp. 208–19.

25 Cf. D. Denby, 'Les croisades aux xviiie et xixe siècle: une historiographie engagéé', in *Les champenois et la croisade*, ed. Y. Bellenger and D. Quéruel (Paris, 1989), p. 170; cf. C. Crossley, *French Historians and Romanticism* (London, 1993), p. 208.

26 A. Beugnot, 'Rapport sur la publication du *Recueil des historiens des croisades*', *Recueil des historiens des croisades: Historiens occidentaux*, I–i (Paris, 1844), i–xv; H. Dehéran, 'Les origines du *Recueil des historiens des croisades*', *Journal des Savants*, n.s. 17 (1919), 260; J. Richard 'Le *Recueil des historiens des croisades*' at www.aibl./fr/fr/travaux/medieval/croisade.html; Richard, 'National Feeling', pp. 213–14.

27 Dakyns, *Middle Ages*, p. 33; Jean de Joinville, *Histoire de Saint Louis*, trans. Natalis de Wailly (Paris, 1865).

28 For the *Salles des croisades*, Chapter 4 note 19 above; for a list of the paintings, Siberry, *New Crusaders*, pp. 208–11 from Constant's 1995 catalogue; for the Courtois forgeries, D. Abulafia, 'Invented Italians in the Courtois Charters', in *Crusade and Settlement*, ed. P. Edbury (Cardiff, 1985), pp. 135–47; Richard, 'National Feeling', pp. 210–13 and refs.

29 M. Marrinan, 'Historical Vision and the Writing of History at Louis Philippe's Versailles', in *The Popularization of Images: Visual Culture under the July Monarchy*, ed. P. Ten-Doesschate Chu and G. P. Weisburg (Princeton NJ, 1994), p. 143; generally pp. 113–43.

30 For Guizot, see Ellenblum, *Castles*, pp. 287–8 and his translations, *Collections des mémoires relatives à l'histoire de France jusqu'à 13e siècle* (Paris, 1823–35); Marquis de Vogüé, 'Le Comte Riant', *Revue de l'Orient*

Latin, 1 (1893), 8; in general and for what follows, cf. Ellenblum, *Castles*, pp. 36–9, 43–9.

31 E. Rey, *Les colonies franques de Syrie au XIIme et XIIIme siècles* (Paris, 1883), pp. vi, 3, 186, 286–91 and chap. 5 *passim*.

32 G. Dodu, *Histoire des institutions monarchiques dans le royaume latin de Jérusalem 1099–1291* (Paris, 1894); D. C. Munroe's review, *Annals of the American Academy of Poltiical and Social Sciences*, 7 (1896), 137–9; Richard, 'National Feeling', p. 219; Ellenblum, *Castles*, pp. 45–6.

33 A. Knobler, 'Saint Louis and French Political Culture', in *Studies in Medievalism*, viii, ed. L. J. Workman and K. Verduin (Cambridge, 1996), *passim*; for a sympathetic account of Lavigerie's schemes, J. Riley-Smith, *The Crusades, Christianity and Islam* (New York NY, 2008), pp. 45–52. Cf. C. M. Andrew, 'The French Colonial Movement during the Third Republic', *Transactions of the Royal Historical Society*, 5th ser., 26 (1976), 143–66.

34 *Archives de l'Orient Latin*, ii (Paris, 1884), 459.

35 C. Enlart, 'L'église des chanoines du Saint-Sépulchre, à Barletta en Pouille', *Revue de l'Orient Latin*, 1 (1893), 562; T. C. Papacostas, 'Western Architecture in Byzantine Lands', in *A Companion to Medieval Art: Romanesque and Gothic in Northern Europe*, ed. C. Rudolph (Oxford, 2006), p. 516; cf. H. Kennedy, *Crusader Castles* (Cambridge, 1994), p. 5.

36 Cf. R. C. Smail, *Crusading Warfare* (Cambridge, 1956), pp. 40–6 and 62–3; Ellenblum, *Castles*, p. 46.

37 Knobler, 'Saint Louis and French Political Culture', p. 168; Kennedy, *Crusader Castles*, p. 5.

38 Barker, 'Crusades', p. 74. D. Hayek, *Le droit franc en Syrie pendant les croisades* (Paris, 1925), pp. 7, 157 cited in J. L. La Monte, *Feudal Monarchy in the Latin Kingdom of Jerusalem* (Cambridge MA, 1932), p. 108, note 1.

39 J. L. La Monte, 'Some problems in crusading historiography', *Speculum*, 15 (1940), 57–8.

40 R. Grousset, *Histoire des croisades* (Paris, 1934–36), i, 287–8, 427; iii, xii, 763; Smail, *Crusading Warfare*, pp. 42–5; E. Sivan, contributing to a symposium in 1984 on 'The Crusading Kingdom of Jerusalem: The First European Colonial Society', in *The Horns of Hattin*, ed. B. Z. Kedar (Jerusalem, 1992), pp. 354, 356; J. Richard, *The Latin Kingdom of Jerusalem* (English trans. Amsterdam, 1979; original French edn 1953), i, v, ix; ii, 463; *idem*, 'National Feeling', pp. 218–19; *idem*, *The Crusades c. 1071–c. 1291* (Cambridge, 1999), pp. xii–xiii.

41 A. J. Toynbee, *Acquaintances* (Oxford, 1967), pp. 187–8.

42 On the development of Arab attitudes, E. Sivan, 'Modern Arab Historiography of the Crusades', *Asian and African Studies*, 8 (1972), 109–49.

43. *De Expugnatione Lyxbonensi*, ed. and trans. C. W. David (New York NY, 1976), p. 48 (Stubbs's Rolls Series edition appeared with the *Itinerarium Ricardi Regis* concerning the Third Crusade, London, 1864); E. Christiansen, *The Northern Crusades* (2nd edn London, 1997), p. 4; La Monte, 'Crusading Historiography', 59; G. G. Perry, *History of the Crusades* (London, 1910), p. 73.

44 J. Riley-Smith, *The Crusades* (2nd edn New Haven CT, 2005), p. 304.

6

The end of colonial consensus

The publication of René Grousset's *Histoire* witnessed the high-water mark of the Franco-German colonial model. New research perspectives and different academic environments combined with growing unease and increasing hostility to the cultural assumptions that had underpinned it. The expansion in range and depth of scholarship came in part as a product of the demands of a burgeoning international historical profession, with its doctorates, academic journals, conferences, proliferation in history departments, job competition and sensitivity to status. The challenge to colonialism and imperialism mirrored the uneven collapse of European hegemony and self-confidence in the half-century from 1914. Local political conditions exerted an influence, as in the caesura in German crusade study after Carl Erdmann's great study on the origins of the idea of the crusade in 1935 or the stimulus to fresh appraisal of Latin Outremer provided by the Jewish settlements in Palestine and the creation of the State of Israel. British negative appraisals of the crusades from the 1940s, at least as regards their impact on the eastern Mediterranean, may have owed not a little to the experience of war and the decline of empire as an ideal as well as a reality. After 1945, the moral and material costs of both looked rather different than they had in the palmy days of the Pax Britannica. The creation of what could almost be regarded as a US school of crusade historians, begun by D. C. Munro in the 1890s, hugely increased the volume and scope of scholarship. Less obvious but as fundamental, accessibility of primary material, in print, libraries and archives, increased internationally in tandem with recognition of its importance, a symptom as well as cause of this new professionalism.

Immediate attacks on Grousset came from two directions: that, despite a work devoted to political history, he had ignored any analysis of the political system in his supposed French state in the Levant and that he had exaggerated or misrepresented the extent of cultural sympathy and synthesis between communities in Outremer. Within a generation, this second assault had developed into a full-scale rejection not of Grousset's colonial assumptions so much as his positive characterisation of Latin Outremer as a tolerant, integrated society. The arguments about crusader settlement still operated within the traditional circuit of liberal economic determinism and the understanding that the Holy Land, as the crusades' main goal, constituted the salient focus for the study of the crusading phenomenon. More radical were those who, from the 1930s, initially in Germany and then France and latterly Britain, set aside the colonial obsession. Instead they investigated the nature of the impulses that gave rise to crusading, swivelling the lens of research from east to west in a return to an earlier sort of cultural self-examination of which nineteenth-century scholars had fought shy. The anti-colonialists were therefore matched by those who, from observing wars on other medieval religious frontiers or from study of western religion and canon law, broke with the Franco-German nineteenth-century consensus completely and restored, consciously or not, the diversity of earlier interests. These latter historians will be the subject of a subsequent chapter. This one looks at the fate of the colonial model itself.

Britain and America

One early reviewer of Grousset's *Histoire*, Frederic Duncalf, a pupil of D. C. Munro, was contemptuous: the first two volumes 'make little or no contribution to our knowledge'.[1] One difficulty, as identified by two nearly contemporaneous reviews by younger scholars, the Oxford art historian and medievalist T. S. R. Boase and John L. La Monte, a Harvard-trained scholar, lay in Grousset's avoidance of any serious analysis of the nature of Outremer society beyond superficial descriptions derived from the narrative sources. La Monte, whose *Feudal Monarchy in the Latin Kingdom of Jerusalem 1100–1291* had appeared in 1932, was particularly severe, although he used Grousset's omissions to argue for a new, collaborative history that would cover all aspects of crusading. Both La Monte and Boase noted the absence of any consideration of what Boase described, very much in the language of Oxford medievalists of the day, as 'the constitutional problem', perhaps better understood as the question of crusader institutions, their nature, scope and imposition. This was a revealing lapse in Grousset's scholarship. In the 1920s, Maurice Grandeclaude had subjected the thirteenth-century law codes of Jerusalem, the *Assises*, to careful analysis to try to determine the survival of any of the pre-1187 legal procedures.[2] Thirty years earlier, Munro had insisted that such law codes could not simply be used to describe twelfth-century circumstances, as Dodu had imagined. In his Lowell lectures at Harvard in 1924, Munro himself had sketched a picture of how Outremer society worked based on sources not sentiment and covering wide aspects of social, economic and commercial life.[3] These critics accepted the Latin states as colonies, a term not yet deconstructed and reviled. However, they sought to integrate study of the Latin East further into mainstream medieval scholarship, both in terms of the critical use of sources and in what would now be called comparative history. Much of the early impetus came from Anglophone scholars.

With the possible exception of Bishop Stubbs and, at a pinch, Charles Mills, almost no English-language work of serious scholarship had been devoted to the crusades for more than a century after Edward Gibbon. The study of crusading had devolved to historical popularisers and literary potboilers. Only slowly did university history departments emerge from the shade of classics and with them some national interest. Thus in Oxford between the World Wars, squeezed in beside a hefty diet of English political, diplomatic and especially constitutional history, there lurked a specialised option on the Third Crusade. Yet even by then, in Britain the most influential works were composed by non-specialists: the historical writer Archer and later medievalist Kingsford; the biblical philologist Stevenson; and the political theorist Ernest Barker (1874–1960), whose 1911 essay for the *Encyclopaedia*

Britannica was reissued in separate book form four times between 1923 and 1939 and was perhaps the most widely read account of the crusades in English of its day. Stevenson (on the First Crusade) and Kingsford (on the kingdom of Jerusalem) reprised their crusade performances for Volume V of the *Cambridge Medieval History* (1926 after an elephantine gestation), where they were joined by a young Cambridge don, E. J. Passant, later a noted expert on the history of modern Germany, whose contribution on the effects of the crusades comprised a feeble mishmash of stale opinion and bombast, its conclusions remarkable for inconclusiveness except for the bracing observation that the crusades provide an excellent example of international cooperation.[4] Perhaps because of the perceived lack of English prominence, and the equivocal standing of the one national crusade hero, Richard I, in the Whig highway of constitutional progress, British writing on the crusades remained, until the 1930s, derivative and provincial. It is notable that none of these authors mentioned confront, let alone react to, the French colonial model – except for Ernest Barker.

Barker, a professional academic, classicist, historian and political scientist, was also a prolific commentator on public affairs. A late Victorian liberal, he enjoyed a conventionally successful career as an Oxford don, head of a London University college and, from 1927, first holder of a chair in political science at Cambridge. An internationalist, libertarian, patriotic critic of nationalism and excessive statism, Barker was unusual in his generation for his emphasis on the positive civic virtues and benefits of organised religion. This was reflected in his essay on the crusades in his eloquent sympathy for the beliefs of individuals. For concision, the application of a classicist's critical eye for texts and lucid style, Barker's essay takes the palm, not least for pithy and, in retrospect, prescient analysis of the phenomenon. For Barker, the crusades formed a central part of a western European religious revival, both holy wars and 'pilgrim progresses', whilst also being the papacy's foreign policy. He saw the First Crusade as 'a penitentiary pilgrimage under arms – with the one additional object of conquering the goal of pilgrimage', Jerusalem. It represented a consecration of the fighting instinct, 'the offensive side of chivalry' (possibly a pun), but rooted in economic circumstances. Here his comparison was less with the British Empire than with

Australian and American gold rushes. Barker drew suggestive and unemotional comparisons and contrasts between Outremer and Norman England and Sicily. His well-honed critical sense provided an acute forensic account of the Jerusalem *Assises*, even though his description of Frankish feudalism tended to follow Dodu. He dismissed the so-called 'Letters of the Sepulchre', reputedly the laws established by Godfrey de Bouillon, as a myth, anticipating by three-quarters of a century recent similar scholarly opinion. His calm assessment of the Fourth Crusade absolved Venice of responsibility for the diversion to Constantinople. In the politest terms, he rejected the French enthusiasm of Rey and Dodu for the Frankish colonists, whose habits he described as 'lawless greed' and their kingdom 'a state of brigands'.[5] In a subsequent reworking of his article, published in 1931, he went further in his dismissal of the Rey–Madelin thesis: 'the absence of any mixture of culture, or indeed of any degree of culture of any kind, in the kingdom of Jerusalem is a striking thing'.[6] While sceptical of the primacy of Outremer as a conduit of eastern culture to the west, preferring Spain and Sicily, Barker nonetheless repeated the cliché of cultural exchange in the context of the immemorial struggle of east and west, although by 1931 he had significantly glossed this crude dichotomy: 'The duel of East and West is a geographical simplification of a complicated series of historical facts.'[7] Well read and intelligent, Barker's *tour de force*, lacking originality of research, exists as an elevated old-fashioned Oxbridge tutor's commentary of the better sort: clever, panoramic, informed, sharp, critical, questioning, accessible and elegant, suggestive as much as definitive. In the high tradition that leads back to Gibbon, its literary virtues are as effective as its academic. The peroration is a triumph of rhetoric over reason, with its talk of 'the majesty of man's incessant struggle towards an ideal good', and of giving thanks for the memory of those 'millions of men who followed the pillar of cloud and fire in the sure and certain hope of an eternal reward'. Yet, in the even older tradition of Fuller, the Congregationalist-turned-Anglican Barker cannot resist a Protestant last word: 'nor can we but give thanks for their memory, even if for us religion is of the spirit, and Jerusalem in the heart of every man who believes in Christ.'[8]

While not entirely free from such literary flights, the group of American crusade scholars that emerged in the 1920s and 1930s adopted a more sober demeanour. At the centre of this circle sat Dana C. Munro, successively from the 1890s until his death in 1933 a professor at the universities of Pennsylvania, Wisconsin and Princeton. His link with German *Quellenkritik* was direct, having studied in Germany in 1889/90 with the prominent medievalist document scholar Paul Scheffer-Boichorst. Munro returned to the USA a crusade enthusiast. While himself publishing little he taught a whole generation of crusade historians of note, including Frederic Duncalf and August C. Krey, later collaborators with J. La Monte in planning a collaborative history, and the authors of a series of pioneering crusade biographies, a form of historical writing of enduring prominence in US academic circles: M. W. Baldwin (Raymond III of Tripoli); C. W. David (Robert Curthose) and R. W. Yewdale (Bohemund of Taranto). Pupils of Munro's own students included R. L. Nicholson (who wrote on Tancred, Joscelin I and Joscelin III of Edessa) and J. H. Hill, editor of Raymond of Aguilers and Peter Tudebode and biographer of Raymond IV of Toulouse. Simply by reciting the topics covered indicates the inherent conservatism of approach, the focus on the material- military, political and colonial. Even the work on Genoese trade by another of Munro's students, E. H. Byrne, and his pupils fitted the familiar frame of investigation, despite the fact that, as in this case, it was novel in exploring a mass of fresh archival material.[9]

No less hidebound was the study of the Frankish monarchy in Jerusalem by John La Monte (1902–49), for all his declared openness to new fields of research. Although not one of Munro's pupils, he became closely associated with his circle after 1930. Like theirs, La Monte's attacks on Grousset were pointed and severe. Reviewing the first two volumes, he accused the Frenchman of neglecting constitutional, social and economic history, of excessive reliance on William of Tyre, and of displaying ignorance of German, English or Italian scholarship. He even lightly hinted at racism, noting – accurately – that Grousset ascribed Saladin's chivalrous behaviour to his being not a Turk but a Kurd and hence 'an Indo-European'.[10] However, La Monte, in neither of his published reviews (in 1935 and 1940), takes issue with Grousset's central Franco-Syrian colonial thesis. He either seems tacitly to accept it or simply avoids the whole issue. This is also apparent in his *Feudal Monarchy*, which is in fact even more narrowly focused than Grousset and as subservient to a highly contestable theory. The question of social, economic or cultural relations between conquerors and conquered never arises, indeed was 'purposely omitted', La Monte contenting himself with referring his readers interested in social history to Rey's *Colonies franques*. Where he is forced to consider the jurisdiction of royal courts over the native population, his commentary is brief, uneasy and derivative, as if he would rather talk of something else (which indeed he does). La Monte's purpose was 'merely to study monarchy', even to the exclusion of what he called the 'private law' of the kingdom of Jerusalem. Given the book's origins in a doctoral thesis, this narrowness of focus is understandable. However, the constitutional and legal arrangements portrayed are not so much a picture as a mirage. La Monte sees Frankish Jerusalem as 'a typical feudal state', subject to *'pure feudalism'* (La Monte's italics), a phrase echoing – hopefully unconsciously – Kingsford's 'purest form' of feudalism in the 1926 *Cambridge Medieval History*. This conviction was based on La Monte's uncritical acceptance of the testimony of the tendentious thirteenth-century Jerusalem law books as evidence for the reality of twelfth-century law and politics, in particular the weakness of the crown *vis-à-vis* the baronage. Yet Munro had exposed the fallacy of this approach in his review of Dodu in 1896, an insight confirmed more recently by the intuition of Barker and the researches of Grandeclaude. Even a clever Oxford undergraduate, in a prize essay of 1937, 'Feudal Society in the Latin States of Palestine and Syria and its Relations to the Saracens', managed a critique of the concept of feudalism and a sceptical scrutiny of the sources that makes La Monte's efforts appear intellectually pedestrian. What makes this even stranger is that La Monte later produced a series of 'fundamental' articles on Jerusalem baronial families.[11]

However, La Monte's legacy was more substantial. As professor at Pennsylvania from 1940, he revived Munro's series of translated sources. He also became the flag-bearer for a scheme to produce a multi-volume collaborative history of the crusades. Munro was the inspiration on two counts, through what he achieved through teaching and research and by failing to complete the massive new interpretation he had planned. With La

Monte, the prime movers for a collaborative history that would achieve what one author could not in breadth and depth of coverage were two of Munro's older pupils, Frederic Duncalf (1882–1963) and August Krey (1887–1961). It was La Monte who provided the impetus, outlining the scheme to the American Historical Association in 1938. After tracing the history of crusade historiography, La Monte explained the two dominant approaches. Either the crusades were seen as an aspect of European history and the confrontation between Christianity and Islam; or studied as agents that created Christian colonies in the eastern Mediterranean. He identified gaps in research, such as the role of the papacy and detailed study of certain individual expeditions, such as the Second and Fifth Crusades. He pointed to recent work by the German Carl Erdmann in crusade ideology and Aziz S. Atiya on the later middle ages and to current research in Grandeclaude's wake on the Jerusalem laws by a very young Oxford scholar mentioned by Boase in his review of Grousset, J. O. Prestwich, the author (although La Monte may not have known it) of the 1937 undergraduate prize essay challenging the idea of Jerusalem feudalism. La Monte referred to a group of willing coadjutors, that included, as well as the core of Munro's pupils already mentioned, the Lebanese Arabist Philip K. Hitti (then at Princeton) and Palmer A. Throop, a late pupil of Munro, shortly to produce his influential, if, in its underlying thesis, highly conventional *Criticism of the Crusade* (1940). The 1938 outline of the projected work conformed to a familiar orthodox model: origins and First Crusade; crusades and crusader states in the twelfth and thirteenth centuries; later crusades and the influence on 'medieval civilisation'.[12] The conservative and narrative structure remained a marked feature of much of the long-delayed finished work.

After early approval from the American Historical Association and the Medieval Academy of America, necessary imprimaturs in the then somewhat deferentially hierarchic world of US scholarship, the Second World War forced the postponement of the enterprise. In 1946, La Monte was appointed editor in chief and his university, Pennsylvania, agreed to underwrite the project. The team of contributors was extended to include foreign scholars. La Monte died in 1949, but his successor at

Pennsylvania, Kenneth M. Setton (1914–95), as general editor, supervised a glacial progress of production. Volumes one and two appeared in 1955 and 1962. The project was then taken over by the university of Wisconsin and four further volumes, alongside reissues of the first two, emerged between 1969 and 1989, over half a century after La Monte's original prospectus. Inevitably, the scope expanded, but rarely systematically. As often with collaborative works, the dispositions owed as much to the interests, availability, productivity and mendacity of individual authors as to the requirements of scholarship.[13] Inevitably, some contributions were out of date when they were published (a few when they were written). Numerous contributors never lived to see their prose in print. While slowly reflecting changes in how the crusades were seen, witnessed by the inclusion of the later crusades in volumes three and six, art and architecture (volume four) and analytical pieces on social, economic and financial aspects (especially in volumes five and six), by relying in the main on established experts there could be little new or innovative about the work produced, nor was there. Narratives by Steven Runciman (in volume one), or studies of Outremer by Joshua Prawer and Jean Richard, were more easily and satisfyingly found elsewhere. With research on crusading witnessing an extraordinary and extravagant protean growth precisely as the US *History* was creeping and grinding its laborious way into bookshops and libraries, the point of the project came into question. The academic landscape was changing so rapidly that synthetic summaries were otiose, a point made as early as 1957 by R. C. Smail.[14] When in 1951 Runciman challenged the 'massed typewriters' of the US work (to which with characteristic insouciance he himself contributed three rehashed chapters) with his solitary pen, in a literary vein he could not fail.[15] More seriously, the US collaborative history was cumbersome in arrangement, marmoreal in tone yet timid in ambition. Seeking inappropriate definition and impossible consensus, it remained forever dogged by the conservatism that attended its birth. For all its industry, weight of material, useful maps, notes on nomenclature, bibliographies and glossaries, it traduced the memories of its dedicatees, Munro, La Monte, Duncalf and Krey, by contributing more or less nothing to the debate on the crusades.

The colonial model under attack: Arabists, Zionists and anti-imperialists

Some of the issues considered by the original planners of the US *History* in the 1930s found rather different treatment by scholars who, while also studying the Latin East, questioned the theoretical bases of their subject. Such attacks on the nineteenth-century 'positive' colonial model came from a number of quarters, deriving not only from fresh scrutiny of the evidence but from the ideological and political stances of the historians. Scholars of the Muslim Near East and Arabic sources combined in criticism with those looking afresh at Frankish Outremer from new perspectives of western scepticism of the virtues of colonialism and the newer still context of the establishment in 1948 of the Zionist State of Israel in the same geographic space. Half a century after Grousset's final volume appeared, very little, if any, of the tradition he represented retained academic credibility. However, this rejection of received interpretation exerted a much more limited impact on popular, public and political attitudes. Equally, as has recently been observed, the critics of the colonial model shared with its creators a concentration on the material features of crusading, its conquests, settlements, and effect on trade, finance, economics, warfare, military and civilian architecture and art. Thus, in a paradoxical manner, they reinforced a 'neo-imperialistic and materialistic interpretation'.[16] It is claimed this continued configuration of crusading as colonialist, even where disapproved of, is shared by liberal, Marxist, Zionist and Muslim commentators alike, to the detriment of seeing the crusades primarily as religious acts. Alternatively, it could be suggested that continued interest in Latin settlements in the eastern Mediterranean flowed from the historical fact of those conquests and their apparent eccentricities. Whatever motivated or compelled Latin settlers, settle they did with concrete results. It is the nature of those results that formed the bone of contention for the critics of the colonialist model.

In his review of Grousset in 1937, Boase had mentioned the recent (1934) critique of Madelin's Franco-Syrian theory by a young French scholar, Claude Cahen (1909–91), whose study of Arabic sources indicated that the Franks had in fact made very little impact on the indigenous population.[17] These ideas he developed over the rest of a career that also embraced studies of the social and economic history of the Near East and pre-Ottoman Turkey. After 1945 successively a professor at Strasbourg and in Paris, for twenty years a member of the Communist Party and a life-long Marxist, Cahen established himself as the most influential western historian of the medieval Islamic Near East in the twentieth century. His work on the crusades, although an adjunct to his chief concerns, was revelatory by placing them in a context that eluded almost all others. Cahen's contempt for Grousset's *Histoire* was profound, regarding it as a work devoid of specialist insight by a popularising author ignorant of 'any of the necessary languages'. But, as he said, this was no laughing matter.[18] For Cahen, a rare Marxist in crusade studies as well as an orientalist, Grousset and the rest who represented the crusades in a positive light, appeared variously as apologists for past social hierarchies, monarchy, colonial mission and for the crusades as precursors of French cultural influence in the Mediterranean since the eighteenth century. His comments on French appropriation of the crusades were particularly dry. Cahen's central criticism was directed at scholarship that looked at the Near East from a wholly western perspective through almost exclusively western sources, an implicit form of patronising western Orientalism. Much of this rested on a near universal ignorance of Arabic among crusade historians before and during much of Cahen's lifetime, but was also a symptom of a wider cultural distortion. Cahen insisted that the crusade settlements in Syria and Palestine should be examined in their local not colonial context, as their colonial nature was itself contestable, conforming neither to classical nor modern types. He insisted that the study of the crusades as a product of western society was one thing; that of the Latin settlements, 'states like the rest', another.[19]

By adjusting the focus to highlight the experience of the Christian, Muslim and Jewish natives as seen through indigenous sources, happy assumptions of cultural exchange disappeared. From this perspective, the Franks were just one more foreign ruling class, like the Turks, whose impact on daily lives was negligible and, Cahen pointedly remarked in a dig at those more interested in the antics of the rich and powerful, 'daily life ... is almost all life'.[20] Indigenous sources indicated no cultural

symbiosis, rather a mutual ignorance and the customary relationships of exploitation by rulers of the ruled. The precise ways in
which exploitation could in fact rely on social contact, drawing
communities together, became a matter of later controversy. In
much of their activities, the Franks excluded locals. They left no
lasting imprint on Syrian or Palestinian society, culture, language
or demographics, their influence marginal and peripheral in the
wider history of the Near East. Almost all the supposed elements
of cultural exchange, in arts, learning and commerce, so lauded in
the colonial model, now appeared illusory, superficial or owing
little specifically to the crusading enterprises. That the crusades
received such attention at all in Arabic sources, Cahen argued,
came as a consequence of the revival witnessed by the Muslim
Near East during the period, but paled in significance beside the
thirteenth-century emergence of the Mamluks and the incursions
of Mongols. In any case, larger geopolitical shifts in the structures
of the Muslim world from the decline of the Abbasid caliphate in
the tenth and eleventh centuries were of far greater moment than
the Frankish occupation of parts of the Levantine littoral. If
nothing else, Cahen deflated the self-importance of western
crusade historiography as well as its sloppy tendency to ill-
informed generalisations about the Muslim world that would not
be tolerated in their own areas of expertise. He also noted that
even by the 1980s Near Eastern scholars were reluctant to take
up the task themselves, a situation confirmed at the very end of
the century by Carole Hillenbrand's innovative *The Crusades:
Islamic Perspectives* (1999), despite her surprising omission of
Cahen in her brief historiographic survey.[21] However, Cahen's
unsentimental, orientalist approach helped change the rules of
engagement even for western scholars unable to read Arabic, not
least in offering new Arabic texts and sterner source criticism of
literatures previously known to most crusade historians only in
translation.

New scrutiny of texts was not reserved to eastern sources;
western texts, many very familiar, came in for radical reassessment at the same time from scholars with equally strong
intellectual and personal motives who nonetheless remained
focused on the Latin East. Some of the new developments are
closely linked to more general revisionism within medieval

studies, moving away from a narrowly political and constitutional approach to a wider appreciation of religious, economic and social contexts and a greater sensitivity to the complexities of understanding the actual workings of legal and administrative institutions from the formal evidence such activities generated. Inevitably, university history faculties provided a focus for such debates which also existed within a wider cultural dimension. After the First World War, in most political societies, whether democracies or dictatorships, much lip-service and public attention was paid to 'the people' and to ideas both of change and of modernisation. This frequently combined with interest in valuing, reshaping or inventing a past attuned to the present, by governments but also by oppositional political factions. Some historians, in places such as Russia, Germany, Italy and Spain, but more subtly in democratic societies, joined or were recruited into such recrafting of history. The rise of Marxist historians in France and Britain is an obvious example. To challenge old-fashioned concentration on the middle ages as a time of kings and castles, knights and battles, churchmen and lawyers surrounded by an undifferentiated, inarticulate and ignored mass of peasantry was not necessarily entirely academic. Militant ideology, war, empire, colonisation, mass conscription, intercontinental conflict and contact all possessed contemporary resonance. The crusades offered scope to all parties, as examples, according to choice, of efficient or, alternatively, inefficient hierarchies; of mass involvement and social cooperation; or as yet another example of material exploitation of followers and conquered; or of the power of faith and ideology to move populations and implement political action across society.

If Cahen attacked the colonial model from without, as it were, others undermined from within the western tradition. In the late 1930s, two young English scholars, John Prestwich at Oxford and R. C. Smail at Cambridge, turned their attention to Outremer. Although he abandoned study of the Latin East, Prestwich, building on his undergraduate prize essay, had essayed a pursuit of Grandeclaude's analysis of the Jerusalem laws to test the prevailing assumptions about the nature of the supposedly 'pure' feudal society established by the Franks in Outremer, untouched by local heterogeneous circumstances. His scepticism, which later he transferred and developed into a forceful critique of feudalism in the Anglo-Norman world, was fuelled by the traditional obsession of English medievalists. Debates about the nature of feudalism and the chronology or even fact of its introduction or not into English society had become and remained a staple of historians' wrangling, exposing fundamental differences in their approach to the past, its sources and the structure of medieval society. This was far from being an English obsession alone; the productive Claude Cahen had himself delivered some pointed comments on accepted orthodoxy in a 1940 book on feudalism in Norman Italy.[22] This concern with the institutions of feudalism was linked to the later nineteenth- and early twentieth-century academic interest in medieval constitutions in general in the context of the development of the contrasting national histories of Germany, France and England. This was also fuelled by the fashionable legalistic bent among medievalists and their interpretations of medieval states and polities. For Outremer as for western Europe, certainties like those of Dodu and La Monte looked increasingly credulous and unconvincing, irrelevant even, when set against the evidence, from chronicles as well as charters and law books, of how societies actually operated in practice and, in particular, of the realities of war. This was to become one of Prestwich's central insights in his post-war work on the Anglo-Norman realm. It also formed the core of what became one of the most effective assaults on the crusader colonial model.

'Warfare is a related part of the whole activity of any society.'[23] Thus, argued R. C. Smail in 1956, examination of how military activity actually operated within Latin Outremer would provide valuable insights into the nature of the settlement and rule. His innovative study of Frankish warfare 1097–1193 explored features, notably campaigning between 1129 and 1187, previously largely ignored by military historians. He established new maxims, most famously that successful defence against aggressors relied on the relationship between adequately manned static garrisons combining with a mobile field army. From this study of Frankish warfare in action, and to some extent picking up a point made by Ernest Barker a generation earlier, Smail concluded that the Franks were never entirely secure in their hold over either territory or native people. Their numbers were too small to engage with the locals in anything beyond a distant and potentially oppressive system of economic exploitation, producing a segregated not integrated society, a view suggested by Cahen and, a century before him, Beugnot. The Franks stayed in their cities, castles and fortified places, their relations with the mass of their subjects fiscal, commercial and seigneurial. The adoption of local habits and dress, as well as the aristocratic contacts across religious and political divides, were essentially superficial. The Rey–Madelin thesis was dismissed as the product of modern French interests in colonialism, a form of self-justification for a contemporary activity for which Smail, in contrast to the French writers he criticised, expressed neither affection nor admiration. Hostility not friendship or cooperation marked intercommunal relations in Outremer, the tacit implication being that the same was, *mutatis mutandis*, likely to be true in modern colonies. In Frankish Outremer there was no superior western culture benevolently to disperse, nor any reciprocal absorption by the conquerors of the sophisticated civilisation of the conquered. Smail took pains to expose the misreading of the sources by those who argued for a Franco-Syrian cultural integration. Thus he contested the old orthodoxy on both historical and historiographical grounds. Late in life, he was content to abandon the term 'colony' altogether as being both too simple and too loaded with inappropriate and complex implications to be a useful descriptive or analytical tool.[24] Although certain links in Smail's argument, such as the distribution of the different local faith communities or the extent of Frankish settlement, were ignored or assumed, his research stemmed from a clearer theoretical grasp on the extensive role of war in medieval society and a consequently broader analysis of the sources. However, in effect, he did not so much reject the colonial model as completely invert it.

If Smail's deconstruction of the colonial model occurred in the circumstances of the twentieth-century end of western European empires in Asia and Africa, a similar attack emerged from the context of a political beginning, the creation of the State of Israel (1948). From the early nineteenth century, study of Frankish Outremer had been conducted almost as a shadow crusade, with writers such as Michaud, de Vogüé, Rey or Prutz making their own *passagia* to the east. The physical remains had similarly been studied by visitors, a process accelerated by the French and British mandates after 1920. Local Arab scholars displayed little interest in serious study of the crusades. Only with the establishment of western-style university history departments in the wake of Zionist settlement (the Hebrew University of Jerusalem was founded in 1925) were the medieval Frankish settlements studied by scholars resident in the same geographic space. Superficial similarities between the plantation of then largely European Jews with the Frankish invaders made a sense of association – even connection – unavoidable even if it was, for some, uncomfortable. Inescapable parallels could speak of rude foreign conquest and impermanent settlement or, alternatively, as negative precursors, warnings from a failed past to guide a different future. For others, as one present-day Israeli historian has put it, by reacting to a form of sentimental empathy, a shared memory born of a shared place, the 'Crusaders ... were transformed simply into another group of former inhabitants of the country, part of its history'. He added, less irenically, 'the fact that the Crusaders had fought the Muslims made this conceptual transformation all the easier'.[25]

In the years immediately after the founding of the State of Israel, attitudes were dominated by a scholar who stood diametrically at the other end of the spectrum of Israeli response to the crusaders' conquest. Joshua Prawer (1917–90), born in Polish Silesia, emigrated to Palestine in 1936 to study at the Hebrew University of Jerusalem. Under the influence of Richard Koebner, a historian of medieval German colonisation and settlement, Prawer concentrated his postgraduate research on the Frankish settlements, almost exclusively in the kingdom of Jerusalem. His approach was far removed from the earlier French school. In a series of major articles beginning in the early 1950s, culminating in three major books, *Histoire du royaume latin de Jérusalem* (Paris, 1969–71), *The Latin Kingdom of Jerusalem: European Colonisation in the Middle Ages* (London, 1972) and *Crusader Institutions* (Oxford, 1980, a collection of revised articles), Prawer examined the social institutions of the kingdom, the power of the kings, the laws, the evidence of settlement, agriculture and economic exploitation, presenting an alternative model that completely contradicted the older colonial theories. Instead of the almost exclusive focus on the noble elites that marked most earlier studies of Outremer, Prawer was drawn to evidence of the whole of Frankish society, notably the free non-nobles, the so-called burgesses. For Prawer, the Frankish settlement was numerically small, restricted to cities, physically and culturally distant from the countryside and its inhabitants except for the few defensive garrison castles. There was no perfect feudal consti-tution holding the kings in aristocratic thrall. Between the new rulers and the indigenous people, very largely Muslim he assumed, unbridgeable gulfs were erected by law, religion and, most sweepingly, by a 'colonial attitude' that rendered the reali-ties of indigenous culture effectively invisible to the western invaders and settlers. The paternalistic benevolent cooperation and synthesis of Rey and Madelin (misguided 'do-gooders') was replaced by a picture of complete separation, of, in a word he used advisedly and often, 'apartheid'. Outremer was a colony but 'there was no fraternization with the local population, there was a refraction with regard to local culture, apartheid with regard to the local population, dependence on Europe in several respects'.[26]

Prawer's opinions complemented and extended the ideas of Smail and, in terms of fresh approach to sources, were matched by others who held somewhat less defined hostility to the older French thesis. Another post-Second World War scholar, the Frenchman Jean Richard (b. 1921), a wide-ranging and innova-tive historian of the county of Tripoli, Outremer lordships, the church, Cyprus, Louis IX and the Asiatic context, retained a profound respect for Grousset while radically reshaping and supplanting Grousset's picture of Outremer in ways that comple-mented Prawer's own work.[27] However, while not explicitly drawing modern parallels, Prawer placed the medieval past in a historical continuum. He linked the colonialism of Outremer, not least as exercised by the Italian maritime cities, with the European expansion of the early modern period in Africa, the Atlantic and the Americas. He noted, pointedly if not mischievously, that Jerusalem had been a capital city for only four of the regimes that had ruled in Palestine: the Israelites, the crusaders, the British Mandate and the State of Israel. More widely, his theories held a clear message for his compatriots. As he wrote in the *Histoire du royaume latin*, 'although it became a homeland (*patrie*) for its inhabitants, the Latin State never became a cradle (*berceau*) of a nation'.[28] The reasons were evident. The Franks never settled in sufficient numbers to secure their survival and, partly as a consequence but also because of their 'colonial mentality', they failed to make the countryside theirs by settling there. Prawer was in a sense answering an unspoken but loud question, one which other Zionists had posed: are the Israelis just like the crusaders and will they suffer the same fate? His work points to a clear answer: no. With its dedication to attract large-scale immigration, and those immigrants' close engagement with the landscape and environment, for example in the *kibbutz* movement, the State of Israel was the antithesis to the Frankish state and so would not share its fate. Only perhaps in the suggestion of the lack, perhaps even impossibility, of cultural synthesis with the other peoples of the region did the Franks provide a direct lesson. Prawer had experienced colonialism at first hand, under the increasingly ragged and unsympathetic British Mandate. He would not have regarded Zionism as a colonial enterprise comparable with those that had penetrated the region before. In 1984 he pointed out that, unlike in European languages where they were called colonies, with all its layers of meaning, the Hebrew word for the Zionist presence in Palestine was *moshavah*, literally 'settlement'.[29] Prawer was a man of affairs as well as a scholar, becoming a central figure in the establishment of Israeli universities and its education system. The modern resonance of his work cannot have escaped him. It certainly did not those of a younger generation, for whom Prawer's work forms one strand in a vigorous debate on Zionism itself.[30] Delegates at a crusade historians' conference in Jerusalem in 1987 were frequently reminded by locals, sometimes casually in the street, that the Israelis were not like the crusaders; they were in the Holy Land to stay.

Central to Prawer's view lay the question of the demography of Frankish settlement and a certain reading of the evidence. Much of the conceptual frame was traditional, even if the picture itself was new. The assumption of colonialism, the generalisations about cultural exchange, even asides on the nature of the crusading enterprise itself – 'one wonders if the whole idea was not polluted at source (*viciée à base*)' – address issues familiar to crusade historians over the previous two centuries.[31] More specifically, in the light of different perspectives and new research, some of it archaeological, Prawer's thesis proved vulnerable on a number of fronts, such as the details of intercommunal relations (closer than he imagined); the extent and location of Frankish settlement (more widespread in the countryside); the structure of indigenous society (more variegated and less exclusively Muslim); the power of Frankish kings (more circumscribed, earlier); and the nature of urban confraternities (faith based rather than political estates). Some of the questions Prawer asked have been superseded by different approaches, such as that of the German Hans Eberhard Mayer (b. 1932). Basing his research on meticulous study of charters and very close reading of chronicles, Mayer has gone further than Prawer in investigating the internal working of secular and ecclesiastical lordships and in exposing both how government worked and how politics operated. Although a wonderfully gifted synthesiser and author of one of the most important and widely read modern general accounts of the crusades, as regards Outremer Mayer looks beyond or perhaps behind the grand structures of constitutionalism in building an impression very much from the bottom upwards.[32] However, more fundamental challenges to Prawer's understanding of Frankish Outremer came from scholars who argued directly against the 'apartheid' model.

Some criticisms operated within the broad Prawer-esque views of the coercive and urban nature of Frankish rule. This did not necessarily confirm a system of 'apartheid'. One of Prawer's former students, Benjamin Z. Kedar, noted that intercommunal relations tended to be stable, partly because of the very lack of Frankish settlement and an attitude of resignation on the part of the Muslim majority. However, while more limited than in Spain or Sicily, Outremer's contribution to 'the transfer of Arabic learning to the West was ... somewhat less negligible than usually assumed'. With his skill at forensic micro-history, as it is sometimes called, Kedar also argued that the apparently racially discriminatory decrees regarding dress and sex issued by the Council of Nablus (1120), in which Prawer had placed great store, were not quite what they had seemed. They had been promulgated in the context of an immediate crisis, may never have been implemented, were not as harsh as similar codes else-where in the Mediterranean, displayed Byzantine not Frankish antecedents and, as another scholar had observed, were not included in the Jerusalem *Assises*.[33] Similar chips came off the Prawer edifice elsewhere. For example, in a series of articles from the early 1970s, the English historian Jonathan Riley-Smith, as well as questioning the extent of royal power early in the twelfth century, argued that the Frankish overlords inevitably had links with the local population through the mechanics of lordship, the administration of manorial estates and the fiscal system, and that these contacts were in no sense necessarily disruptive or hostile. Pursuing this idea of continuity, he further suggested (implausibly in Mayer's view) that Frankish bureaucracy inherited the previous Fatimid system. Pointing to the number of sites of shared worship and religious veneration and to a social relationship equivalent to the Muslim *dhimma* system, which allowed for religious freedom in return for a poll tax and certain legal restrictions (a point also made for example by Kedar), Riley-Smith argued for peaceful if not harmonious relations between the communities, including the Franks. In some ways this represented a reworking of the insights of Claude Cahen that portrayed the Franks as yet another foreign ruling class. Riley-Smith's recognition of active administrative borrowing and continuity for indigenous institutions cut near the heart of Prawer's model of absolute segregation and 'colonial mentality', whatever that implied.[34]

More fundamental to the Prawer–Smail interpretation is the size and distribution of the Frankish population and the military, economic and social circumstances of the settlement. The Israeli historian and archaeologist Ronnie Ellenblum has argued in two recent works, *Frankish Rural Settlement in the Latin Kingdom of Jerusalem* (Cambridge, 1998) and *Crusader Castles and Modern Histories* (Cambridge, 2007), that what he calls the anti-colonial-ist segregation model of Prawer and Smail is fatally flawed. By re-examining the written evidence, the cultural assumptions of previous historians and fresh archaeological material, Ellenblum constructs a very different picture of Frankish society. He suggests that there were proportionately more western settlers than previously admitted; that native Palestinians included signif-icant communities of local Christians; that it was in these

Christian areas, for instance north of Jerusalem, that numerous Frankish villages were established; that in consequence Frankish society was far from being the urbanised ghettoes of Prawer's imagination; that the Franks did engage directly with the rural landscape and its agriculture as more than absentee landlords; that the security situation of the Franks for most of the mid-twelfth century at least was not so very precarious; that the spread of castles across the often peaceful landscape was for economic and not solely military and defensive purposes; that earlier interpretations had been coloured by their advocates' personal attitudes towards colonisation in general. Ellenblum draws comparisons with Latin emigration and settlement in southern Europe.

This is far from a return to the Rey–Madelin fairy tale. Communities were divided by religion; Franks did not settle in predominantly Muslim rural areas. Militarisation increased as the political balance shifted against the Franks in the generation before Hattin. It is however a root and branch rejection of the Prawer–Smail thesis. Prawer himself was dismissive of Ellenblum's findings when first presented. Much of Ellenblum's account rests, as with previous interpretations, on assumptions about texts, demographic models and material remains more or less unprovable. Even among archaeologists, Ellenblum's theories have not gone unchallenged. Denys Pringle, perhaps the most learned modern scholar of all types of Frankish architecture in Palestine, has pointed out that even on Ellenblum's own evidence, the idea of Franks settled in the countryside in fortified villages, houses and towers hardly contradicts the Prawer–Smail thesis of the permanent tension of an occupying elite. Similarly, the evidence for lack of numbers, as for example produced by Smail, is scarcely refuted in Ellenblum's model, which may not be as radical a departure as it appears. Mayer commented a generation ago that the number of burgesses 'who settled in the countryside should not be underestimated'.[35]

There is another connection with older theories, the influence of the writer's own intellectual and social context. Ellenblum himself provides a clue at least to one element in his own cultural influences. After describing anti-colonial and Zionist views of the Frankish states, he argues that the invention of any national history is determined by a selection of past episodes within that nation's geographic space. Consequently, societies that have no obvious affinity with previous occupants of their space nonetheless find some selective identification, as with the British interest in and preservation of their island's Roman past. By using the Frankish incursion as 'a sort of reverse pre-figuration' for the State of Israel, the crusader episode was recognised as part of the history of the Holy Land and therefore of Israel, a view reinforced by the powerful testimony of the physical remains in the Israeli landscape, 'part of the history of the Israeli nation ... part of my own country, and to a certain degree, as part of my own history'.[36] This is a telling contrast to the colonial rejectionism of Prawer's generation. Yet it too speaks of its time, at once more confident of established belonging, full ownership of the territory and its history yet with an awareness of persistent threats. The identification with the Franks (or its rejection) cannot be conceived within the sort of colonial matrix that occurred naturally to an older generation of immigrants. Yet the absorption and Israelification of the Palestinian landscape that Ellenblum's almost elegiac response suggests in fact derives from one of Prawer's main concerns, the engagement with the land. There may be a further ironic twist that speaks to emotions similar to those expressed by Ellenblum, although leading in a very different direction to his scenario of accommodation. It has recently been observed (or argued, according to taste and political persuasion) by one Israeli former crusade historian that Israel's crusader past is seen as more acceptable than its Arab one. Ummayad remains and posh formerly Arab houses are rebranded as 'crusader', just as archaeological periods have become attached to invaders rather than indigenous inhabitants. Better to immortalise the 1096 killers of Rhineland Jews than acknowledge Arab civilisation.[37] Such things are not neutral, and potentially just as corrosive as the most rancid application of colonialism.

In the context of debates about crusading, perhaps the chief significance of such new approaches is the extent to which they represent a genuine abandonment of all western European perspectives on the Frankish conquests, whether orientalist, nationalist, imperial, colonial, anti-colonial or, as originally, crusader. The models of integration or segregation exist as part of arguments borrowed from separate historical, political or cultural discussions. These are tenacious. Carole Hillenbrand's landmark study of Islamic evidence in 1999, where she exposes the extensive rhetoric of external and émigré Muslim hostility to the Franks, sits securely in this tradition; both Stevenson and Runciman ('an excellent starting point') are cited approvingly.[38] Hans Mayer's elegant and lucid chapter on 'the Latin East 1098–1205' in volume four of the *New Cambridge Medieval History* (2004) is a masterpiece of concision. Yet it deals exclusively with the 'Latin' rather than the 'East', constrained by space to concentrate on the political, legal and constitutional history of the immigrant *Staatsvolk* 'to the exclusion of the Muslims and Syro-Christians, not to mention the minorities of the separated eastern churches or, even smaller in number, the Jews'.[39] Merely acknowledging the absence exposes the distortion, like studying Norman England without the English, Anglo-Norman Ireland without the Irish, Norman Sicily without the Muslims or the German conquest of Prussia and Livonia without the Prussians and Livs. Similar historiographical traditions, dating back to medieval apologists, surrounded western European expansion in northern, eastern and southern Europe. Yet the Frankish conquest displayed special features as well as a markedly different history when contrasted with the Baltic or Sicily or Andalusia. Observing that non-Latin locals existed and then excluding them tacitly accepts a segregation model if only as a literary convenience. Kedar, an extremely original and sensitive student of intercommunal relations in Outremer, still felt the need to play with concepts of colonial 'fragments'.[40] Even Ellenblum, while seeking to subvert the colonial and anti-colonial models alike by demonstrating a more complex set of relationships, appears somewhat conceptually trapped by the theory he is attacking.

Others are pursuing more radical abandonment of the colonial/segregation argument. The work, for instance, of Cahen and Richard indicate other possibilities, especially in Cahen's idea that the Frankish states need to be distinguished from the crusades and placed in their proper historical context as Near Eastern polities without any intrusive neo-colonial model. Once that model has been entirely discarded, as distorting, then other parallels and analytical techniques can be introduced, derived

from or contrasted with studies of other multi-communal societies. One recent attempt at this has been Christopher MacEvitt's
(2008) description of relations between the Franks and local
Christian communities as 'rough tolerance'. This MacEvitt char-
acterises by three prime features: 'silence', or a lack of
intercommunal engagement, of the sort witnessed by the absence
of local Christians from William of Tyre's history of twelfth-
century Outremer; permeability – of people but not ideas or
learning – across social and religious divides; and localisation.
This last point emphasises the previous tendency to generalise
and lump together both the different communities and their
detailed experiences of each other. It is suggested that in fact
social relationships were marked by a disinterest in rigid categori-
sation or delineation of or between neighbouring communities.
Thus MacEvitt rejects an idea favoured by anti-colonial historians
that the Franks treated Muslims and others as *dhimmi*, pointing
out that, in contrast to the system in Muslim lands, the non-Latin
communities possessed no recognised hierarchies or leadership,
their groupings remained undifferentiated in the eyes of their
conquerors and were dealt with on a local *ad hoc* basis not a
formal legal one.[41] Whatever view is taken of such ideas, which
only apply to Frankish–Christian relations, chiefly in the northern Frankish territories, and are still in the process of articulation,
they counter westernised assumptions that have determined most
previous interpretations, and promote understanding that the
habit of determinist generalisations tends to mislead, whether
conditioned by inappropriate analogies, the study of elites or
theories of multiculturalism. In positing an intrinsic difference,
uniqueness even, in Outremer's experience that owes nothing to
general schemes of colonialism or the interplay of civilisations,
the challenge to familiar approaches is clear, radical and potentially liberating. It is a model, almost an anti-model, which
implies that, properly observed and understood, Outremer
society, as opposed to its conquest, is actually irrelevant to
debates on the crusades: an end of consensus indeed.

Notes

1 F. Duncalf's review of Grousset vols. i and ii, *American Historical Review*, 41 (1935–36), 124–6.

2 T. S. R. Boase, 'Recent Developments in Crusading Historiography', *History*, 22 (1937), 110–25; J. L. La Monte, 'Some Problems in Crusading Historiography', *Speculum*, 15 (1940), 57–75.

3 Revised and published posthumously, D. C. Munro, *The Kingdom of the Crusaders* (New York NY, 1935).

4 *Cambridge Medieval History*, v, ed. J. R. Tanner *et al.* (Cambridge, 1926), chaps vii–ix.

5 E. Barker, *The Crusades* (London, 1923), esp. on Letters of the Sepulchre, p. 42, note 1; on Franks as brigands, p. 50.

6 E. Barker, 'The Crusades', in T. Arnold and A. Guillaume, *The Legacy of Islam* (Oxford, 1931), p. 54; cf. p. 46.

7 Barker, 'Crusades', p. 40.

8 Barker, *Crusades*, p. 104.

9 In general, H. E. Mayer, 'America and the Crusades', *Proceedings of the American Philosophical Society*, 125 (1981), 39–45; K. Setton, 'Foreword' to 1955 edn of *A History of the Crusades*, i (Madison WI, 1969), xiii–xviii; G. Constable, 'Crusading Studies in America', in his 'The Historiography of the Crusades', in his *Crusaders and Crusading in the Twelfth Century* (Aldershot, 2008), pp. 32–42.

10 J. L. La Monte's review of Grousset's *Histoire des croisades* vols i and ii, *Byzantion*, 10 (1935), 685–700; the Indo-European reference appears in R. Grousset, *Histoire des croisades* (Paris, 1934–36), ii, 535–6. It is notable that La Monte ignores the colonial dimension completely.

11 J. L. La Monte, *Feudal Monarchy in the Latin Kingdom of Jerusalem* (Cambridge MA, 1932), pp. vii, ix, 108–9, 243, 244; cf. C. L. Kingsford, 'The Kingdom of Jerusalem 1099–1291', in *Cambridge Medieval History*, v, 303; J. O. Prestwich's Lothian Prize essay was published posthumously, *Feudal Society in the Latin States of Palestine and Syria and its Relations to the Saracens* (Centre for Medieval and Renaissance Studies, Durham, 2006); cf. M. Prestwich, 'Foreword' to J. O. Prestwich, *The Place of War in English History* (Woodbridge, 2004), pp. xi–xii; for Munro's 1896 review, above, pp. 147, 154; Mayer, 'America and the Crusades', 42.

12 La Monte, 'Some Problems in Crusading Historiography'.

13 At least one invited contributor serially lied to Setton about a chapter he claimed was nearing completion of which not a word seems to have been penned. Setton clearly possessed enormous patience and capacity to forgive; he and the contributor – who never did write the chapter – remained friends.

14 R. C. Smail's review of the then Pennsylvania *History of the Crusades*, vol. i, alongside Runciman's complete *History of the Crusades*, to which the comment was equally applied, *English Historical Review*, 72 (1957), 687.

15 S. Runciman, *A History of the Crusades* (Cambridge, 1951–54), i, xii–xiii.

16 J. Riley-Smith, *Crusades* (2nd edn New Haven CT, 2005), pp. 303–4.

17 Boase, 'Recent Developments in Crusading Historiography', p. 112 referring to C. Cahen, 'Indigènes et croisés', *Syria*, 15 (1934), 351–60.

18 C. Cahen, *Orient et Occident aux temps des croisades* (Paris, 1983), pp. 6,

257, note 3; cf. *idem*, 'Notes sur l'histoire des croisades et de l'Orient Latin', ii, *Bulletin de la Faculté des Lettres de Strasbourg*, 29 (1950–51), 286–310.

19 Cahen, *Orient et Occident*, p. 208 and *passim*.

20 Cahen, 'Indigènes et croisés', 359.

21 Cahen, *Orient et Occident*, p. 7; C. Hillenbrand, *The Crusades: Islamic Perspectives* (Edinburgh, 1999), pp. 10–13; cf. E. Sivan, 'Modern Arab Historiography of the Crusades', *Asian and African Studies*, 8 (1972), 109–49.

22 Prestwich, *Place of War*, pp. xi–xii; cf. J. C. Holt's chapter 'English History 1066–1272', in *A Century of British Medieval Studies*, ed. A. Deyermond, (Oxford, 2007); C. Cahen, *Le régime féodale de l'Italie normande* (Paris, 1940), p. 64. For the continuing debate of Outremer feudalism, S. Reynolds, 'Fiefs and Vassals in Twelfth Century Jerusalem', *Crusades*, 1 (2002), 29–48; P. Edbury, 'Fiefs and Vassals in the Kingdom of Jerusalem: From the Twelfth Century to the Thirteenth', *Crusades*, 1 (2002), 49–62; J. Rubin, 'The Debate on Twelfth Century Frankish Feudalism', *Crusades*, 8 (2009), 53–62.

23 R. C. Smail, *Crusading Warfare* (Cambridge, 1956), p. 16; cf. pp. v, 2 and *passim* for what follows.

24 R. C. Smail, 'Crusading Kingdom of Jerusalem: The First European Colonial Society?', in *The Horns of Hattin*, ed. B. Z. Kedar (Jerusalem, 1992), pp. 342–7.

25 R. Ellenblum, *Crusader Castles and Modern Histories* (Cambridge, 2007), p. 61.

26 Smail, 'Crusading Kingdom of Jerusalem', p. 366; cf. pp. 364 and 360–6; J. Prawer, *The Latin Kingdom of Jerusalem: European Colonisation in the Middle Ages* (London, 1972), pp. ix, 524 and generally pp. 469–533; *idem*, *Histoire du royaume latin de Jérusalem* (2 vols. Paris, 1969–71), i, 6–8 for current parallels; Ellenblum, *Castles*, pp. 57–9 for a view of Prawer and Zionism; cf. B. Z. Kedar, 'Joshua Prawer (1917–90), Historian of the Crusading Kingdom of Jerusalem', *Mediterranean Historical Review*, 5 (1990), 107–16; B. Z. Kedar et al., *Outremer* (Jerusalem, 1982), pp. 1–4.

27 J. Richard, *The Crusades c. 1071–c. 1291* (Cambridge, 1999), pp. xii–xii, xiv; *idem*, 'National Feeling and the Legacy of the Crusades', in *Palgrave Advances in the Crusades*, ed. H. Nicholson (Basingstoke, 2005), pp. 218–19; *Dei Gesta per Francos: Etudes sur les croisades dédiées à Jean Richard*, ed. M. Balard et al. (Aldershot, 2001), pp. ix–x for the impact of Grousset on the adolescent Richard; in 1947 Grousset provided the preface for Richard's youthful *Histoire du royaume latin de Jérusalem*.

28 Prawer, *Histoire*, i, 7, 13.

29 *Horns of Hattin*, p. 361.

30 Apart for Ellenblum above, cf. A. Arkush, 'The Jewish State and its Internal Enemies', *Jewish Social Studies*, 7 (2001), 178–9; D. Ohana, 'Are Israelis the New Crusaders?', *Palestine–Israel Journal of Politics, Economics and Culture*, 13:3 (2006), 36–42; Z. J. Asali, 'Zionist Studies of the Crusade Movement', *Arab Studies Quarterly*, 14 (1992), 45–59.

31 Prawer, *Histoire*, i, 9.

32 H. E. Mayer, *The Crusades* (Eng. trans. J. Gillingham, 2nd edn Oxford, 1988); for appreciation and bibliography only to 1997, *Montjoie: Studies in*

Crusade History in Honour of Hans Eberhard Mayer, ed. B. Z. Kedar *et al.* (Aldershot, 1997), pp. vii–xx.

33 B. Z. Kedar, 'The Subjected Muslims of the Frankish Levant', in *Muslims under Latin Rule*, ed. J. M. Powell (Princeton NJ, 1990), pp. 135–74, esp. pp. 165–6, 174; for an appreciation and bibliography, *In Laudem Hierosolymitani*, ed. I. Shagrir *et al.* (Aldershot, 2007), pp. ix–xxiii.

34 J. Riley-Smith, *The Feudal Nobility and the Kingdom of Jerusalem* (London, 1973), pp. 40–98; *idem*, 'Some Lesser Royal Officials in Latin Syria', *English Historical Review*, 87 (1972), 1–26; *idem*, 'The Survival in Latin Palestine of Muslim Administration', in *The Eastern Mediterranean Lands in the Period of the Crusades*, ed. P. M. Holt (Warminster, 1977), pp. 9–22; *idem*, 'Further Thoughts on Baldwin II's *établissement*', in *Crusade and Settlement*, ed. P. Edbury (Cardiff, 1985), pp. 176–9; Mayer, *Crusades*, p. 165.

35 D. Pringle's review, *H-France Review*, 8 (2008), 180–3; Mayer, *Crusades*, p. 156.

36 Ellenblum, *Castles*, pp. 60–1.

37 M. Benvenisti, *Scared Landscape: The Buried History of the Holy Land since 1948* (London, 2000), pp. 192–3, captions to illustration nos. 18 and 23, pp. 299–303, 309–10.

38 Hillenbrand, *Crusades*, pp. 11 and 13.

39 H. E. Mayer, 'The Latin East 1098–1205', in *New Cambridge Medieval History*, iv–ii, ed. D. Luscombe and J. Riley-Smith (Cambridge, 2004), 666 and generally 644–74.

40 *Horns of Hattin*, pp. 350–2.

41 C. MacEvitt, *The Crusades and the Christian World of the East: Rough Tolerance* (Philadelphia PA, 2008), esp. pp. 13–26.

7

Erdmann, Runciman and the end of tradition?

The two most influential books on the crusades written in the twentieth century could hardly have been more different, the one academic, conceptually seminal, the preserve of scholars; the other literary, conceptually nugatory and a world bestseller. The writer of the first died obscurely and young, in the unwelcome military service of a despotic, disapproving regime he despised; the writer of the second lived to be ninety-seven, bathed in golden opinions and laden with public honours, a multi-millionaire. Separated by less than twenty years but an intellectual universe, Carl Erdmann's *Die Entstehung des Kreuzzugsgedankens* (*The Origins of the Idea of Crusading*, 1935) and Steven Runciman's *History of the Crusades* (1951–54) display the janus-like characteristics of crusade study, the contrasting, often contradictory interests and enthusiasms of the specialist scholar and of the intelligent browser. Erdmann reopened investigation into the nature and origins of the phenomenon, largely ignored or assumed by the functional materialist focus on the crusaders' conquests. Runciman perpetuated the epic grand narrative, a drama of good and evil, heroism and villainy, civilisation and barbarism. Their perspectives could not be more different, a refined abstract study of ideas versus an almost filmic imaginative recreation of experiences and events. Yet both spoke directly to their own times, one analysing how wars become legitimate, the other suggesting their human cost.[1]

Erdmann and holy war

Carl Erdmann (1898–1945) was a historian of ideas and an expert on medieval letter writing, a form of literature central to the communication of intellectual arguments as much as information. Focusing on the eleventh century, Erdmann concentrated on material generated by the Investiture Contest and the reformed papacy. However, his somewhat unorthodox career lent him a perspective that differed from the many German scholars who tilled that rich field of political, institutional and ideological conflict. Born in Dorpat/Tartu, Estonia, and raised in Saxony, having abandoned plans to become a Lutheran pastor, Erdmann spent some years after university in Portugal as a private tutor. While there he conducted research on crusading in Portugal which formed the basis for his first doctorate. When he was later recruited by the Prussian Historical Institute in Rome, among other things he worked on papal correspondence with Portugal. There, too, he began work on the ideas behind the First Crusade. Already some of the elements that distinguished his great book were in place: a view of the instrumentality of the papacy in western society and thought; an understanding that ideas and practice of church-approved war concerned more than campaigns to the Holy Land; an awareness that the wars begun in 1095 formed part of a wider change of intellectual climate. Experience of the fringes of southern Europe, the early medieval frontline of Christendom against Islam, as well as his sharp (and apparently bitter) personal family memories of the problems of the German plantation in the north-eastern Baltic, encouraged a subtle view of conflict between and within societies. Shortly before his death, Erdmann declared himself a 'true humanist' who hoped he knew how to die '*en philosophe*'. This, combined with not coming from a Roman Catholic background, may have allowed Erdmann the freedom displayed in his unblinking assessment of the steps taken by succeeding popes, and especially Gregory VII ('as much a warrior as a priest and politician'), in constructing the theory and practice of Christian holy war. Even Gregory the Great failed to avoid censure for promoting aggressive religious missionary wars, a 'dubious direction' (*bedenklichen Schritt*) for Christian doctrine.[2]

Erdmann, who had lost two brothers in the First World War, held no admiration or approval of the subject he chose for his *Habilitationsschrift* of 1932 that became the *Entstehung* in 1935. Behind the detailed study of the medieval texts suitable in a scholar now (from 1934) employed by the *Monumenta Germaniae Historica*, lay a much larger question, 'the historical foundations of the Western ethic of war and soldiering'.[3] Coupled with this was an understanding that the Christian warfare of the crusades was no sudden aberration, violence in the name of a good cause being as old as western European civilisation itself. Nor was it a consequence either of elite or of popular impulses alone, but a potent conjoining of the two, in this case the ideology of the church and the psychology of the knightly classes. Such issues were scarcely neutral or irrelevant in the Germany of the early years of the Third Reich, even if some modern attempts to cast the *Entstehung* as a coded critique of Nazi fanaticism and militarism underestimate the purely academic drive behind the work.[4] It was less its coolness towards war that struck early readers than its departure from the usual objects of crusade study and its explicit challenge to the underlying assumptions of that prevailing orthodoxy. Erdmann turned decisively away from regarding the crusades as material exercises of foreign conquest and colonisation in favour of examining their western ideological roots. In doing so, he denied the cherished centrality of the Holy Land.

For all his unassuming scholarly style and tone, Erdmann was combative. An initial sally, 'to regard the belief that Christianity was destined to world domination as the root of the crusading idea is an exaggeration', is footnoted with reference to a paladin of German crusade scholarship, Hans Prutz.[5] By locating a continuum of ecclesiastical responses to elite warrior culture that stretched back to the emperor Constantine and the doctrines of Augustine of Hippo, Erdmann reduced the uniqueness of crusading, depicting it as merely one form of holy war particularly developed by the eleventh-century papal reformers. The concentration was on holy war, not pilgrimage or the Holy Land which were only later 'to fertilize the war upon the heathen'.[6] Originally, wars fought as a religious act, or related to religion in some way, had taken the form of state wars against enemies or heathen, as in the wars of Charlemagne against the Saxons. Patristic teaching had allowed for warfare in defence against the church's enemies, such as heretics. However, acknowledging a direct debt to Ranke, Erdmann distinguished between official state and church policy and the more popular generalised Christianisation of the Germanic *Heldenethik*, 'ethics of heroism', through the early middle ages, accelerating in the tenth and eleventh centuries. Thus, this *populäre Kreuzzug* developed in parallel with official policy.[7] In the eleventh century, the reformed papacy, notably Gregory VII and the theorists in his circle, openly justified aggressive wars against enemies, both heathen and, during the Investiture Contest, political and doctrinal opponents, who could be characterised as heretics and schismatics. Conversely, supporters, such as the Milanese gang leader Erlembald in the 1060s, could be cast as saints, and papal soldiers promised spiritual rewards. 'Pre-crusades' were fought against Christian enemies of the papacy and the Moors in Spain. Knights were recruited through local Peace of God initiatives and directly by Gregory VII's abortive *militia sancti Petri*. However, this holy war as a means of discipline and defence – the *hierauchischen Kreuzzugsidee* – was not widely attractive.[8] It took Urban II's association of ecclesiastical war with the popularity of pilgrimage and his use of Jerusalem as a secondary recruiting device, to harness the knightly ideas of the *ritterlichen Kreuzzug* – the chivalrous crusade – to the hierarchical to produce the First Crusade.[9]

In tracing the Christianisation of war, Erdmann subverted contemporary crusade orthodoxy. As he noted, his approach was not entirely original. In *Die abendländisch-hierarchische Kreuzzugidee (The Western Hierarchical Idea of the Crusade*, dissertation, Halle, 1905), O. Volk had used Ranke's distinction between the hierarchical and the popular crusade and had broken with the Jerusalem/Holy Land-centred interpretation of the nineteenth-century Franco-German school. Erdmann went further. 'The general idea of crusade, far from being confined to wars actually directed towards the Holy Land, could be found in the most varied theatres of combat.' In a sense this was a revival of the old 'feudal violence' construct, except that Erdmann, in the tradition of German *geistesgeschichte* – history of ideas – had a clear view that ideologies underlie actions. Freed from any innate or necessary association with pilgrimage or Holy Land, Erdmann's crusade was distinctive because 'religion itself provided the specific cause of war, unencumbered by considerations of public welfare, territorial defence, national honour or interests of state'.[10] The historical development of this form of holy war, an 'aggressive war of religion' *deo auctore*, led to a further, more precise inversion of orthodox thinking.[11] Erdmann regarded the wars, debates and theories of war surrounding the Investiture Contest as crucial stages in the formation of the crusade idea of 1095, as significant as the contemporary campaigns against the infidel in southern Europe. These debates revolved around wars against deviant or dissident Christians, in an elaboration of Augustinian war theory. Thus 'war against pagans was very rarely and only incidentally mentioned ... the true war of the church was to be directed against heretics and schismatics, excommunicates and rebels within the church'. In case there should be any misunderstanding, Erdmann continued: 'There is no truth to the common opinion that the idea of a crusade against heretics (*Ketzerkreuzzugs*) was a corruption of the Palestinian crusade. On the contrary, such a crusade against heretics was envisioned from the start.'[12] The wars against pagans grew in clerical theory from those against heretics not vice versa.

Erdmann did not in fact pursue this reformulation consistently, partly because of his interest in the non-clerical popular crusade enthusiasm combined with a peculiar reluctance to stick to a simple, single working definition of 'crusade'. While the 1095 war was described as distinctive, at other times Erdmann's crusade seems a synonym for an amorphous range of religiously inspired war. His methodology imposed other constraints. In his reconstruction of Urban II's plan, Jerusalem could never be more than the *Marschziel*, the physical goal of the campaign, rather than the object of the war, the *Kriegsziel*, which he identified as the liberation of the eastern church, a direct extension of the papal ideology of the Investiture Contest.[13] However, the detail of Erdmann's thesis was perhaps of less immediate historiographic importance than the topic and approach. The Franco-German model had taken the crusaders' religious militarism somewhat for granted, as had eighteenth-century and earlier writers. Where recognised, the paradox of Christian warfare had escaped systematic study, being largely dismissed as hypocritical or deluded cover for fanaticism, greed and adventure. By contrast, Erdmann sought to explain crusade ideology as a genuine force. The narrative of the First Crusade had long attracted detailed scrutiny. Now its social, intellectual, political and psychological springs took centre stage. Erdmann gave the crusades back to the west and ideology back to the crusaders.

He was not entirely alone. He noted local debts, for example to Walther Holtzmann's research into the reformed papacy's policy towards Byzantium.[14] In France, Etienne Delaruelle, a historian of religious life rather than simply ideas, had written a thesis at the Institut Catholique in 1935 on the formation of the crusade idea, although he did not start to publish his findings until 1941, and only then in instalments spread over more than a decade. Delaruelle's *Essai sur la formation de l'idée de croisade* emphasised the religious context, as expressed in the liturgy and Christian art, and the spiritual power of Urban's message offering a means of salvation. One standing criticism of Erdmann was his lack of emphasis on the penitential dimensions of the enterprise despite his association of the First Crusade with pilgrimage. Delaruelle also probed the social features, from the increasingly prominent role of the nobility in wars on the frontiers of Christendom to the crusade as a means through which the church reached out to the laity.[15] The responses of the laity that Erdmann had explained in essentially top-down terms – the lead coming from church, state and nobility – had also been the subject of lectures by Paul Alphandéry at the Ecole des hautes études before his death in 1932. These were only edited, completed and published by Alphonse Dupront in 1954 and 1959, but show that Erdmann was not working in isolation in redefining the subject. Alphandéry sought to expose the crusaders' psychology, even though, like others trying to do the same thing, he was forced to rely on the filtration of clerical chronicles, especially such loaded texts as Raymond of Aguilers's miracle collection. In contrast to Erdmann, Alphandéry's crusade was a mass popular movement inspired by intense eschatalogical enthusiasm centred on the image of Jerusalem. Here, the key to understanding lay in collective mass psychology.[16]

The extent to which Erdmann's *Entstehung*, or the works of Delaruelle and Alphandéry, constituted tracts for their times is less clear. Erdmann dedicated his book to the memory of his father 'who lost a professorship at Dorpat in 1893 for remaining true to his mother tongue', and to his dead brothers 'with unshaken faith in the future of the German spirit'. German nationalism and resentment occasionally peeps out from the *Entstehung*, as in the wistful contrasting of German bravery and Italian cowardice at the battle of Civitate in 1053 and the ironic comment that crusading seemed destined 'not for the German *Volk* but only for their adversary', that is, the French.[17] Although denied promotion for his undisguised lack of enthusiasm for the Nazi regime, Erdmann was hardly an active dissident. He was even offered a professorial title, which he was able to decline without immediate drastic repercussions. Erdmann's published work would have been scrutinised for seditious intent, not least by its publishers. Yet he was allowed to continue working for the *MGH*, until, despite his indifferent health, he was conscripted during the Second World War. On service as a translator in the Balkans he died of typhus in March 1945. The *Entstehung* can be read as a critique of the acceptance of militarist ideology by elites and society at large, as one later reviewer put it, 'a protest of the human spirit against fanaticism and aggression in any age'. It is not a condemnation of Nazism *per se* but an analysis of how such ideologies could be constructed and disseminated, remaining studiously moderate in judgement. The treatment of ideology has been depicted by some as oddly un-ideological, perhaps reflecting the need for discretion.[18] However, the contemporary issue for Erdmann, and perhaps for Delaruelle and Alphandéry, was not so much the fascism of the 1930s, but the ethics of militarism that had led to the First World War, ideologies of violence that had received overt and active promotion by churches and states with extensive public support. Erdmann discovered in the crusades the political workings of the clerical elite and the psychology of the ruling class; Delaruelle the force of collective faith; Alphandéry the power of popular culture. From each, contemporary parallels could be drawn, and personal political persuasions inferred, but far less crudely than some associated with the colonial crusade model. The central issue that Erdmann returned to the forefront of the debate was the one that had proved the most awkward, the problem of religious or ideological violence distinct from *raisons d'état*. While such phenomena challenged post-Renaissance and Enlightenment expectations, they spoke directly to the experience of the twentieth century.

While many admired Erdmann's scholarship and recognised the 'rich theme' he had explored, a number quibbled over his emphases. The Byzantinist Louis Bréhier criticised both the psychological analysis and the very idea that the First Crusade possessed a long lineage. W. Holtzmann took issue with Erdmann's opening distinction between holy war in general and crusading as a specific genre of religious violence. La Monte, who seemed flummoxed by the absence of traditional political history, adopted an unreflective supercilious condescension towards 'German scholarship', ending with one of the least prescient of comments: 'both the content and the style forbid its ever becoming either popular or widely influential'.[19] Yet increasingly, the old explanations of the First Crusade as a result of politics and diplomacy appeared inadequate. This mirrored a growing breadth in research into medieval canon law and religiosity, seen not simply in terms of ecclesiastical structures and politics but as systems of belief. It also perhaps reflected the contemporary mid-twentieth-century familiarity with wars of ideas, fought or threatened. Erdmann's trail was followed by Paul Rousset's *Les origines et les caractères de la première croisade* (Neuchâtel, 1945), that attempted to reconstruct – somewhat disapprovingly – the religious crusading mentality as revealed by sources in the fifty years after 1095. One reviewer drew a precise contemporary parallel. La Monte entirely rejected what he described as Rousset's attempt 'to re-establish the old thesis of the crusades as essentially a religious movement', accusing Rousset of naivety in taking the religious language of his texts – such as *militia Christi* – as demonstrating that religion 'was the essential cause of the crusade'. This was 'like accepting the statements of *Pravda* that the USSR is only altruistically interested in establishing "truly democratic peoples' governments"'.[20] The date was 1948. By contrast, fifty years later, a leading British crusade historian could remark, apparently without irony, 'all of us, although with different emphasis, now know that the subject of crusading is a religious one, whatever other elements were important to it'.[21] La Monte believed in 1948 that 'recent research has been steadily moving' away from the religious interpretation. That this has not proved so owes much to Erdmann. His approach, however flawed in practice, encouraged others to overcome any distaste at the concept of religious war and to take the ideological origins and religious impulses seriously, regardless of the undoubted pitfalls in the evidence. While Rousset studied religious rhetoric, in *La croisade: essai sur la formation d'une théorie juridique* of 1942 Michel Villey, later a noted conservative, Roman Catholic legal historian and philosopher, pioneered the modern examination of the crusade as a juridical theory.[22]

Not that Erdmann's analysis and conclusions have necessarily commanded agreement. As well as the contrasting perspectives of Delaruelle and Alphandéry, Rousset argued that the First Crusade differed from 'pre-crusades' before 1095 in Sicily, Spain or North Africa in certain key characteristics, such as the imagery of the Cross and the Jerusalem indulgence. Villey noted the absence of evidence for the legal acceptance of the new form of aggressive war against pagans. Further investigation of the policies and ideas of Gregory VII, Urban II and theorists of the Investiture Contest wholly modifies Erdmann's sketch. The genesis of penitential war has been more precisely located in the 1080s. Erdmann's relegation of Jerusalem to an incidental feature of Urban II's scheme was effectively challenged by John Cowdrey in 1970. More sweepingly, Erdmann's chronology of changing attitudes to holy war and his reading of the shift of opinion amongst canonists have both been demolished, for example in a series of articles by John Gilchrist. The Spanish 'pre-crusade' has been questioned and the role of the Peace of God widely dismissed.[23] Since the 1930s, the nature and development of knighthood have grown almost into a separate sub-discipline. More recently new attention to charters has sought to exhume secular beliefs at a local level that contradict Erdmann's rather hierarchic assumptions about the transmission of ideas, indicating less sophisticated levels of devotion and the desire for penance.[24] Even admirers indulge in considerable modification. Thus Mayer stresses the part played by pilgrimage and the indulgence and Jean Flori, who has reasserted the Erdmann-esque centrality of holy war, nonetheless predates the church's embrace of violence and ascribes to Jerusalem a key part in the creation of the crusade.[25] In his biographical study of Urban II, Becker recasts the whole argument by rejecting the association with pilgrimage and locating Urban II's conception of the First Crusade firmly in the pre-1095 eleventh-century tradition of Christian reconquest in Spain and especially Sicily. Yet, oddly, despite his disagreement with the characterisation of the First Crusade as an armed pilgrimage, Becker has been accused of being a neo-Erdmannite, presumably because of his lack of emphasis on spiritual ideology and his implication of continuity rather than innovation in Urban's 1095 plan.[26] Most fundamentally, if imprecisely, Erdmann has been criticised for misunderstanding or underestimating the very core of his own thesis, ideology. He is accused of adopting too rational and elitist a view of the spiritual fears, ideals and ambitions of knights and too political an interpretation of the ideas of the papacy; in short, of minimising the power and importance of faith.[27]

Yet amidst the rubble, Erdmann's thesis survives. To dismiss it as of little value is to forget Bernard of Chartres's hackneyed maxim of dwarfs on giants' shoulders. As his translators said, he defined a subject. Unlike Prutz, Röhricht, Stevenson, Barker, Grousset, Munro or La Monte, the *Entstehung* continues to exert an influence and remains a necessary point of reference. The mere fact of its translation into English in 1977 is indicative. His interest in symbols, such as papal banners, and liturgies blessing violence, appears strikingly modern. Even its weaknesses have proved fruitful. His failure to define a crusade has helped inspire one of the livelier late twentieth-century debates on the crusades. Erdmann's determination to place 1095 in a long social, political and intellectual perspective demythologised the crusade. It also persisted in shaping opinion. For example, Ernst-Dieter Hehl's study of canon law and war in the twelfth century, *Kirche und Krieg im 12 Jahrhundert* (Stuttgart, 1980) is Erdmann-esque in arguing that theory follows practice and in adopting a very general view of the relationship of holy war and crusading. Three generations after his premature death, Erdmann's ideas continue to arouse intense scholarly interest, even in criticism. Despite some attempts to belittle his continued importance, as John Cowdrey remarked, 'all subsequent enquiry has in the last analysis sprung from' Erdmann. American scholars such as Paul

Chevedden are critically revisiting some of his views, on, for example, pre-crusades (or, as they may prefer, pre-1095 crusades) and Urban II's Mediterranean policies.[28] Most significant to the historiography of the crusades, Erdmann offered a contrasting method and substance to moralising assumptions about motives and to the obsession with superficial political narrative.

Runciman and crimes against humanity

Nobody could accuse Steven Runciman's *History of the Crusades* (1951–54) of lacking either moralising or narrative. Even when published, dated in technique, style and content; derivative, misleading and tendentious; a polemic masquerading as epic; Runciman's three volumes represent the most astonishing literary phenomenon in crusade historiography since Michaud. Almost sixty years after the publication of the first volume, in educated circles in Britain, if anyone talks about the crusades 'Runciman' is almost certain to be invoked. Across the Anglophone world he continues as a base reference for popular attitudes, evident in print, film, television and on the internet. However much scholars may grind their teeth, there are sound, non-academic reasons why this should be so.

Runciman himself explained: 'I believe that the supreme duty of the historian is to write history, that is to say, to attempt to record in one sweeping sequence the greater events and movements that have swayed the destinies of man,' adding, significantly, 'Homer as well as Herodotus was a Father of History.'[29] These certainties, value judgements and literary flourishes may grate, but they are carefully directed to illustrate central themes. Runciman, a Byzantinist, pitches his story on two parallel levels: the clash of civilisations – western European, Byzantine Greek and Muslim – at different stages of development; and the motives of people, individuals and groups. Each level is only properly understood in relation to the other. Individual participants are vividly portrayed in deft, if slightly predictable, character sketches, psychological stereotypes that illustrate their cultural progress; westerners brave, wilful, rough and rude; Greeks adult, sophisticated, touched with decadence; Muslims two-dimensional in their faith, martial vigour and oriental manners. The weaving of the overarching conflict of societies, Gibbon's World's Debate, with the dramas of immediate human experience renders the account both coherent and accessible. The narrative is lent a dimension of timelessness, as in the notorious summing up: 'the Holy War itself was nothing more than a long act of intolerance in the name of God, which is a sin against the Holy Ghost'.[30] The whole work is shot through with literary device, from imagining the thoughts of the actors to inventing fictitious scenes of action. In this, Runciman is the true heir of Michaud, but also of medieval chroniclers whose narratives never left the service of their didactic purpose.

This didacticism provides Runciman's *History* with its lasting immediacy. In Gibbonian style, he discourses on the eternal foibles of human nature. The perspective is Olympian, speaking with the cultural confidence of a man of great wealth, high intellect and enormous curiosity. His approach and style were shaped by synthesising writers such as the nineteenth-century historian of Greece George Finlay and, especially, J. B. Bury (1861–1927), his mentor at Cambridge. Runciman claimed (inaccurately) to have been Bury's first and only pupil. They shared a taste for scholarship over a wide period and space (in Bury's case mainly in the later Roman Empire and Byzantium), sympathy with Victorian liberal values and a desire to write accessible prose. Nurtured in a cosmopolitan intellectual and cultural elite (his family money came from shipping; both his grandfathers were successful businessmen; both his parents were Liberal MPS, his father a Liberal Cabinet minister), his position as a private scholar from his early thirties allowed him complete academic freedom. He addressed himself to urgent contemporary issues in a very particular manner, spurning the 'massed typewriters' of the USA and attacking professional academic history, 'where criticism has overpowered creation', dominated by 'the minutiae of knowledge' (not seen by Runciman as a particularly good thing) in articles and theses, 'small fortresses that are easy to defend'.[31] Runciman's view of the past rejected the dehumanised (and he would have thought dehumanising) theories of Marx, Freud or Weber, the statistical aggregate or the determinism of economics. Clad in the full cultural armour of his liberal classical education at Eton and Trinity, Cambridge, *A History of the Crusades* argues in defence of that culture and education, regarded as quintessentially civilised and humane. The mass movements of his own lifetime, which spanned almost the entire twentieth century (1903–2000), were not only personally anathema but had brought the world near to destruction. He had little time for the tyranny of numbers, the equality of the herd or horde. The responsibility and importance of the individual looms large. 'By the inexorable laws of history, the whole world pays for the crimes and follies of each of its citizens.'[32] To an audience gripped by the impersonal forces of the Cold War, this seemed to soften causation to the explicable, to human agency.

The message was clear. Once the values of moderation, learning, high culture and reason become overlaid or undermined by passion, ignorance, greed or violence, civilisation is imperilled. Look, Runciman says, at what the crusades did to those they first set out to assist, the eastern Christians and the cultivated world of Byzantium. These they destroyed through ignorance, allowing the Turks to subjugate half of Christendom. Good intentions are not enough; 'faith without wisdom is a dangerous thing' whether, the implication seems to be, that faith is in God, gods, Mammon, economic nostrums or political creeds.[33] Unlike Michaud, Runciman betrays no nationalism or even a preference for western European ideals. It was not part of his intellectual milieu. Narrow national or cultural partisanship had reaped a dreadful harvest in his lifetime; his first Cambridge pupil was Guy Burgess (although they had a number of things in common, treachery he would have thought vulgar and dishonourable). For Runciman, the best of the west came from the east which the west wilfully and witlessly had cast down. In one of his most famous lines, anger touched his lament at Byzantium's tragedy: 'there never was a greater crime against humanity than the Fourth Crusade'.[34] Published in 1954, its message stood in sombre relief: it was less than a decade after Hiroshima; the concentration camps; the Holocaust; and the Nuremberg trials that first defined crimes against humanity. As an example of man's avaricious inhumanity and as an episode with untold, unforeseen and, in Runciman's eyes, catastrophic consequences, 1204 may appear a suitable subject for horrified sermonising. However, the hyperbole reaches beyond the author's passionate Hellenophilia. Byzantium stands for western civilisation itself, inherited from the classical past, rational, tolerant and humane. The crusaders are the barbarians within: energetic, self-righteous, semi-educated, driven by appetites not reason. The unspoken relevance is loud.

If *A History of the Crusades* is a threnody for a lost world – Runciman's as well as Byzantium – its compelling force is surprisingly crude in construction. Its concerns and assumptions are rigidly traditional: the Holy Land crusades, with excursions mainly restricted to related wars against Islam – Moors or Ottomans; Outremer a Frankish colony.[35] The tone is consistently romantic in following the fates of nations through the actions of individuals. One caustic modern critic has commented that Runciman's account 'was almost what Walter Scott would have written had he been more knowledgeable'.[36] There is a tendency to divide people into good and bad, to assume transparency of motive, however devious. Oddly, Runciman's Greeks are as two-dimensional in their suave sophistication as are his Franks in their boorishness. His Muslims parade as figures from an orientalist's sketch-pad. Shirkuh's 'features revealed his low birth'. The epithets showered on Saladin – cunning, ruthless, courteous, generous, considerate, tolerant, merciful, gentle in manner, simple in tastes, disliking coarseness and ostentation, well read, a lover of both hunting and intellectual discussion, modest – have the strange effect of sucking individuality from the sultan, reducing him to a catalogue of nineteenth-century English upper-class virtues.[37] At times, Runciman comes close to self-parody, perhaps deliberately given his highly refined sense of humour. By the device of misplacing her famous physical description of Bohemund of Taranto from 1108 to 1097, he imagines the teenaged Anna Comnena admiring Bohemund of Taranto's 'good looks' despite his sinister demeanour and fearsome reputation, Anna 'being, like all Greeks down the ages, susceptible to human beauty'.[38] Here, perhaps, the hidden text is not too hard to read.

These literary touches, more journalistic than novelistic, fit the almost unwavering avoidance of serious historical analysis. The complexity of the narrative comprises events sustained by a running commentary of judgement – fateful, tragic, evil etc. – that substitutes for reflective discussion of cause, motive and consequence. However, this is one reason why Runicman's *History* survives. Readers are invited to think that they are seeing what actually happened, an exercise in imaginative transportation, their response unimpeded by the uncertainties of evidence and interpretation beyond a few throwaway comments suggesting Runciman's almost personal acquaintance with the medieval writers. The absence of doubt is combined with the skilful creation of a convincingly fabricated world inhabited by his recognisable stereotype cast. Such was the conviction behind this literary performance that others have plundered it almost as a primary source. Runciman's *History* is the last chronicle of the crusades.

Yet those passages that are not pure invention are often uncritically and occasionally unadmittedly derivative. The first volume, on the First Crusade, is heavily dependent for content and structure on Ferdinand Chalandon's posthumously published *Histoire de la Première Croisade jusqu'à l'élection de Godefroi de Bouillon* (Paris, 1925). The narrative, largely following the *Gesta Francorum*, with accurate chronology provided by Hagenmeyer, treats the chronicle evidence as a sweetshop of good stories. Runciman's method – the broad sweep, the summary generalisa- tion and the memorable human cameo – is here displayed at its smoothest. It is no coincidence that it was later reissued as an autonomous book. The second volume, subtitled *The Kingdom of Jerusalem and the Frankish East*, takes the story to 1187 largely by copying William of Tyre, with shades of Stevenson's *Crusaders in the East*. Despite his best prose, this volume lacks the coher- ence of the first or the set-piece dramas of the third and, like its model William of Tyre, can be rather hard to follow. The treat- ment displays little engagement with any fresh areas of research, although Cahen and Prawer feature in the footnotes and bibli- ographies. Runciman was widely read, even if he appears to have lacked the Arabic necessary to penetrate below the surface of the *Recueil* translations of the nineteenth century. The handling of Islam reflects this lack of sympathy or understanding of religion as other than an adornment of high (or low) culture. This appears to contradict Runciman's stated purpose to 'understand not only the circumstances in western Europe ... but perhaps still more, the circumstances in the East that gave to the crusaders their opportunity and shaped their progress and their withdrawal'.[39] Much of his secondary reading remained in the nineteenth and early twentieth centuries. This suggested not a lack of industry but a rather optimistic view that the subject was settled and thus ripe for some definitive synthesis. The third volume, *The Kingdom of Acre and the Later Crusades*, contains the furious description of the Fourth Crusade, relying on Byzantine sources such as Nicetas Choniates. Otherwise, the continuations of William of Tyre and the *Gestes des Chiprois* provide the material, with Grousset's own final volume lurking not far in the background. The central judgemental dynamic beats loudly: 'the misguided crusades'; crimes and follies in Outremer and the west; the Latins castigated for failing to ally with the non-Muslim Mongols.[40] A cursory nod is given to crusading after 1291 (as had Fuller and Gibbon). Runciman's personal interests may lie behind the unexpectedly elaborate genealogies of the royal and noble families of Outremer that complete the final volume.

Nobody writes like Runciman today. Very few did even fifty years ago. The scholarship is wide but not deep; the literary technique effective in short stretches but taken in large doses tends to indigestion. A review by Erdmann might have been worth reading. Contemporary academic critics were not slow to cast aspersions, noting variously the lack of analysis, originality or concern for spiritual motives beyond the external manifestations of pilgrimage, *jihad* etc. Smail, after a positive welcome to the first volume, offered some very dry criticisms of the finished work, especially of Runciman's prejudices, his exaggerated devotion to Byzantium, his caricature of Latin Christianity, the absence of analysis and his omission of any serious consideration of the crusade as a reflection of western religious life. Smail also questioned the timing of the book, along with the Pennsylvania project: 'an odd time to halt and summarize' given that new areas of research (not least Smail's own) were being explored and many others awaited investigation. In the light of all this, how did Runciman's *History* become such as public *succès d'estime?* Why is it still revered, with even a modern academic author describing the book – apparently without irony – as 'an excellent starting point'? Smail hinted at an explanation. As a history for the 'general reader', he argued, it constituted: 'a remarkable achievement of literature and scholarship ... distinguished by its breadth of design and boldness of generalization' which, combined with extensive reference to primary sources, made it 'the best scholarly survey of the subject by a single author', that 'will always remain the first considerable work of its kind in the English language'. Even twenty years after the appearance of the first volume, Hans Mayer could, with justice, comment that for Anglophone readers Runciman was 'indispensable for anyone who wishes to study the crusades at all seriously', not least because there was no competition. However, Mayer's description of it as a *tour de force* of English historical writing' perhaps contains just a suspicion of irony.[41] Readable, opinionated but well-informed, engaging both in its style and in the coherent world it conjures into existence, what Smail wrote in 1953 was true: Runciman's *History* was the first of its kind in English. It was also the last.

It would be unfair simply to ascribe Runciman's success and influence to the literary tricks of an ersatz novelist alone, even though he himself insisted that 'he was not a historian, but a writer of literature'.[42] He certainly was a showman, in life as in words. However, all was not just trickery and verbal legerdemain. Like almost all the greatest or most significant crusade historians, he expressed a clear view of his subject. The crusades formed part of a process whereby western European civilisation became globally dominant through the transfer of power from Byzantium and the Arab caliphate. Far from the agent of beneficent exchange, the crusades acted as a destructive force. The (in Runciman's eyes) civilised, tolerant empires of Abbasid Baghdad and Orthodox Byzantium were replaced by harsher regimes in east and west. He makes the whole subject easy by setting it up as a conflict between east and west, Christianity and Islam. In the service of clarity, he ignores the awkward issues of ideology raised by Erdmann or the complex tensions within Europe that made crusading a feature of the heartlands of western Europe not just its frontiers. Runciman presented a very English vision of history, avoiding triumphalism, self-deprecatory when discussing western society, the glamour of the past tempered by shafts of sceptical irony, the romance and passion coloured by an abidingly gloomy view of the human condition. The virtues of Runciman's characters are almost invariably balanced by vices. He has no time for militarism, but accepts its historical importance.

Oddly for one hardly attuned to the age of the common man, his liberal cynicism resonated with modern, post-war prejudices. His characters are not really medieval at all, but recognisable modern, pre-Freudian people in medieval clothes. Consequently, they are not distanced from his audience. In language of sonorous high seriousness, great events are reduced to a human scale without ever diminishing their significance; Homer indeed. The closer his text resembles a novel, the more engaging it is. Above all, he panders to the two most potent sirens of popular history: the sense that people in the past were essentially just like people in the present; and that, partly as a consequence, the past can be judged according to hindsight and modern schemes of value, ethics and morality.

Despite this, Runciman's *History* merits inclusion in any study of crusade historiography not simply as a final representative of a *belles lettres* tradition, but also because his book exerted a profound influence on the subject in the Anglophone world which, unexpectedly, came to occupy a leading position in the academic study of crusading. More than once, it has been posited that this explosion of research interest in Britain indirectly owes something to Runciman. Certainly few British historians of the crusades over the next half-century were not exposed to or brought up on Runciman; fewer still would have entirely escaped the excitement of his style, narrative and generalisations. Reading Runciman could be immensely enjoyable, not a charge that can be levelled at all works on the crusades. Irritation at his lingering influence beyond the academic world may be fuelled by envy, disdain at his patrician insouciance, or professional axe-grinding. Yet the subject as described by Runciman is now almost wholly unfamiliar except as a relic of past modes of thought and of an approach to the writing of history that has long since ceased to make much sense, not least his confident construction (invention might be a better word) of a historical narrative. For all his not entirely unsuccessful attempts to keep abreast of research literature, Runciman failed to predict or embrace the signs of wholly new directions in research. He may not have cared. The points he wished to make and the impact he sought to leave were of a different order.

New perspectives, old issues

In the more than half-century since Runciman's *History*, the study of the crusades has been transformed. The weight of publications has been complemented by changes in how the subject has been understood and its integration into other areas of research, from psychohistory to gender studies. Whole new national traditions of crusade scholarship have sprung up, for example in parts of eastern and northern Europe. Parallel and antithetical to this renaissance of learning has been the association of the crusades with competing modern political discourses concerning relations between Islam and the First World, the establishment and development of the State of Israel, the relationship of the east Baltic with western Europe and tendentious theories of 'the clash of civilisations'. The divergence between professional and popular history, witnessed by Runciman's continued reputation and the 'impotence of academic critics' to influence public perceptions of the past, has never been so acute.[43] Yet many of the familiar accounts – Michaud, Prutz, Grousset, Runciman – encourage a settled view of the crusades as culture wars. Similar impulses sustain both academic and popular concern; the interest in ideological warfare as a function of society; the ramifications of institutionalised belief systems; objective awareness of the sincerity and force of popular and individual spirituality; multiculturalism; the historic divergence of the development of different faith communities; the condemnation of imperialism and colonialism; the efficacy, corruption or compromises of political idealism; the role of historical memory. In a violent century, fascination with war remained part of the cultural furniture, perhaps especially after 1945 in societies that experienced the luxury of peace. For all the freshness of new research, many of the broad interpretive schemes scarcely differed from earlier opinions: the colonial debate; the crusades as exemplars of medieval religion/fanaticism; the theme of economic opportunity; the balance sheet of waste. However, one difference has marked most modern scholars from their predecessors: a prevailing academic relativism that has tended to outlaw overt anachronistic judgementalism so prominent in previous historians and so beloved of the reading public.

The extent to which the new waves of crusader research after the 1950s had the potential to alter the geography of the subject can be illustrated by comparing two post-war surveys of the terrain less than a decade apart. In 1948, reviewing Rousset's *Origines*, La Monte appeared wedded to the 'political, military or social' aspects. He listed four prominent explanations of the First Crusade – holy war, pilgrimage, the effect of Cluniac reform and papal policy – with three auxiliary influences: the reconquista, union of eastern and western churches and Byzantine policy. He explicitly rejected a return, as he saw it, to an outdated view of crusading as 'essentially a religious movement'.[44] By contrast, in his prescient 1957 joint review of Runciman's *History* and of the first Pennsylvania volume, Smail pointed to three broadly defined areas of interest: the expeditions themselves; the Latin East; and the relation of crusading with western religious life. He also indicated possible subjects that needed exploring: the military orders, largely untouched since Delaville Le Roulx's work on the Hospitallers and Prutz's on the Templars; the Jerusalem *Assises* building on the pioneering work of Grandeclaude; and, following Erdmann and Rousset, the ideas and emotions that underpinned the whole phenomenon. His conspectus did not ignore traditional topics, reviving some and suggesting new perspectives on others.[45] It now seemed possible to examine these issues free from confessional or, in western Europe at least, heavily nationalistic bias. To this catalogue could have been added new methods of economic history unfettered by moralising snobbery towards the motives and morality of those involved in trade; the use of new techniques of archaeology, anthropology, sociology; and a redefinition of cultural history to include the mass not just the articulate elite. No longer did the excesses of the colonial enthusiasts or the overblown disdain of Runciman convince.

From the mid-1950s, the subject was reshaped in a string of major reinterpretations. Some, such as Smail's own *Crusading Warfare* of 1956, Prawer's 'apartheid' or Mayer's institutions, remapped familiar territory. Others, such as Giles Constable's seminal 1953 article on 'the Second Crusade as seen by contemporaries', began to extend the conceptual as well as evidential scope of the subject, in this case beyond the focus on campaigns to and in the Holy Land.[46] Long-standing assumptions regarding commercial exchange, western economic exploitation and colonial systems that reach back to Robertson and Heeren, were entirely recast by detailed and innovative use of the archives of Italian maritime cities, notably David Jacoby's extraordinary sequence of studies of Romania and Venetian involvement in the eastern Mediterranean; and Michel Balard's exploration of the Latin diaspora, in particular Genoese commerce and presence in Greece, Outremer and the Black Sea. Here, the crusades were located within a far wider scheme of reference regarding economic change and the development of urban western European mercantile communities and of their overseas *comptoirs* or trading posts.

What was true for commerce applied to war and chivalry. Knightly attitudes, of central concern at least since Sainte-Palaye in the eighteenth century, increasingly formed part of a much wider debate about the origins of western knighthood, its nature, impact and chronology. Beyond discussions of whether the association of crusading and chivalry was either complementary or contradictory, or whether chivalry as a code or social signifier could be said to have existed at all before the twelfth century, the crusades have been incorporated as symptoms of contested social change. These arguments bled into disputes over feudalism and the alleged radical changes in local power structures, especially the authority of lords and knights, in the years (or centuries even) around the year 1000, a so-called *mutation* that, its proponents argue, transformed the political, social, legal, fiscal and even geographic landscape in favour of regional *seigneurs*. The prominence of non-royal commanders and their *milites* has made the early crusades an obvious battleground in this debate, with clear potential implications for the origins of the crusade. Thus, Riley-Smith and his pupil Marcus Bull have identified the pressures that produced the enthusiasm for the First Crusade in the collapse of public, centralised authority in western Francia, the subsequent internecine violence producing a reaction of guilt and anxiety that could be channelled by the clergy or driven by the lay knights themselves towards penitential holy warfare. Others, such as Jean Flori, appear less convinced by this theory of disruption.[47] While the certainties on the very concept of 'feudalism', let alone its application in Outremer, assumed by La Monte in the 1930s, have been fractured, largely by non-crusade historians, the relevance of such revisions is obvious.[48] If there was no coded chivalry and no feudal system in 1095, the First Crusade could not have been the product of the former or exported the latter.

The centrality of war in medieval society has also kept attention on the concrete aspects of crusading: tactics, castles, sieges, recruitment and logistics. The old concerns with the exchange of tactics and military architecture across opposing frontlines and cultural differences have been refashioned. Smail's ideas have been applied widely. John France's military account of the First Crusade, *Victory in the East* (Cambridge, 1994) emphasises the adaptable eclecticism of crusade commanders and fighters. By contrast, Ronnie Ellenblum's discussion of crusader castles is dominated by a challenge to a set of theoretical assumptions that portray castles primarily in terms of military defence.[49] Much work has dwelt on preparations rather than fighting, using the crusade to illumine western society's engagement with the wider economic, social, political and fiscal repercussions of war in western Europe. More widely still, crusading has been incorporated as one of the forces producing what has been called 'the expansion of Catholic Christendom' or even 'the Making of Europe'.[50] In such studies, tactics of individual battles, a staple of a certain type of military historian, assume a distinctly secondary role. However, elsewhere, study of numbers of troops, the ratio of casualties and the details of the conduct of campaigns have deepened understanding of what fighting a crusade may have been like. Highly innovative research on logistics, on land and, notably, at sea, by J. H. Pryor and others, has demonstrated that what happened on the march, sea voyage or battlefield cannot be seen as entirely discrete subjects. Pryor's work on Mediterranean currents and winds as well as the ships themselves has provided concrete explanations for much that previously was taken for granted.[51] Such studies tackle not just questions of supply and how armies operated over long distances, but reveal perhaps unexpected vistas on the determinants of strategy, the policies and mentalities of commanders, the level of military intelligence and expectations, even the geographical awareness of would-be leaders. What emerges is a picture of much greater complexity than the old models would allow. Images of optimistic *ingénus* blundering about a world they did not understand in a near-permanent state of violent myopia now appear hopelessly crude.

This has also proved the case with an issue that concerned both Erdmann and Runciman: the role of Byzantium. The growth in Byzantine studies may have been stimulated by Runciman, although, even in English, he 'was hardly a pioneer'.[52] Much of the establishment of a distinct modern Byzantine historical identity was the work of French art and literary scholars, such as Charles Diehl (1859–1944) and Louis Bréhier (1868–1951), who also edited and translated the *Gesta Francorum* (Paris, 1924). The political cycles of Byzantine contraction and recovery became familiar through books that no longer treated Byzantium in the Gibbonian manner as an effete decadent mockery of its ancestor the Roman Empire, for example *The History of the Byzantine State* (first German edition 1940; English 1957) by the Russian-born Yugoslav scholar George Ostrogorsky (1902–76). The role of the crusades as agents of decline, and in 1204 destruction, rested on acceptance of a high political narrative largely the creation of Greek authors such as Anna Comnena and Nicetas Choniates and sustained by the persistent assumption of culture wars. This was lent added definition by a conceptual frame that showed civilisations being plotted on a graph of rise and decline set against some, presumably classical, standard of excellence. Traditionally, this essentially Enlightenment idea of cultural progress cast crusaders as bumptious destroyers of a decadent relic, an increasingly feeble guardian of classical heritage. While the Greeks tended to be described as in some senses superior to the crusaders, the future seemed to lie, through conflict as much as contacts, with the rise of the west. This formed a sort of subsidiary east versus west narrative to shadow that played out in the Levant. Despite a subtler understanding of Byzantium, crusaders continued to be cast as inevitable opponents, an interpretation reflected in studies bearing titles such as *Byzantium Confronts the West*.[53]

This combination of the teleology of hindsight, inherited stereotypes – cultivated Greeks, malign western thugs and avaricious Italian merchants – and a concentration on the surface of high politics only began to be undermined from the 1960s. With further research on the Byzantine economy, for example by

Michael Hendy among others, and detailed investigation of trade, commercial links with Italian traders and western settlers in thirteenth-century Greece, as by Jacoby, Balard and Ralph-Johannes Lilie, the old image of conflict became seen as too simple, misleading or irrelevant.[54] The trend to place Byzantine crusader relations in a wider context of multivalent contacts in time, space and circumstance has been matched by fresh scrutiny of the famous confrontations. The diplomacy of the twelfth century has been reviewed outside the traditional shadow of the inexorable path to 1204, as in Lilie's *Byzanz und die Kreuzfahrerstaaten* (Munich, 1981, Eng. trans. *Byzantium and the Crusader States*, Oxford, 1988 and 1993). New interpretations of the First and Fourth Crusades, while not diminishing the misunderstanding, tensions and hostility generated by these events, escape the traditional paradigms. Jonathan Shepard has since the 1980s recast the First Crusade as in part a consequence of Byzantine diplomacy and pre-1095 Latin penetration of Byzantium, with Bohemund as a Greek-speaking enemy, turned potential ally, turned enemy; rather above the heads of those, like Runciman, merely content to gloss Anna Comnena.[55] Similarly, the dominance of Nicetas Choniates in blaming the disaster of 1204 on western greed, Venetian duplicity and supercilious Byzantine imperial folly has been confounded on two fronts. The decline of Byzantium as a military force and cohesive polity now seems less inevitable and of shorter gestation; and the Fourth Crusade has been rebranded as a series of accidents rather than a concerted conspiracy of intent (the old idea of an actual formal plot – still pedalled by unwary students – being a curious nineteenth-century canard based on textual misreading). The Venetians, it is argued, were no less susceptible to crusade idealism than other Europeans and actually invested considerably more in it than they did.[56]

This reluctance of modern historians to adopt the confident cultural diagnoses of the past or accept the determinism of fate owes much to new techniques of textual scholarship that unravel and to a degree deconstruct the chronicle narratives. Suspicion of sources is also matched by an anxious secular relativism that denies forces of history as determining whether individuals or groups have been on winning or losing sides. Especially in those regions less in thrall to a Cold War Manichean outlook on life, in the second half of the twentieth century contingency and the equality of experience tended to replace the patterned, predictive and hierarchic schemes of Whigs or Marxists. It is true that recently in certain parts of the academic world, primarily but not exclusively North American, a fresh Whiggish scheme of Western Destiny has emerged in response to the end of the Cold War and the coming of effective Islamist terrorism, a new teleology that once again threatens to privilege certain elements of crusade history. However, the earlier fracturing of interpretive models has allowed greater prominence to aspects of the crusades that once appeared tangential to what theorists call the meta-narrative, the big issues of the rise and fall of civilisations. Two examples may suffice here: the history of the military orders; and the crusades of the later middle ages.

As Smail noted in 1957, for over fifty years little study had been devoted to the military orders, institutionally or ideologically, despite their being one of the most original, prominent, distinctive and adhesive consequences of the crusades. This may have been a function of unease at the overt institutionalisation of an apparent oxymoron of confessed religious dedicated to butchery. More specifically there perhaps existed a lingering suspicion of entrenched hypocrisy encouraged by literary slanders and the often misleading images of the lurid perjuries of the Trial of the Templars, the brutal conquests and regimes of the Teutonic Knights in the Baltic, or the effete aristocratic Hospitaller rulers of eighteenth-century Malta swept away by Napoleon in 1798 in a gesture of apparently cleansing modernity. By the mid-1970s this reticence had changed completely. Surveys and monographs were appearing, by, among others, Jonathan Riley-Smith and Antony Luttrell (on the Hospitallers), Marie-Louise Bulst-Thiele, Alan Forey and Malcolm Barber (on the Templars) and William Urban (on the Teutonic Knights). Each of these and other studies, such as Werner Paravicini's seminal work on the Teutonic Knights and the Baltic Crusade from the late 1980s, rehabilitated the study of the military orders as institutions of considerable significance in the development of religious orders, elite and popular spirituality and the relations between ecclesiastical corporations and society.[57] In Britain, much of the impetus in studying the institutional history of military orders came from a circle of medievalists gathered as pupils and colleagues by a vigorous academic entrepreneur and Professor of Medieval History at the University of St Andrews, Lionel Butler (1923–81), a group that included at various times Riley-Smith, Forey, Luttrell and Peter Edbury, historian of Frankish Cyprus, the Jerusalem *Assises* and the texts of the continuators of William of Tyre. Butler himself, although a spasmodically industrious archival scholar, published nothing of substance on his chosen area of the Hospitallers in Rhodes. However, he noted the riches and potential of the Maltese Hospitaller archives and drew others to them. The institutional approach was very characteristic of the secular post-war Oxford tradition in which Butler was raised, and was applied to ecclesiastical as to lay history. However, latterly, in the past twenty years or so, the ideological implications of the personal and religious commitment of the Military Knights have come to be integrated into their history, another sign of the greater willingness to confront the belief systems of the middle ages on their own terms.

Study of the military orders inevitably helped shift the geographical and chronological emphasis, as many of them survived as active political and ecclesiastical corporations for centuries after the loss of the Holy Land. The heyday of the Teutonic Knights' *Ordenstaat* ('Orderstate') in the Baltic and of the Hospitallers' in Rhodes belonged to the later middle ages. That crusading had continued long after the evacuation of mainland Palestine in 1291 was obvious to early modern and Enlightenment historians. Only with the emergence of the models of colonialism and culture wars did the focus narrow. The crusades of the later middle ages, tending to be localised affairs conducted by those on the frontiers of Christendom, scarcely fitted either. They also displayed a rather messy narrative, hard to weld into a clear story. If the crusades were regarded as the wars over the Holy Land, campaigns elsewhere, even if against Muslim enemies, simply did not fit; still less did the wars fought as crusades within Christendom against enemies of the papacy, notably in Italy. Later medieval conflicts with the Ottomans were hardly popular subjects for study. They highlighted Christian failure as well as raising issues that possessed awkward contemporary resonance well into the twentieth century, while simultaneously drawing attention away from the reassuring familiarity and distance of the Palestine wars. Yet the obvious presence of wars of the cross after 1291 had not been entirely ignored. Delaville le Roulx had written about campaigns in the fourteenth century, perhaps unsurprising for a historian of the Hospitallers.[58] The abundance of surviving fourteenth- and fifteenth-century theoretical, technical and propagandist crusade texts stimulated interest from the Romanian Nicolai Iorga (*Philippe de Mézières 1327–1405 et la croisade au XIVe siècle*, Paris, 1896), the Italian Arturo Magnocallo (*Marin Sanudo il Vecchio e il suo progetto di crociata*, Bergamo, 1901) to the German G. Dürrholder (*Die Kreuzzugspolitik unter Papst Johann XXII 1316–34*, Strasbourg, 1913). Some of these texts had appeared in the *Recueil des historiens des croisades: Documents Arméniens* (vol. ii, Paris, 1906) – and indeed in Bongars's *Gesta Dei Per Francos* in 1611 – as well as many published in the *Revue de l'Orient Latin* by luminaries such as Charles Kohler. However, such literary investigations could be incorporated into an argument of decline and decadence, ineffectual wishful imaginings compared with the central dramas played out in the Levant between 1097 and 1291. The west, fructified by its contact with the east and the experience of conquest and settlement, was imagined to have decisively turned its back on the crusades in preparation for the Renaissance.

However, it was apparent that these literary texts were matched by general later medieval action which, as Aziz Suryal Atiya (1898–1988) noted in his groundbreaking *The Crusade in the Later Middle Ages* (London, 1938), altered the conception of the whole subject beyond its old chronological, Holy Land boundaries. Atiya, an Egyptian and exceptionally gifted linguist, had extensive experience of the academic world in Germany and England before going on to hold chairs in Egypt and the USA. His interests in the crusades went alongside pioneering research into Coptic history and eastern Christianity in general. His first book, on the Nicopolis crusade of 1396 (London, 1934), sought to place later medieval crusading practice, planning and propaganda in the wider setting of 'relations between East and West', including pilgrimages and missions to the Tartars as well as military campaigns. He was later to develop theories of counter-crusades.[59] His perspective – and many of his sources – reflect his unusual personal and academic position straddling the cultural and linguistic divide that formed the core of his crusade research. The bulk of his evidence, as it had been for Delaville le Roulx and Iorga, remained literary. Only with new archival material could the later medieval crusade fully come into its own. One appeal of the earlier crusades for historians lay in the comparatively restricted range and type of source material, primarily chronicles. Few royal, seigneurial or urban archives survived from before the thirteenth century. With the exception of Gregory VII's, only from Innocent III did the run of extant papal registers begin. Only later in the twentieth century was the substantial corpus of charters employed by crusade historians. Given that the later middle ages, with comparatively less rich chronicle material, have left far more archival documentation, sifting through it for the thread of crusading appeared daunting, especially before these archives were edited or calendered.

After the Second World War, Atiya's conceptual inclusion of the later middle ages was matched by an explosion of archival work, especially on Italian mercantile cities and, crucially, the papacy. In the vanguard of this research was Kenneth Setton, whose interests, like those later of Jacoby or Balard, significantly were not constrained in a crusade model. In certain ways, his *Catalan Domination of Athens 1311–1388* (Cambridge MA, 1948) continued the old tradition of William Miller, *Latins in the Levant* (London, 1908). More directly, his enormously erudite *The Papacy and the Levant* (Philadelphia PA, four volumes, 1976–84) was in many respects, especially in the early volumes, 'essentially a history of the later crusades'. However, by adopting the fashionable US style of narrative history, the use of a huge range of Greek, Italian and papal documents placed the crusade in a dense weave of contemporary events; aptly Setton described himself as a 'mosaicist'.[60] What was incontestably demonstrated was that the subject existed on a scale far more extensive than previously explored, but one that could not be approached shackled by the old models that contrasted dramatically with Setton's long, multi-volume account. In his third volume of nearly 500 pages in 1954, Runciman, heavily dependent on Atiya, produced a cursory survey of anti-Muslim warfare and planning, just over forty pages to cover 1291–1464. Given his Byzantinist perspective, this may appear peculiar, even on his own terms. Just over a decade later Hans Mayer deliberately ended his account in 1291, signalling a clear view that crusading properly delineated concerned the wars and settlement in, around and for the Holy Land, a position that he consistently maintained thereafter which inevitably excluded the later middle ages.

One incentive to extend the range of study came with a rejection of his assumption. Atiya's broad definition in some ways represented a return to the Enlightenment model of generalised cultural contact. Another was the growing interest in their medieval pasts by historians of and from regions that had been on the periphery of Latin Christendom. One of the more subtly restrictive features of crusade historiography has always been its narrow geographic, often essentially Franco-centric bias. Medievalists of and from Scandinavia and the Baltic, some stimulated by the end of the Cold War and issues of national identity and relations with an apparently resurgent European community, could hardly avoid studying crusading in the later middle ages. In the territories of the Teutonic Knights, the emergence of Christian Finland and the consolidation of a royal and national Danish identity, the place of crusading institutions and motifs could not be ignored.[61] Elsewhere, from the 1970s, a group, initially primarily of British historians, articulated refinements of the pre-nineteenth-century inclusive interpretation. Wherever a crusade, defined by its familiar panoply of privileges and ecclesiastical, propagandist and fiscal institutions, was discussed, proclaimed, organised and conducted it came within the legitimate ambit of crusade history.[62] Some were pragmatically drawn to this simply by the evidence of continued active as well as passive interest in what later medieval contemporaries described and understood as crusades. For others this shift in emphasis betokened what was argued as being a more sensitive empathy with the aspirations of the time in a reassertion of the centrality of religious idealism. What pragmatists and idealists shared was a rejection of the orthodox historiography of decline that charted an increasing lack of popular enthusiasm and a rise in secularism, cynicism and indifference towards crusading amongst both rulers and subjects. Some regarded the argument about unpopularity as crudely configured; others as false. These new perceptions, while neither united in attitude nor universally accepted, produced a series of monographs and general surveys that extended the work of Setton and the historians of the later medieval military orders, prominently Norman Housley's quartet of studies *The Italian Crusades 1254–1343*, *The Avignon Papacy and the Crusades 1305–78*, *The Later Crusades: From Lyons to Alcazar 1274–1580* and *Religious Warfare in Europe 1400–1536* (Oxford, 1982, 1986, 1992 and 2002 respectively).

From a rather different angle, the chronological limits of medieval crusading have been further extended by scholars of humanist literature, such as Robert Black, Robert Schwoebel, James Hankins and more recently Nancy Bisaha and Margaret Meserve, whose research decisively challenges one of the most cherished and venerable conventions of crusade scholarship. The crusades have been branded as quintessentially 'medieval'; that is what gave them their diagnostic edge for their Enlightenment critics. Now it is clear that the subject obsessed humanist writers of the Renaissance just as seriously as their supposedly benighted medieval ancestors. The 400 or so humanist crusade texts by fifty different authors produced between 1451 and 1481 constitute a volume of work 'at least equal to all the surviving crusade literature of the high Middle Ages'.[63] This fact sits awkwardly with the construct of the crusades as a representative aspect of the culture that the Renaissance was supposed to have abandoned. It challenges the facile, crude demarcation of 'medieval' and 'modern', a pattern of historical progress and change that united most of the major influential writers on the crusades, from Grousset and Runciman back to Gibbon and Robertson. Just as study of the military orders raised issues of taking seriously medieval systems and institutions of belief, so the extension of scrutiny into the later middle ages seemingly discarded some of the strongest hoops that bound the subject together.

Notes

1 C. Erdmann, *Die Entstehung des Kreuzzugsgedankens* (Stuttgart, 1935), trans. M. W. Baldwin and W. Goffart, *The Origins of the Idea of Crusading*

(Princeton NJ, 1977); S. Runciman, *A History of the Crusades* (3 vols. Cambridge, 1951–54).

2 *Origins*, pp. 10, 181, and for Gregory VII and war generally, pp. 147–81; *Entstehung*, p. 8 for *bedenklichen Schritt*; for Erdmann's career, *Origins*, p. ix based on the memoir by F. Baethgen in his collection of Erdmann's work, *Forschungen zur Ideenwelt des Frühmittelalters* (Berlin, 1953) and the author's own comments, pp. xxxv–xxxvi; G. Constable, 'The Historiography of the Crusades', *The Crusades from the Perspective of Byzantium and the Muslim World*, ed. A. Laiou and R. P. Mottahedeh (Washington DC, 2001), pp. 10–11; Erdmann's self-description is quoted by H. E. J. Cowdrey in his review of *Origins*, *International History Review*, 1 (1979), 121–5. cf; the rather misleading account by N. Cantor, *Inventing the Middle Ages* (New York NY, 1991), pp. 402–4.

3 *Origins*, p. xxxiv.

4 E.g. Cantor, *Inventing the Middle Ages*, pp. 403–4.

5 *Origins*, p. 4

6 H. E. Mayer, *The Crusades* (Eng. trans. J. Gillingham, 2nd edn Oxford, 1988), p. 14; cf. *Origins*, p. 331.

7 *Origins*, pp. xxxv, 20, 269; *Entstehung*, pp. 17, 250.

8 *Entstehung*, p. 250.

9 *Entstehung*, p. 26.

10 *Origins*, p. 3.

11 *Origins*, pp. 9–10; *Entstehung*, p. 8.

12 *Origins*, p. 265; *Entstehung*, p. 246.

13 *Origins*, pp. 332, 368 and Appendix pp. 355–71; *Entstehung*, pp. 363–77.

14 See esp. the notes to chap. X on Urban II.

15 E. Delaruelle, 'Essai sur la formation de l'idée de croisade', *Bulletin de litérature ecclésiastique*, 42 (1941), 24–45, 86–103; 45 (1944), 13–46, 73–90; 54 (1953), 226–39; 55 (1954), 50–63; published as a book (Turin) 1980.

16 P. Alphandéry, *La chrétienté et l'idée de croisade*, ed. A. Dupront (Paris, 1954–59).

17 *Origins*, p. 125; Cantor's tendentious reading of the book as a seditious tract fails to convince, *Inventing the Middle Ages*, pp. 402–3.

18 Cowdrey's review of *Origins*, p. 125. J. Riley-Smith, 'Erdmann and the Historiography of the Crusades 1935–1995', in *La primera cruzada*, ed. L. Garcia-Guijarro Ramos (Madrid, 1997), pp. 17–29.

19 Reviews by T. Boase, *History*, 22 (1937), 112–14; L. Bréhier, *Revue d'histoire ecclésiastique*, 32 (1936), 671–6; W. Holtzmann, *Zeitschrift für Kirchengeschichte*, 56 (1937), 152–4; J. L. La Monte in *Speculum*, 12 (1937), 119–22; Z. N. Brooke, *English Historical Review*, 54 (1939), 108–10.

20 J. L. La Monte in *Speculum*, 23 (1948), 328–31, esp. 329–30.

21 Riley-Smith, 'Erdmann', p. 329.

22 M. Villey, *La croisade: essai sur la formation d'une théorie juridique* (Paris, 1942).

23 H. E. J. Cowdrey, 'Pope Gregory VII and the Bearing of Arms', in *Montjoie: Studies in Crusade History in Honour of Hans Eberhard Mayer*, ed. B. Z. Kedar *et al.* (Aldershot, 1997), pp. 21–35; *idem*, 'Pope Urban II's Preaching of the First Crusade', *Past and Present*, 55 (1970), 177–88; J. Gilchrist, 'The

Erdmann Thesis and Canon Law', in *Crusade and Settlement*, ed. P. Edbury (Cardiff, 1985), pp. 37–45; *idem*, 'The Papacy and War against Saracens', *International History Review*, 10 (1988), 174–97; *idem*, 'The Lord's War as a Proving Ground of Faith', in *Crusaders and Muslims in Twelfth Century Syria*, ed. M. Shatzmiller (Leiden, 1993), pp. 65–83; M. Bull, *Knightly Piety and the Lay Response to the First Crusade* (Oxford, 1993), but cf. H. E. J. Cowdrey, 'From the Peace of God to the First Crusade', in *La primera cruzada*, pp. 51–61.

24 G. Constable, 'Medieval Charters as a Source for the History of the Crusades', in *Crusade and Settlement*, ed. Edbury, pp. 73–89.

25 Mayer, *Crusades*, esp. pp. 23–37; J. Flori, *La guerre sainte* (Paris, 2001).

26 A. Becker, *Papst Urban II (1088–99)*, ii, *Der Papst, die greichische Christenheit und der Kreuzzug* (Stuttgart, 1988); J. Riley-Smith's review, *Journal of Theological Studies*, 41 (1990), 281–2; *idem*, 'Erdmann', p. 18.

27 Riley-Smith, 'Erdmann', pp. 17–29; cf. the comments on the fate of Erdmann's ideas by N. Housley, *Contesting the Crusades* (Oxford, 2006), pp. 30–6.

28 Riley-Smith, 'Erdmann'; Cowdrey's review of *Origins*, p. 125; P. Chevedden's two articles on 'Canon 2 of the Council of Clermont', *Annuarium historia Conciliorum*, 37 (2005), 57–108, 253–322; *idem*, 'The Islamic View and the Christian View of the Crusades: A New Synthesis', *History*, 93 (2008), 181–200; cf. the implication in B. Bachrach, 'From Nicaea to Dorylaion', in *Logistics of Warfare in the Age of the Crusades*, ed. J. H. Pryor (Aldershot, 2006), p. 51; in general cf. B. Hamilton's review of the 1977 English translation, *History*, 64 (1979), 443–4.

29 *History of the Crusades*, i, xiii.

30 *History of the Crusades*, iii, 480; cf. p. 469: 'Seen in the perspective of history, the whole Crusading movement was a vast fiasco.'

31 *History of the Crusades*, i, xii–xiii; the 'massed typewriters' referred to Setton's Pennsylvania *History* to which Runciman unblushingly contributed; for Runciman's career, see his own memoir, *A Traveller's Alphabet* (London, 1991); Averil Cameron's biographical entry in the *Oxford Dictionary of National Biography*, ed. B. Harrison *et al.* (Oxford, 2004, online edition); G. Constable, 'Sir Steven Runciman', *Proceedings of the American Philosophical Society*, 147 (2003), 95–101. One of Bury's other pupils was the Byzantinist, Norman Baynes.

32 *History of the Crusades*, iii, 480.

33 *History of the Crusades*, iii, 480 and, generally, pp. 469–80

34 *History of the Crusades*, iii, 130; perhaps significantly he altered the phrase in his memoirs (published in 1991) to 'there is no greater tragedy in history than the Fourth Crusade', as if to underline his awareness of the precise implications of his 1954 judgement, *Traveller's Alphabet*, p. 90. He also conceded that the Frankish occupation of the Morea 'had its compensations'.

35 *History of the Crusades*, esp. iii, 367–86.

36 J. Riley-Smith, *The Crusades* (2nd edn New Haven CT, 2005), p. 300; cf. the same authority's rather grumpy review of yet another reissue of Runciman's first volume, *Crusades*, 6 (2007), 216–17.

37 *History of the Crusades*, ii, 383; iii, 77–8.

38 *History of the Crusades*, i, 157–8.

39 *History of the Crusades*, i, xi.

40 The 'misguided crusades', the title of Book II of the third volume, included the Fourth, Children's, Fifth, Frederick II's, Theobald of Navarre's and Richard of Cornwall's crusades.

41 R. C. Smail's reviews appeared in the *English Historical Review*, 68 (1953), 85–9 and 72 (1957), 680–7; cf. a similar trajectory from M. J. Tooley in *History*, 37 (1953), 67; 38 (1954), 104–5; 40 (1955), 330; C. Hillenbrand, *The Crusades: Islamic Perspectives* (Edinburgh, 1999), p. 13; Mayer, *Crusades*, p. vii.

42 Quoted by Riley-Smith, *Crusades*, 6 (2007), 217.

43 Riley-Smith again, *Crusades*, 6 (2007), 216.

44 J. L. La Monte's review of Rousset *Speculum*, 23 (1948), 328–31.

45 Smail, *English Historical Review*, 72 (1957), 687.

46 G. Constable, 'The Second Crusade as Seen by Contemporaries', *Traditio*, 9 (1953), 213–79.

47 J. Riley-Smith, *The First Crusade and the Idea of Crusading* (London, 1986), esp. pp. 9–12; Bull, *Knightly Piety*; idem, 'The Roots of Lay Enthusiasm for the First Crusade', *History*, 78 (1993), 353–72; Flori, *La guerre sainte*; Housley, *Contesting the Crusades*, pp. 24–38. For the feudalism debate, see, as an example, that conducted between T. Bisson, D. Barthélemy and C. Wickham in *Past and Present*, 142 (1994), 6–42; 152 (1997), 196–205; 155 (1997), 196–207 and 208–25.

48 E.g. E. A. R. Brown, 'The Tyranny of a Construct', *American Historical Review*, 79 (1974), 1063–88; S. Reynolds, *Fiefs and Vassals* (Oxford, 1994).

49 R. Ellenblum, *Crusader Castles and Modern Histories* (Cambridge, 2007).

50 Titles of books by J. France (London, 2005) and R. Bartlett (London, 1993).

51 E.g. J. H. Pryor, *Geography, Technology and War* (Cambridge, 1988); ed. *Logistics of Warfare*.

52 Constable, 'Sir Steven Runciman', p. 97.

53 By C. M. Brand (Cambridge MA, 1968).

54 E.g. M. Hendy, *Studies in the Byzantine Monetary Economy c. 300–1450* (Cambridge, 1985); D. Jacoby, 'The Encounter of Two Societies', *American Historical Review*, 78 (1973), 873–906; idem, *Recherches sur la Méditerranée orientale du xiie au xve siècle* (London, 1978); idem, *Trade, Communities and Shipping in the Medieval Mediterranean* (Aldershot, 1997); idem, *Commercial Exchange across the Mediterranean* (Aldershot, 2005); M. Balard, *La mer Noire at la Romanie génoise* (London, 1989); idem, *La Romanie génoise* (Rome, 1978); idem, *Les Latins en Orient* (Paris, 2006).

55 E.g. J. Shepard, 'When Greek Meets Greek: Alexius Comenus and Bohemund in 1097–98', *Byzantine and Modern Greek Studies*, 12 (1988), 185–277; idem, 'Cross-Purposes: Alexius Comnenus and the First Crusade', in *The First Crusade: Origins and Impact*, ed. J. Phillips (Manchester, 1997), pp. 107–29.

56 In general, D. Queller and T. Madden, *The Fourth Crusade* (2nd edn Philadelphia PA, 1997); M. Angold, *The Fourth Crusade* (London, 2003); J. Harris, *Byzantium and the Crusades* (London, 2003).

57 J. Riley-Smith, *The Knights of St John in Jerusalem and Cyprus c. 1050–1310*

(London, 1967); A. Luttrell (whose pioneering work has appeared in myriad, often obscure journals), as, e.g., in collected studies, *The Hospitallers in Cyprus, Rhodes and Greece and the West 1291–1440* (London, 1978); *The Hospitallers of Rhodes and their Mediterranean World* (Aldershot, 1992); *Studies in the Hospitallers after 1306* (Aldershot, 2007); M. L. Bulst-Thiele, *Sacrae Domus Militiae Templi Hierosolymitani Magistri: Untersuchungen zur Geschichte des Templeordens 1118/19–1314* (Göttingen, 1974); A. Forey, *The Templars in the Corona de Aragon* (Oxford, 1973); M. Barber, *The Trial of the Templars* (Cambridge, 1978); W. Urban, *The Baltic Crusade* (DeKalb IL, 1975), the first of many; W. Paravicini, *Die Preussenreisen des europäischen Adels* (Sigmaringen, 1989–).

58 J. Delaville le Roulx, *La France en Orient au xive siècle* (Paris, 1885).

59 A. S. Atiya, *The Crusade in the Later Middle Ages* (London, 1938), esp. pp. vi–vii; *idem, Crusade, Commerce and Culture* (London, 1962).

60 K. Setton, *The Papacy and the Levant* (Philadelphia PA, 1976–84), i, p. vii.

61 E.g. A. V. Murray, ed., *Crusade and Conversion on the Baltic Frontier 1150–1500* (Aldershot, 2001), esp. K. V. Jensen's introduction and the essays by Axel Ehlers on Lithuania and Thomas Linkvist on Sweden; K. V. Jensen, 'Denmark and the Second Crusade: The Formation of a Crusader State?', in *The Second Crusade*, ed. J. Phillips and M. Hoch (Manchester, 2001), pp. 164–79; S. Ekdahl, 'Crusades and Conversion in the Baltic', in *Palgrave Advances in the Crusades*, ed. H. Nicholson (Basingstoke, 2005), pp. 172–203; J. M. Jensen, *Denmark and the Crusades 1400–1650* (Leiden, 2007); various articles in T. M. S. Lehtonen and K. V. Jensen, *Medieval History Writing and Crusading Ideology* (Helsinki, 2005).

62 Below, Chapter 8; the ur-text for this approach is J. Riley-Smith, *What Were the Crusades?* (London, 1977; 3rd edn Basingstoke, 2002).

63 J. Hankins, 'Renaissance Crusaders', *Dumbarton Oaks Papers*, 49 (1995), 112 and note 3 and 117, and generally 111–207; R. Black, *Benedetto Accolti and the Florentine Renaissance* (Cambridge, 1985); R. Schwoebel, *The Shadow of the Crescent: The Renaissance Image of the Turk* (Niewkoop, 1967); N. Bisaha, 'Pope Pius II and the Crusade', in *Crusading in the Fifteenth Century*, ed. N. Housley (Basingstoke, 2004), pp. 39–52; *eadem, Creating East and West* (Philadelphia PA, 2004); M. Meserve, 'Italian Humanists and the Problem of the Crusade', in *Crusading in the Fifteenth Century*, pp. 13–38.

8

Definitions and directions

In the past sixty years, the study of the crusades has flourished as never before, now the subject of courses at major universities from the eastern Mediterranean to the western seaboard of North America to the Antipodes. Research has reached far beyond traditional confines and occupies the attention of dozens of scholars worldwide. An international society, The Society for the Study of the Crusades and the Latin East, was founded in 1980. It boasts over 400 members from thirty countries, dwarfing its nineteenth-century predecessor, Riant's elite Société de l'Orient Latin. In keeping with modern academic fashion, since 2002 the society has had its own niche journal, *Crusades*. After two centuries of academic debate, this raft of modern scholarship challenged certain traditional perceptions of the crusades and crusading, not least regarding the nature of the phenomenon itself. Erdmann's attempt at definition had merely added diversity rather than clarity. These issues caught a historiographical moment, exposing divergent perceptions as to how medieval Europe worked, how medieval evidence could be used and, indeed, how historians operate. Simultaneously, the crusades were placed more firmly than ever within non-crusading contexts of religion, society and economy. New approaches to sources appeared. The range of material studied expanded from records of government and diplomacy, property transactions (charters) to liturgical and academic legal texts. Arabists, like their distant Maurist predecessors, once again became interested in texts relevant to crusade history, opening clearer new perspectives to scholars from a western tradition. Critical responses sharpened, for example as regards the nature and authority of narrative as a genre and narratives as witnesses. New models were applied, borrowed, for example, from literary theory and gender studies. In a climate of revived public religiosity, empathy for actions determined by faith, even violent ones, no longer appeared necessarily eccentric or a remnant of the Christian verities of the *ancien régime*. In such contexts, discussion of the nature of the crusades could appear somewhat abstract and even, on occasion, old-fashioned, as if the battles of the Enlightenment and Romantics were being refought. Elsewhere, much of what was sometimes proclaimed as representing fresh insights, in essence rehearsed some rather hoary interpretations, such as Fuller's theory of waste or Michaud's empathy.[1]

One of the oldest features of crusade historiography had been its relation to contemporary cultural and political attitudes. This association was given fresh impetus in the six decades from the end of the Second World War. The power of ideology as a motive of political action was inescapable in the ruined aftermath of the wars against fascism and during the subsequent Cold War. After 1945, concepts and institutions of international law were applied at least rhetorically to the legitimacy of the use of force and the notion of war crimes. In Europe, the fall of the Soviet Empire after 1989 recreated states as well as granting new independence to existing ones. Their inevitable redefinition of identity encouraged engagement in a non-Communist vision of history. In many cases – such as Hungary, Poland, the Baltic States – this included the crusades. The simultaneous enlargement of the European Community stimulated fresh consideration of supranational identity, with various implicit and explicit references to a medieval past. Conflicts surrounding post-1945 decolonisation in Asia and Africa raised issues of legitimate violence as did struggles against oppressive regimes in Latin America, stimulating the development of Liberation Theology in the 1960s and 1970s. The Second Vatican Council (1962–65) discussed the role of papal authority and the nature of relations between Roman Catholics and other denominations and faiths. In the 1990s, from the carcass of the collapsed Yugoslavia, there emerged ethnic cleansing laced with religious contest and prejudice. In Serbia, Bosnia and Kosovo, propaganda and violence opposing Christian and Muslim once more became features of politics and war. With them came a selective historical memory of holy war against the Turks. The failings of secular political movements in the Near and Middle East, in Egypt, Syria, Iraq and, in different register, Iran, encouraged dissident movements based on politically radicalised Islamic agendas, both Sunni and Shia. These movements were initially aimed at reforming or destroying what they saw as the corrupt Muslim regimes before turning their focus more intently on western influence in the region, symbolised in the continuing unresolved conflict between the State of Israel and the Palestinians. Most dramatically, in the first decade of the twenty-first century the extension of these conflicts to global terrorism invited a new public spotlight to be shone on the medieval wars of the cross. The facile historical parallelism this stimulated found receptive audiences not just in the Near East but in the First World as well, notably but not exclusively in the United States of America among certain elements in fundamentalist evangelical groups, the religious Right and even constitutional conservatives. Once again, as Hume observed 250 years ago, the crusades engaged the curiosity of mankind.

Defining the definers

The last quarter of the twentieth century was also marked by a multifaceted debate on defining what a crusade actually was and, thus, the scope of the subject. Before Erdmann, little serious attention had been paid to the matter. The assumption prevailed that the crusades were Christian wars directed initially at recovering Jerusalem. Other subsequent theatres of religious warfare – in Spain, the Baltic, Languedoc, against papal enemies in Italy and Germany or against the Ottomans – were variously included by early modern and Enlightenment writers without much reflection. The nineteenth-century Franco-German concentration on the Holy Land hardly touched issues of category. Yet Erdmann's focus on crusading as a constructed political ideology and feature of western society, not a glorified frontier war, by challenging accepted conventions, invited debate. The various eschatological, spiritual, legal and liturgical emphases of Alphandéry, Delaruelle, Villey and Rousset combined with the reshaping of older Holy

Land interpretations by Cahen, Richard and Smail to further cloud the picture for those, like Hans Mayer in 1965, seeking a uniform, clear model and theory or, as he put it, an 'unambiguous, lucid and generally accepted definition of the term "crusade"'.[2]

What was a crusade? Were crusades synonymous with all or any Christian religious or holy war? If not, what distinguished them in nature, institutions or conduct? Were they defined by being expeditions to regain or retain Jerusalem and the Holy Land? If so, were they a special form of penitential war separate from other campaigns against infidels such as those in Sicily or Spain? Did that difference lie in the combination of warfare and pilgrimage and/or in a unique indulgence? Or were all and any campaigns proclaimed by popes crusades that attracted features associated with the Jerusalem wars, such as cross, indulgence, preaching, taxation, special liturgical support and temporal privileges? What was the status of wars against infidels or enemies of the church granted lesser papal privileges, such as in early thirteenth-century Livonia? Was there an official or unofficial hierarchy of crusades, with Jerusalem at the top and others following according to papal, political or popular mood? Could there be 'unofficial' crusades, such as those apparently essayed against papal crusaders in England in 1263–65 and Germany in 1240?[3] If not, can these and other incidents with explicit crusader trappings be excluded? What of unauthorised expressions of popular enthusiasm for the recovery of the Holy Land, such as the Children's Crusade (1212) or the Shepherds' Crusades (1251 and 1320)? Where, in a strict view of crusading as an institution, do the military orders fit, especially where their activities strayed far from the Holy Land or even holy war; the order-states of Prussia, Livonia and Rhodes or the hospitaller function of the Knights of St John? Should definition be dependent on papal decree, medieval academic opinion or popular response?

Merely by stating this far from exhaustive list of questions identifies some of the difficulties inherent in historians' attempts to provide a satisfactory response to Mayer's request. Concepts and categories, medieval or modern, repeatedly fall foul of medieval action. It is probably fair to observe that none of the arguments offered in the post-1965 debate provides solutions to all the conceptual and practical conundrums. None commands universal agreement, which is perhaps as it should be, given the diversity of medieval witness. It may be wondered whether in fact there was much point to the attempt to construct a universal definition in the first place. The range of views recorded by the canonist and crusade promoter Hostiensis among others in the thirteenth century indicates that consensus may in any case be fundamentally anachronistic, even unhistorical.[4] However, in some ways, the debate acted as a device to promote a certain methodological approach as much as a means to reach a commonly agreed definition. It also allowed an otherwise disparate parade of research to march under one crusading banner, from theology to archaeology, from liturgy to logistics, from institutions to mentalities, from the early middle ages to the sixteenth and seventeenth centuries. Whatever view is taken of the ubiquity of the influence of the crusades, its collective label has immeasurably assisted its prominence in the academic world.

Mayer's appeal for a definition was propelled by his challenge to those who disagreed with his own. Mayer championed a traditional, 'narrow' interpretation, regarding crusading in origin and essence as holy wars concerned with the Holy Land. The struggle for Jerusalem lay at the centre, both militarily and spiritually, the determining feature of the crusade indulgence. Crusades directed elsewhere either lacked the full panoply of privileges afforded the Jerusalem expeditions or represented an abuse. While not denying that non-Holy Land crusades were authorised by popes, justified by canonists and fought by *crucesignati*, Mayer commented that 'what is at issue is not Church doctrine but the extent to which society found that doctrine acceptable'.[5] He rejected attempts to characterise vociferous opponents of non-Holy Land crusades in the thirteenth century as a self-serving biased minority by historians who simultaneously accepted, more or less at face value, the equally self-serving claims of promoters of these crusades for their popularity. Mayer was less interested in interior emotions or the self-referential theorising of the papal curia or university lawyers and canonists. He saw an institution originally devised for the Jerusalem campaign being used for different purposes under the disguise of some theoretical association with the Holy Land. Consequently,

Mayer's definition tended to exclude crusades away from the Holy Land and wars of the cross in the later middle ages.

Mayer's challenge was taken up in 1977 by Jonathan Riley-Smith (b. 1938) who proposed a far more embracing definition.[6] An increasingly dominant figure in Anglophone crusade scholarship, in outline his approach mirrored earlier general, inclusive formulations, the vagueness of which had in part prompted Mayer's search for clarity. However, Riley-Smith, in discussing what he dubbed 'first principles', sought precision which he found essentially in papal authority.[7] Crusades were a particular form of Christian holy war that addressed the needs of the universal church as defined by Christ's representative and head of Christendom, the pope, whose authority ordered, legitimised and, in spiritual terms, controlled the exercise. Some, at least, of the participants took a vow, signalled by the receipt of a cross, and in consequence enjoyed certain specified privileges, including protection of the church. The war was regarded as waged for Christ and therefore itself holy, not merely just, and, for those involved, a penitential act. Consequently, crusaders were granted full remission of sins, later standardised as plenary indulgences. These privileges and institutions, as well as the language used by and about crusaders, were closely associated with pilgrimage. These formulae and thus this form of holy war was not restricted to the Holy Land or the eastern Mediterranean but was applied to warfare in Spain, the Baltic, against heretics, schismatics, Greek orthodox and political enemies of the papacy, branded rebels against the church. However, 'when they were not engaged in war in the East, the remission of sins or indulgence was related to those given to crusaders in the Holy Land'.[8] This last point was particularly delicate, as it implied to some an acceptance of the centrality of Jerusalem that the thrust of Riley-Smith's thesis sought, at the very least, to qualify. This sensitivity may be reflected in the account of Riley-Smith's definition by two of his pupils in the *festschrift* for their mentor that omits any mention of the place of the Holy Land in his description of the crusade indulgence.[9]

The force behind Riley-Smith's definition is religious. Mayer looked at the material objectives of crusading and at motives largely in institutional terms, although he highlighted 'the obstinate simplicity of the believer's heart' that drove them towards Jerusalem. Riley-Smith was centrally concerned with the faith that inspired crusaders and, he argued, initiated crusading. Thus he castigated Erdmann's apparent lack of feeling for genuine ideological and spiritual commitment.[10] Defining crusading as a canonical institution, much in the fashion of Villey, allowed Riley-Smith geographically and chronologically to incorporate far more than Mayer. Where there were papally authorised institutions instigating wars of the cross, there were crusades. This led Riley-Smith to consider in detail technical aspects of the theology constructed around crusading, somewhat in the tradition of Delaruelle, Rousset and of German scholarship, such as that of Hehl. However, it was the empathy for the beliefs of the crusaders that colours this definition. This was allied to fierce opposition to the habit of historical judgementalism, so often the rhetorical prop of those who have written on the crusades, not least Runciman whose legacy Riley-Smith subjects to some distinctly acid criticism. While admitting the difficulty in grasping the 'discredited' 'amalgam of piety and violence, of love and hate', Riley-Smith has no room for 'moral repugnance felt by liberal thinkers' which he sees in part as a legacy of Protestant disapproval of Roman 'Catholic bigotry and zealotry'.[11] Here, the alert may catch faint echoes of Michaud. Given that crusading is thus seen to reflect the inner aspirations of so many Christians in medieval Europe, its wider significance becomes unmistakable, not just in studying the church and popular religion, but also in the habits of the aristocracy, the conduct of war and the development of medieval society in general, 'a movement which touched the lives of the ancestors of everyone of European descent'. Or, as another contemporary British historian not particularly associated with Riley-Smith's views claimed: 'the effects of the crusading movement were almost limitless', playing a major role 'on the stage of world history'. For obvious reasons, few crusade historians were or are as dismissive as the distinguished French medievalist Jacques le Goff, who declared that the crusades' chief contribution to western culture was the introduction of the apricot. However, not all follow the maximalist analysis. Some regard the crusades as less homogeneous or distinct as phenomena, as effects rather than causes.[12]

In 1988, Riley-Smith claimed his interpretation had 'won the day', partly because of shifts in contemporary cultural attitudes that tended to a greater awareness and understanding of ideological violence; and partly through the promotion of his theory in his own works and those of his pupils. One of those pupils subsequently reflected that this assertion of victory had been made 'somewhat hubristically'. Nonetheless, a decade later there was the confident revelation that 'all of us now know that the subject of crusading is a religious one, whatever other elements were important to it'.[13] As far as that went, that was hardly controversial, but it could be said that it did not go very far. All previous crusade historians had acknowledged the role of religion. Where they differed was what that actually meant in operation, what it implied for cause, motive and conduct. Some critics suggested that Riley-Smith and his followers seemed wedded to an acceptance of the significance of often self-referential texts from sections of the clerical elite. From this there flowed both an insistence on the primacy, sincerity and truth of religious commitment on the part of crusaders and a rejection of the evidence of contemporary criticism. The Riley-Smith definition was thought by some to be too neat and theoretical, at times parodying papalist apologia (Riley-Smith himself noted that its proponents 'follow the medieval popes'), arguably a very partial reading of the middle ages.[14]

However, different interpretations not only persisted but gained new advocates. Erdmann's opinion that the crusade was another form of holy war *deo auctore* remained attractive, for example in the work of E.-D. Hehl in the 1990s and, by implication, in K.V. Jensen's categorising of all Danish wars against pagans.[15] The Danish scholar J. M. Jensen and others challenged the centrality of pilgrimage, at least in the origins of crusading, a line followed in part by Jean Flori.[16] However, Flori revives elements of Alphandéry's eschatological analysis, while emphasising the importance of Jerusalem. Gary Dickson has focused with subtlety and insight on popular crusades that Riley-Smith's original definition awkwardly excludes. Dickson shows how a set theoretical definition of crusading, of whatever sort, can still miss some of its protean aspects.[17] More recently, the American Paul Chevedden has sought to emphasise the external political elements in crusading as a response to the threat of Islam, returning circuitously to one of the oldest historiographical tropes. For Chevedden, the crusades began with the papally sponsored invasion of Muslim Sicily in 1060.[18] This recent revival of interest in crusading as part of a political as much as a religious contest with Islam is tinged with more than a hint of historical parallelism. More potentially challenging to existing fashions has been, on the one hand, a recent attempt to apply a historical materialist analysis of the First Crusade and, on the other, a widening of perspective towards a context of religious war.[19] All the while, Mayer's view has retained adherents and Mayer himself has recently vigorously taken up cudgels against those followers of what they claim as the 'now predominant' view of crusading and attempts to belittle his approach.[20]

Internationally, perhaps most crusade scholars have not been led by theory. The question of definition, especially where it excludes elements so obviously associated with the Jerusalem wars, is not always a *sine qua non*. Even on the territory most churned up in the definition debate, much, in any case, comes down to different assessments of particular pieces of evidence, not some meta-theory of human or divine inspiration. One such area surrounds the key issue of popularity. Were the Jerusalem crusades more, or more consistently, popular than the others regardless of the similarity of benefits on offer? This answer has much to do with accepting the competing bias in the evidence. It also is determined by attitudes to the extent of papal power and how far attitudes in Christendom followed or were accurately reflected in papal diktats or not. Even historians who recognise the legal validity of papal crusades wherever fought, have, like Mayer, taken account of varying popular responses. The insistence of some of Riley-Smith's pupils not just on the sincerity of religious response but on the ubiquitous popularity of all crusading, has not universally been found convincing. Yet the differences between Riley-Smith's interpretation and those he seeks to revise may also be exaggerated. By arguing that an equation with the Jerusalem war was integral to the crusade indulgence, Riley-Smith, as Mayer pointed out, was putting 'Jerusalem squarely back at the heart of things'. Furthermore, some historians found it entirely possible to acknowledge the legal validity of all papal crusades while noticing the continuing primacy – in the policy of many popes, in liturgy, in literature, in rhetoric and in public responses – of Jerusalem. As Riley-Smith wrote: 'everyone accepted that the crusades to the East were the most prestigious and provided the scale against which the others were measured'. This was precisely the point argued not only by critics but latterly by some close supporters of the Riley-Smith definition. There may not have been a formal 'league table of crusades', but at least some popes, such as Innocent III in his handling of Livonian pagans and the Albigensian heretics, recognised the prior claims of Jerusalem. The technical efficacy of identical privileges may not have varied according to different military targets, but participants inevitably were aware of the difference on the ground.[21]

This is merely one example of how theoretical definitions come apart when faced by the reality of research and the developing ideas of scholars. Thus there is something inherently artificial in the recent attempt by Giles Constable to define the definers. In 1953, Constable, a leading historian of twelfth-century monasticism and religion, had long anticipated Riley-Smith's inclusive definition in his study of the Second Crusade (1146–49) where he argued for the coherence of the various crusading fronts in Iberia and the Baltic as well as the eastern Mediterranean. A quarter of a century later, he pointed the way to how charters could be used by crusade historians to investigate attitudes, finances and prosopography.[22] In an influential article on crusade historiography published in 2001, Constable proposed four categories into which he judged contemporary crusade scholarship roughly fell.[23] Traditionalists were primarily concerned with where the crusades were directed and, like Mayer, restricted authentic crusades to those aimed at recovering or defending Jerusalem. Pluralists, such as Riley-Smith, emphasised how crusades were initiated, authorised and organised, including all campaigns conducted by those who had taken legitimate crusade vows and enjoyed crusade privileges, not just wars for the Holy Land. Popularists Constable described as those, such as Alphandéry and in a different manner Delaruelle, who identified the collective prophetic and eschatological elements as of the essence, a conclusion largely derived from regarding the First Crusade as 'a moment of collective exaltation'. Unlike the pluralists, this interpretation included the popular demonstrations of the Children's Crusade and the Shepherds' Crusades. Finally, Constable classified those, like Hehl, who regard the crusades simply as a holy war, *deo auctore*, as generalists, potentially admitting into the definition a far wider category of warfare even than the so-called pluralists.

While his classifications have been widely accepted, Constable himself sounded an immediate note of caution. Although described as a pluralist, he noted he was 'reluctant to exclude the "popular" crusades or to deny that at least a spiritual orientation toward Jerusalem was an essential aspect of crusading'.[24] The attempt to label scholars invites caricature of both scholarship and categories in a *reductio ad absurdum* that argues over the classification not the history. Thus Riley-Smith regards Jean Flori as a popularist while Norman Housley sees him as a traditionalist. In a related example, traditionalism can be traduced because two scholars so designated (not by themselves but by others) disagree, even though neither fit neatly into the boxes chosen for them, the one because of popularist elements, the other through adopting a pluralist frame.[25] Constable applied his categories cautiously to recent historiography, but others have extended the classifications backward in time. Erdmann may illustrate the wider point. For some, Erdmann is a generalist, in placing the crusade firmly in the pre-existing tradition of war *deo auctore*. Yet he emphasises the Rankean contrast between the hierarchic crusade and the popular, with its eschatalogical dimensions. For Erdmann, the novelty of Urban II's call lies in Jerusalem and pilgrimage, a traditionalist claim. Yet put the other way round – pilgrimage first, Jerusalem second – is to touch on pluralist territory.

The debate over definition may have petered out, perhaps because the expanding range of research, source material and consequent interpretations and interests render such definitions irrelevant or redundant. Moreover, enthusiasm for 'schools' of interpretation is fashionable only in some not all academic traditions and institutions. For many, mainly but not exclusively non-British historians, the definition debates appeared of little consequence. Even in Anglophone scholarship, it impinges but little if at all, to take a few random examples, in recent work on attitudes to Islam by John Tolan, on John Pryor's studies of logistics, on Gary Dickson's examination of crusading 'mythistory', on Ronnie Ellenblum's or Denys Pringle's archaeology, on Benjamin Kedar's historiographical exposés, on Peter Edbury's analysis of the legal texts of the thirteenth century and the translations of William of Tyre, or on Jay Rubinstein's reappraisal of First Crusade sources. German or French scholarship seems relatively unaffected. In Italy, Franco Cardini, for example, or Elena Bellomo's work on Genoa discuss definition, but are not framed by it.[26]

Even as shorthand, Constable's categories seem to raise as many difficulties as they solve. Perhaps a less constricting approach might avoid unnecessary ideology, theory and confusion. Crusade historians vary one from another and even within their own published research. Some are led by the need for a pre-existing model; others, more critically empirical, are not: the idealists and the pragmatists. Some historians prefer to see in the evidence the workings of an overarching, almost mechanical process, the discovery of which is a collaborative endeavour striving towards agreed consensus, even a 'truth'. Others are less eager to identify consistency in the historical record or insist on uniformity in historical interpretation. Scepticism over the extent any medieval evidence can provide unmediated access to the thoughts of the laity limits the attraction of any theories based on examining the responses of the inarticulate. It encourages suspicions that much of what passes for revealing information as to the existence, progress, popularity of crusade ideas are part of internalised debates within self-validating elites. More simply, much, perhaps most, research on topics related to wars of the cross does not depend for its intellectual coherence or integrity on adopting a position on any abstract definition but rather on the critical interrogation, assessment and interpretation of the sources. Definition that implies exclusion may seem, *a priori*, a peculiar place from which to proceed. Beyond that, despite, perhaps because, of the claims for the ubiquity of crusading as a socially normative phenomenon, it is often unprofitable to impose discrete boundaries between crusading and its context. The real vitality in the debate on definition in fact lay paradoxically less in an attempt to find agreement over 'first principles', but rather in the promotion of a particular way of looking at the medieval past in order to dispel any lingering modern condescension, a project that came to characterise a vociferous group of younger crusade historians centred from the 1960s in Britain.

The British school and the rehabilitation of crusading

Possibly the least predictable development in crusade studies in the past fifty years has been the unmistakable explosion of academic interest and scholarly achievement amongst British medievalists. To give this too much prominence risks the charge of insularity. However, it represents perhaps the most notably cohesive and extensive national network of active crusade scholars since the inter-war US school, if only in the weight of publication demanding notice and academic posts obtained. Its genesis depended on groups of individuals but also on certain extrinsic academic influences: the availability of translated texts for teaching purposes; the revival in the study of medieval religion and ideas; the abundance of increasingly available literary and archival evidence, both published and in manuscript; the growth in the size and number of university departments and the consequent increase in the numbers of students in search of doctoral topics. Here, the excitement of Runciman's narrative, however meretricious, may have played a role. It should be remembered that, in contrast to many continental European nations, notably Germany, or to the USA, a formal research culture including postgraduate training in methods and skills or supervised doctorates, was for long unknown among arts subjects in the oldest, grandest and richest of English universities, Oxford and Cambridge. Most of the most distinguished late nineteenth-century medievalists were not professional academics, having begun or remained private gentleman scholars. This only began to change after the First World War and only gathered momentum a generation later. In that sense, the rise of crusades from 1960 conformed to a general eruption of postgraduate research. In Britain, too, the crusades seemed to carry less awkward, less current baggage than in France, Germany or Italy, let alone Franco's Spain. While ideological warfare had returned to the agenda of civilisation, British observers could apparently regard it with greater equanimity. Perhaps the self-satisfied and rather smug British myth of measured, moderate detachment, evident from Fuller to Hume and Gibbon to Runciman, rendered the crusades less polemic, less toxic. In this vein, Richard I was an ideal British crusade hero: one of ours yet not; a regal absence, his crusading a presence always somehow just off-stage.

However, there was and is no single or uniform British coterie of crusade historians. The difference between clusters of crusade historians in part reflected different approaches to teaching and research, possibly to history itself. There emerged a distinct and remarkably cohesive 'school' of explicitly crusader studies primarily associated with the universities of Cambridge and London that proved notably successful in colonising British university history departments. This is not necessarily a common experience in universities that teach crusading history. To take just one contrasting example, in Oxford, where the crusades became an optional specialist subject for undergraduates in the late 1960s, crusading was incorporated into wider study of the middle ages, driven by a variegated empiricism that hardly saw 'The Crusades' as a whole subject apart. A number of very distinguished Oxford medievalists, none of whom were 'crusade specialists', nonetheless taught the course and, as offshoots of both teaching and their other research, published often significant articles on crusading: Karl Leyser on money and supplies on the First Crusade; Colin Morris on the Fourth Crusade; John Prestwich on Richard I on crusade; John Cowdrey on the intellectual, institutional and spiritual origins of the First Crusade; Henry Mayr-Harting on Odo of Deuil and the Second Crusade; Maurice Keen on fourteenth-century crusaders. Another contemporary Oxford scholar, Eric Christiansen, has written innovatively and imaginatively on the Baltic crusades. Yet, despite some individual theses – such as Randall Rogers (a Leyser pupil) on twelfth-century crusading siege warfare and Simon Lloyd (a Prestwich pupil) on thirteenth-century England – there was and is no Oxford crusade school.[27] This is not to privilege the Oxford experience, merely to note its eclecticism as illustrative. Another British example lies with Bernard Hamilton at Nottingham and his pupils, notably Malcolm Barber of Reading and John France of Swansea, three of the most effective recent British crusade historians, whose research in this area has also been conducted on an individual basis, in a non-ideological context, and as part of larger portfolios of interests and publications.

Rather different was the study of the crusades in Cambridge. In part this reflected, specifically as opposed to Oxford, the subtly different structure of academic employment and history syllabus that allowed for more pedagogic specialism, academic focus and research concentration. It may have also demonstrated certain features of the Cambridge history school in general. The Cambridge system encouraged the creation of intellectual schools around university lecturers who dominated certain reaches of the past, or tried to. Equally, from the 1930s, there developed in Cambridge a concern for the importance of ideas in politics and society, a sort of filtered *geistesgeschichte*. This rejected equally the sentimental determinism of Whiggish materialism, the mechanistic materialism of the Marxists, and the institutional and prosopographical materialism of Lewis Namier of Manchester (originally of Oxford). This 'revisionist' Cambridge school became associated with figures such as J. H. Plumb and Quentin Skinner. Amongst medievalists, Walter Ullmann provided his own logical explanations of how ideas operated in the way the middle ages worked, likened by one colleague to his fascination with the internal combustion engine.[28] In such an atmosphere, that the crusades were essentially of interest for their demonstration of powerful ideology would come as no surprise.

Ironically, the flag-bearer for the crusades in post-war Cambridge, R. C. Smail, could not have been less domineering in personality, manner or scholarship or more sceptical of abstractions. Nonetheless, his influence was profound beyond his own studies. In his 1957 review of Runciman, Smail had mapped out three areas for future research: the military orders; the Jerusalem *Assises*; and crusading ideas and motives. As his pupil Riley-Smith remarked fifty years later, Smail brilliantly 'foresaw the direction of crusade studies for the next half-century'.[29] This becomes less remarkable when it is remembered that Riley-Smith's own academic pilgrimage followed precisely Smail's agenda, taking him from the military orders, to the institutions of the kingdom of Jerusalem, including the *Assises*, to the ideology and motives of crusaders. Yet whilst Riley-Smith admitted owing his greatest academic debt to Smail, their take on the crusades differed. Smail was never finally a convinced pluralist. He was wedded to the tradition of close textual scrutiny, German-style *Quellenkritik* and suspicious of categories: 'the more complex the phenomenon, and the wider the differences of opinion about its nature, the less useful a one-word label'.[30] Although referring to colonies, his remark could be applied to the crusade as well.

While Smail gave Riley-Smith his initial direction, inspiration and doctoral topic on the Hospitallers in the east, the Cambridge–London 'pluralist' school was very much the creation of the pupil. Second to Smail as a mentor came Lionel Butler, a representative of a very different academic tradition, a pupil of the intellectually austere K. B. McFarlane, whose approach was defiantly secular, influenced by both Marx and Namier. Butler gave Riley-Smith his first job, at St Andrew's, and later helped his move to a chair in London. Butler's own work on the Hospitallers foundered, but, primarily from his Department of Medieval History at St Andrew's, he exerted a subtle influence on the development of crusade studies, conveyed largely through personal engagement with colleagues, undergraduates and graduate pupils. He left no school, and his pupils came to adopt very different approaches to the crusades.[31] However, true to his own academic training under McFarlane, Butler grounded in his pupils the importance of archives, not up to that point a marked feature of Anglophone crusade scholarship. By contrast to Butler's urbane, eclectic *laissez faire*, at Cambridge (where he returned after St Andrew's), then London, then Cambridge again, Riley-Smith built up an unsurpassed équipe of crusade scholars as his graduate students, attracted by his skilful, green-fingered identification of research topics, clarity of vision, generosity of nurture and infectious enthusiasm. Few areas or aspects of crusading were ignored. The pluralist agenda was pursued through studies of political crusades, crusading in the Holy Land, the Baltic and Greece, the organisation and motivation of crusades. Some characteristic features are discernible: a reliance on papal evidence; the preparedness to hear authentic medieval voices in often formalised texts; the search for an early coherence and achronological consistency in crusade theology. These were concerns shared by Riley-Smith himself, notably in studies of the ideas surrounding the First Crusade and response to them of the First Crusaders in which he stresses the absence of material incentive and seeks to demolish the fancy of crusaders as greedy land-grabbers or feckless impecunious younger sons on the make.[32]

Riley-Smith's vision of the crusades was that of a movement possessed of almost anthropomorphic patterns of youth, maturity and old age. The spiritual was central. In some of his pupils this produced an almost mechanical insistence not just on the crusades' narrow canonical legitimacy, but on the sincerity and weight of religious inspiration behind them. Personal conviction is repeatedly insisted upon. Axiomatic is the approval afforded crusading at the time. Riley-Smith's own work has been infused by a desire to understand the crusaders' motivations on their own terms, however alien or contradictory those motives may appear to modern eyes. Increasingly, the penitential aspect is identified as crusading's 'most important defining feature'.[33] As two of his more senior pupils have identified, this 'process of imaginative engagement' has been informed by Riley-Smith's beliefs as a Roman Catholic and Knight of the Sovereign Military Order of Malta and the Venerable Order of St John. 'Always earthed by Jonathan's professionalism', this empathy 'plays a large part in yielding some of his richer insights and observations.'[34] It also makes him especially alert to historians with other frames of reference, past and present. As with many prophets, Riley-Smith is an eager and robust disputant. He has a proselytising enthusiasm for his ideas and his approach. Others are judged accordingly almost as if in a search to expose those who stray from the path of true doctrine. Erdmann is dismissed as lacking sufficient ideological sympathies. Runciman, like Riley-Smith a product of Eton and Trinity College, Cambridge, but so very different in so many ways, is taken to task for his romanticism and judgementalism but also, it seems, for his religion, 'another Lowland Calvinist' (the other being Walter Scott). Runciman's Calvinism, though sincere, was scarcely of the puritanical or disapproving sort and his dislike of the crusaders hardly sprang from religious taste or distaste. Jean Richard's 'visceral attachment to the Holy Land' is lamented. Materialism and the condescension of Protestants, Marxists and liberals are especially to be rooted out.[35] The 'pluralist' stance and empathetic engagement become almost totemic. Like many sectarians, Riley-Smith and his 'pluralist' school can indulge in exhaustive mutual endorsement and dismissive polemic against dissidents. Observing from across the North Sea, Hans Mayer, himself a target for Olympian pluralist disdain, recently teased: 'in England it is really dangerous not to be a pluralist'.[36]

Of course, such knockabout is the stuff of historical debate. Historians are notoriously disputatious. It cannot be denied that the stimulus given by Riley-Smith and other British crusade scholars in the past half-century has helped transform the subject. Constable's definitions have in fact served usefully to expose their own limitations. Many of the articles of faith, even among pluralists, have admitted of modification. Anxiety has been expressed that the desire to empathise minimises the difficulties in teasing out authentic witness of belief and detailed events in formalised medieval texts, from chronicles and vernacular literature to no less artificial charters and trial records.[37] The much harked-upon dichotomy between spiritual and material motives seems increasingly either misconceived or old hat. An increased awareness of the roots of the historiography has shifted perceptions. Anyone reading Knolles or Fuller or even Wilken might not find pluralism so novel. Anyone reading Michaud would appreciate the value of controlled empathy. More widely, the increasing academic interest in historiography as a subject of cultural history in its own right has thrown new light on past and developing interpretations of the crusades, what might be called the historicism of history. The crusades remain a barometer of attitudes both to the sort of history each generation regards as worth exploring and of the wider social response. Thus the twentieth-century interest in the legitimacy of violence has become subsumed in a renewed focus on the crusades as examples of inter-faith conflict and of cultural and political imperialism.

New lamps for old?

It is trite but true to say that any historian will 'see the crusades filtered through the material of his own mind'.[38] Revision is, or should be, as inherent in the study of history as interpreting evidence. This book is about the past. However, it may be worth considering pointers to future debates on the crusades and how they conform to patterns already revealed. Within what might be described as traditional crusade scholarship, familiar themes remain attractive: papal records; the military orders; attitudes of theologians, canon lawyers, preachers; the study of liturgy and popular religion. There is a renewed activity in assessing how the western settlement in the Holy Land fits the context of multi-faith Mediterranean societies.[39] It is probable that there will be a reaction against the prevailing religious emphasis in explaining the crusades towards a more nuanced materialist approach. Hitherto, such initiatives have tended to be misjudged, eccentric or mutton dressed as sushi. Some rely on highly speculative if not contentious and partial readings of imprecise texts or a set of very generalised but equally speculative determinist theories, such as the American 'Frontier' thesis or Lynn White Jnr's once fashion-able thesis of technological development producing a force that the crusades released.[40] Old saws receive ill-fitted new clothes. The hardly novel idea that crusading resolved the crux of Christian doctrines of sin confronting the social reality of violence reappears as psychological tension resolutions. When added to millenarian anxiety and the perceived Muslim threat, the First Crusade is rebranded in sociological terms as a remedial 'disaster reaction' in accordance with 'Disaster Theory'. Some economic theorists in the 1990s regarded the crusades as 'an essential part of a wealth-maximising strategy'; the church gained a monopoly over salvation in the face of the threat from Islam and crusaders sought their fortunes through war and conquest. As Constable noted in his restrained account of these developments, 'the views of Voltaire and Gibbon have thus been revived'.[41]

Materialism will probably have its day again with convincing analysis of the sources and a defter use of the models of social science. However, other fresh directions are suggested by new academic approaches beyond either the crusades or even the middle ages. New techniques of source criticism borrowed from literary critical theory are being applied not just to explicitly imaginative literature, such as vernacular poems and songs, but also to chronicles. The process of composition and the techniques of narrativity are also complemented by ideas derived from Pierre Nora and others; crusading as confected memory.[42] Study of the transmission of literary and historical images is matched by that of art, notably the nature of the stylistic forces at play in the plastic arts in Outremer, especially architecture, the decorative arts and manuscript illumination.[43] This feeds naturally into the wider debates about cultural exchange, increasingly seen in non- or post-colonial ways. As yet in its relative infancy, the methods of gender studies have begun to produce intriguing commentaries on the distinctive experiences and images of women in their varied relationship with crusading, hitherto largely neglected.[44] Further removed from classical crusade studies, in books such as *Medieval Film* and *Queer Movie Medievalisms*, the genre of film studies argues for the inclusion of this popular medium as conveying serious interpretive messages, from Cecil B. de Mille's *The Crusades* (1935) to Ridley Scott's *Kingdom of Heaven* (2005), the latter's fundamental, meretricious historical errors nonetheless attracting the fury of Muslim activists and right-wing Christians alike.[45]

The Crusades and politics

Such reactions to Scott's lamentable film provide just one demonstration of the unavoidable recent development: the politicisation of the crusades. This is not primarily an academic issue in so far as few serious historical studies are predicated on interpretations derived from modern politics. However, the crusades have been elevated into models of oppression and proclaimed as a continuing force in the politics of the First World in its dealings with Muslim countries. Western colonialism in the nineteenth century revived, or, some argue, created interest in previous Christian European penetration of the eastern Mediterranean, an interest unfortunately fed by the fashionable, available and predominantly neo-colonial vision of writers such as Michaud. The collapse of the Ottoman Empire and the succession of the British and French mandates in Syria and Palestine consolidated the neo-colonial interpretation, not least in western scholarship and Near Eastern politics. Post-war conflicts in the Near and Middle East, from the creation and defence of the State of Israel from 1948 to the Lebanese wars in the 1980s to the Iraq wars of 1990–1 and 2003 and beyond, have attracted claims of crusading precedents, almost exclusively from Muslims. The exception of G. W. Bush's notorious *faux pas* of 16 September 2001 lent such views a phoney credibility. The crusades had ceased to be a subject for disagreement between academics; they were thrust back into the arena of public debate and often violent and bloody political action.

While imperative to insist that the medieval wars of the cross were of a different nature, in a different time and between different peoples, and have nothing directly to say to modern problems, the recent adoption of a caricature of them as a parallel and model for our times cannot be ignored, even in a study of largely academic historiography. As should now be evident, historical parallelism often sits at the centre of writing history, the subject of this book. It is only within the past eighty years, perhaps only fifty, that such facile comparative habits have been replaced by a historical relativism that judges the past on its own terms not ours. This at least is true in the hitherto dominant European and North American historiographical tradition. One potential new direction of crusade studies lies with non-Europeans, in particular Arab and Turkish scholars whose historiographic legacy, in part derived from nineteenth-century Europe, has in the past displayed marked discrepancies from the trends analysed above. In his pioneering 1972 study of what he called 'Arab historiography of the crusades', Emmanuel Sivan described the umbilical link between Near Eastern politics and the study of the crusades since the 1860s.[46] Such little Arabic academic study that there was before 1945 seemed to follow ideas of east–west conflict developed by governing elites. This was further encouraged by Arab nationalists during and after decolonisation from the 1930s and 1940s who sought to deflect attention from indigenous problems and define a new political identity against an oppressive and exploitative external force, the western Mandate powers. In the early 1930s, Palestinian nationalists celebrated the 'Day of Hattin'. One division of the Palestine Liberation Army bore the name 'Hattin'. For those, like General Nasser of Egypt, wishing to promote a pan-Arab unity in the region, heroes of the resistance to the crusaders, such as Saladin or the Mamluks (both conveniently based in Egypt), supplied powerful historical models. The role of the French and the

British, from the mandates of the 1920s to the Suez invasion of 1956, invited further comparison with the western invasions of the crusades. To this was added the creation of the State of Israel in 1948. Consistently supported by western powers, Israel provided a ready excuse for historical parallelism, the Zionists as new crusaders occupying the Muslim homelands, the *dar al-Islam*. Thereafter, it became commonplace to regard the crusades, as one Syrian writer noted in 1948, as providing 'a major link in the chain connecting the past and the present'.[47] While drawing on a long intellectual tradition of extrapolating present moral lessons from history, this parallelism suggested that history was actually repeating itself, a lesson of hope to Arab nationalists.

The debate over the crusades in the Arab world had been stimulated intellectually by the interpretations of western writers of the nineteenth and twentieth centuries (Ernest Barker's essay was translated into Arabic twice, in 1936 and 1960). Partly originating among the Christian intelligentsia of the Lebanon and Egypt, the academic study of the crusades remained largely secular: 'the west today is still waging Crusading wars against Islam under the guise of political and economic imperialism', this from an Egyptian book published in 1934.[48] Following the French colonial school, the crusades were depicted as driven by materialism confronting the idealism of their Muslim opponents. This idealism was interpreted by secular-minded nationalists after 1945 in terms of 'Arabhood' rather than religious faith. Within this could be subsumed non-Arabs in the crusade story – including Saladin and Baibars – and hence in modern political agendas. This trope of conflict was not just a feature of crude political polemic. The central irony within Arab historiography is that it derived so directly from the European Enlightenment and Romantic tradition filtered, in part, through the cultural influence of precisely those invading powers – France and Britain – that were being branded neo-crusaders. From India to Cairo, which, from the 1920s, with Damascus, acted as the focus for what Near Eastern crusade research there was, intellectual circles absorbed a western model of a clash of civilisations as, for example, in the work of A. S. Atiya.[49] Revival of interest in the crusades was thus doubly a product of empire.

The secular approach reversed the post-Enlightenment debate

about western superiority. It has been argued that Arab writers used the crusades as a means of 'uprooting the inferiority complex created as a result of their encounter with the modern west'.[50] The issue of the apparent transfer of economic, technological and cultural supremacy from east to west had been a staple of western analysis from the seventeenth century onwards. In this process, the crusades were variously regarded, from being central to peripheral. Although many Islamicists and Arabists argued that the crusades were of only tangential significance to medieval Islam, the idea re-emerged that the crusaders' contact with the east had civilised the west. Such reheating of tired western clichés scarcely furthered either a political or an academic agenda. It did, however, speak to a sense of frustration and victimisation fuelled by colonialism, continued western interference and the political capital local regimes made from both. Any sense of inferiority was hardly assuaged by comments such as Sivan's in 1972, describing Arab historiography: 'the account it renders is essentially an emotional one', stemming from an 'unintellectual approach'.[51] In the same issue of the journal of the Israel Oriental Society, perhaps tinged with post-1967 triumphalism, Hava Lazarus-Yafeh, a distinguished Israeli scholar of Islam, wrote of 'the lack of intellectual and emotional maturity in the Arab world today' which she found in the judgemental dualism and extreme, inappropriate language of Arab textbooks. She continued: 'Imperialism, like Israel, reminds the Arab world daily, hourly, of its backwardness, of the loss of its splendour and greatness,' adding that, 'Islam is the embodiment of the glorious national past and the source of national pride'.[52]

Since the 1970s, the political dimension to the Arabic study of the crusades has been radically altered in two significant ways. First, the dominance of the secular, materialist interpretation of crusading has given way to a more stridently religious understanding of the past conflicts which have been projected forward to the present day. Second, the jihadism and jihadist attitudes that this has produced have been turned from being mainly directed against corrupt regimes within the Near East to a confrontation with western powers who, in Iraq and elsewhere, have once more intervened violently into the Muslim world. In 1972, Sivan looked forward to a more sophisticated Arab historiography. The current context makes this more difficult. Much of the impetus for the study of the Arab world invaded by the crusaders still comes from Arabist scholars based in the west where new debates about the nature of Islam, the medieval Islamic threat to Europe and the extent of cultural conflict have arisen, products of the same sense of anxiety and renewed combat.[53] The scene has shifted. In his well-known study *Orientalism* in 1978, Edward Said argued that at least since the eighteenth century, western cultural attitudes, public policy and academic scholarship towards Islam and the Arab world have rested on convenient self-interested, ignorant, inaccurate, hostile and patronising caricatures. Yet in his lengthy polemic, Said gave the crusades only fleeting cursory mention.[54] Such indifference would be unlikely in any similar investigation today, a point presciently emphasised by Amin Maalouf's widely read *The Crusades Through Arab Eyes* (1983 original French edition; the often creaking and clumsy English translation 1984).

Maalouf (b. 1949), a Lebanese Christian writer and journalist living since 1976 in exile in Paris, provided what he called a 'true-life novel' of the eastern crusades, an essentially uncritical and in places imaginative and sentimental narrative based largely on Arabic sources to challenge the Eurocentric vision of the classic accounts of Grousset or Runciman. As if to underline this imbalance of traditional perspective, the majority of his primary sources exist in western European editions. In its superficial populist approach, Maalouf's *Crusades* implicitly demonstrates the paucity of contemporary Arab scholarship and its dependence on western research. If inconsequential and occasionally inaccurate as a historical study, Maalouf's work nonetheless clearly and deliberately exposes the inescapable contemporary resonance of his subject. The commentary on the First Crusade focuses on Arab humiliation and the sense of violation by the barbaric western invaders encapsulated in the experience of Palestinian refugees 'determined never to return until the occupiers had departed for ever and ... resolved to awaken the consciences of their brothers in all the lands of Islam'. The modern parallel needs no pointing. Nor does the argument that the jihadist revival of the twelfth century came not from the political elites but from 'a ground swell' beginning in the streets and mosques, a force mobilised by Nur al-Din, the 'Saint King', and Saladin who directed Muslims morally, militarily and through propaganda to recover 'the occupied territories'.

However, from his non-Muslim Arab Lebanese perspective, Maalouf achieves some objectivity in skilfully reconciling the final telling irony of the book and, he implies, of the history of the Near East. The Muslim world won the crusades and repelled the invaders, yet this presaged the rise of western Europe and the eclipse of Arab civilisation. Maalouf's take on this hoary paradox involves an unblinking critique not so much of what the west gained from contact with the east as of the structural weaknesses within Arab society itself, a subject far less studied. Among the causes for the decline of Arab power Maalouf identified disunity, the predominance of foreign leaders, the lack of stable civic institutions, the reliance on the arbitrary power of rulers over the rule of law and the consequent failure to develop strong traditions of individual rights. Some of these issues remained 'on the agenda in scarcely altered terms in the latter part of the twentieth century'. The struggle to defeat the crusaders produced an insularity that rejected openness to new still less foreign ideas. This militated against innovation, intellectual, scientific or commercial, leading to 'long centuries of decadence and obscurantism'. More corrosively, Maalouf argued, the creation of a solipsistic culture of embattled victimhood encouraged the Muslim world to regard progress and modernism as alien. Western colonialism exacerbated the sense of grievance and persecution, as the options presented veered from imposed westernisation to the embrace of obsessive 'xenophobic traditionalism'. Either way the modern west appeared an enemy, with the crusades the obvious precursor, the legitimate resistance of Saladin or Baibars against one seeming to validate supposed vengeance against the other. Maalouf concluded that 'there can be no doubt that the schism between these two worlds dates from the Crusades, deeply felt by the Arabs, even today, as an act of rape'.[55] While adding nothing to the understanding of the medieval phenomenon, Maalouf helps explain why rational academic study of the crusades in the Arab world seems so difficult.

Yet the refashioning of the crusades into a modern jihadist banner of hate is not without western parallels. Any visit to the world wide web can reveal apparently serious western historians arguing over the intrinsic violence of Islam and consequently that the crusades were a necessary defensive measure against Turco-Islamic barbarism, a debate joined enthusiastically by a motley coalition of right-wing secularists, conservative libertarians, biblical fundamentalists, evangelists and Christian bigots. While possibly beginning to exert an influence in the direction of crusade studies back towards more political, material considerations, this new – actually rather old – political and cultural stance prompts a final observation, if one of absence.

The study of the crusades has rarely attracted historians of the political or intellectual Left. The oppositionist critique of the crusades by the *philosophes* was not sustained. Partly this has been a function of the appeal of medieval studies, not just the crusades, for Roman Catholic scholars, not least, but not only, in countries where confessional higher education remained prominent. While German nineteenth-century liberals may have taken to *Forschung* and *Quellenkritik* in some degree to escape the stultification of hierarchy and confessional orthodoxy, the crusades hardly lent themselves in any country to radical championing. The Enlightenment characterisation of crusading as one of the most bewildering and depressing aspects of the middle ages and, by extension, its *ancien régime* hangover, left an indelible impression. Where the crusades were not seen as reactionary obscurantism, their identification with either nationalism or colonialism confirmed their place in a world of the powerful not the powerless. In the twentieth century, with the exceptions of writers such as Alphandéry and Dickson, the popular dimensions of crusading have generally been seen as adjuncts to hierarchical promotion. Erdmann's attention to the *populäre Kreuzzug* was Rankean; his whole approach was dictated by a liberal humanism.

Yet, given crusading's popular elements, the grandiose material and cultural claims made on its behalf, not least as a vehicle of social change, and its association with social institutions or constructs such as feudalism, its avoidance by Marxist and socialist historians is notable. Claude Cahen was a distinguished exception. Yet there was no serious scrutiny by members of the *Annales* school in any of its incarnations. Given the wide embrace of crusade studies, and its increasing admittance of theoretical models, this may appear a peculiar omission. Perhaps more recent interpretations emphasising religious devotion and the public acceptance of ecclesiastical orchestration of beliefs, what Beryl Smalley called 'deep acquiescence', has taken for granted a form of medieval social deference.[56] This may appear highly questionable when set beside evidence of medieval scepticism, dissent and popular action, some of it crusading. Perhaps interest in the sociology of crusading will encourage different approaches. Yet, whatever the direction of new research and whoever, wherever, conducts it, one conclusion is evident. The crusades have been reinvented by each new generation; so will they be in the future.

Notes

1 On historiographic parallels, see C. Tyerman, *The Invention of the Crusades* (London, 1998), p. 125.

2 H. E. Mayer, *The Crusades* (Eng. trans. by J. Gillingham of 1965 *Geschichte der Kreuzzüge*, 1st edn Oxford, 1972), pp. 281–6; cf. 2nd edn Oxford, 1988, pp. 312–13.

3 On anti-papal crusades, Tyerman, *Invention*, pp. 32, 45, 77–8, 87 and refs.

4 Cf. Mayer's brief but pertinent commentary on Hostiensis, *Crusades* (2nd edn 1988), pp. 320–1.

5 Mayer, *Crusades* (2nd edn 1988), p. 313. Leading figures in the debate on popularity include P. Throop, *Criticism of the Crusades* (Amsterdam, 1940) and, attempting to dismiss or minimise evidence of hostility, E. Siberry, *Criticism of Crusading* (Oxford, 1985).

6 J. Riley-Smith, *What Were the Crusades?* (London, 1977).

7 Riley-Smith, *What Were the Crusades?* (3rd edn Basingstoke, 2002), p. xi.

8 Riley-Smith, *What Were the Crusades?* (3rd edn Basingstoke, 2002), p. 88.

9 N. Housley, with M. Bull, 'Jonathan Riley-Smith: An Appreciation', in *The Experience of Crusading*, ed. N. Housley and M. Bull (Cambridge, 2003), i, 4–5; cf. Mayer's review of *What Were the Crusades?* in *Speculum*, 53 (1978), 841–2.

10 J. Riley-Smith, 'Erdmann and the Historiography of the Crusades 1935–1995', in *La primera cruzada*, ed. L. Garcia-Guijarro Ramos (Madrid, 1997).

11 Housley, with Bull, *Experience of Crusading*, i, 9; Riley-Smith, *What Were the Crusades?* (3rd edn 2002), pp. xii–xiii; cf. *idem*, *The Crusades* (2nd edn New Haven CT, 2005), pp. 303–4.

12 Riley-Smith, *What Were the Crusades?* (3rd edn 2002), p. xiii; S. Lloyd, 'The Crusading Movement and the Historians', in *The Oxford Illustrated History of the Crusades*, ed. J. Riley-Smith (Oxford, 1995), p. 64; J. Le Goff, *La civilisation de l'Occident medieval* (Paris, 1964), p. 98; but cf. M. Balard's summary, 'Notes on the Economic Consequences of the Crusades', in *Experience of Crusading*, ed. Housley and Bull, ii, 233–9.

13 N. Housley, *Contesting the Crusades* (Oxford, 2006), pp. 18–19 and note 74 for ref.; in general this is an eloquent apologia for a particular, 'pluralist' view of the crusades masquerading as an objective study of recent historiography; Riley-Smith, 'Erdmann', p. 29.

14 Riley-Smith, *The Crusades*, p. 309; cf. Tyerman, *Invention*, pp. 1–6.

15 E.-D. Hehl, 'Was ist eigentlich ein Kreuzzug?', *Historisiche Zeitschrift*, 259 (1994), 237–336; K. V. Jensen, 'Denmark and the Second Crusade: The Formation of a Crusader State?', in *The Second Crusade*, ed. J. Phillips and M. Hoch (Manchester, 2001), pp. 164–79. Cf. J. M. Jensen's similar approach, '*Sclavorum expugnator*: Conquest, Crusade, and Danish Royal Ideology', *Crusades*, 2 (2003), 55–81.

16 J. M. Jensen, 'War, Penance and the First Crusade', in *Medieval History Writing and Crusading Ideology*, ed. T. M. S. Lehtonen and K. V. Jensen (Helsinki, 2005); C. Tyerman, *God's War: A New History of the Crusades* (London, 2006), pp. 71–4; J. Flori, *La guerre sainte* (Paris, 2001), pp. 316–20.

17 G. Dickson, *The Children's Crusade* (London, 2008); cf. his collected studies, *Religious Enthusiasm in the Medieval West* (Aldershot, 2000).

18 P. Chevedden, 'Canon 2 of the Council of Clermont', *Annuarium historia Conciliorum*, 37 (2005), 57–108, 253–322; cf. *idem*, 'The Islamic View and the Christian View of the Crusades: A New Synthesis', *History*, 93 (2008), 181–200.

19 C. Kostick, *The Social Structure of the First Crusade* (Leiden, 2008); N. Housley, *Religious Warfare in Europe 1400–1536* (Oxford, 2002).

20 H. E. Mayer, *Zwei deutsche Kreuzzugsgeschichten in Züricher Sicht: Eine Replik* (Kiel, 2008); the quotation is from Christoph Maier's collusive review of N. Jaspert, *Die Kreuzzug* (Darmstadt, 2003), *Crusades*, 4 (2005), 177–8 at p. 177.

21 Mayer's review, *Speculum*, 53 (1978), 841–2; J. Riley-Smith, 'The Crusading Movement and the Historians', in *Oxford Illustrated History*, p. 9; Tyerman, *Invention*, pp. 2–3; *idem*, 'The Holy Land and the Crusades of the Thirteenth and Fourteenth Centuries', in *Crusade and Settlement*, ed. P. Edbury (Cardiff, 1985), pp. 105–12; N. Housley, *The Later Crusades* (Oxford, 1992), pp. 3–4 (but cf. his more nuanced later work, *Fighting for the Cross*, London, 2008); cf. I. Fonnesberg-Schmidt, *The Popes and the Baltic Crusades 1147–1254* (Leiden, 2006); M. Lower, *The Barons' Crusade: A Call to Arms and its Consequences* (Philadelphia PA, 2005); R. Rist, *The Papacy and Crusading in Europe 1198–1245* (London, 2009).

22 G. Constable, 'The Second Crusade as Seen by Contemporaries', *Traditio*, 9 (1953), 213–79; *idem*, 'The Financing of the Crusades in the Twelfth Century', in *Outremer*, ed. B. Kedar *et al.* (Jerusalem, 1982), pp. 64–88; *idem*, 'Medieval Charters as a Source for the History of the Crusades', in *Crusade and Settlement*, ed. Edbury, pp. 73–89.

23 G. Constable, 'The Historiography of the Crusades', reprinted in *idem*, *Crusaders and Crusading in the Twelfth Century* (Aldershot, 2008), pp. 3–32.

24 Constable, 'Historiography', pp. 12–13.

25 Riley-Smith, *What Were the Crusades?* (3rd edn 2002), pp. 101–2; Housley, *Contesting the Crusades*, pp. 2 (and note 4), 5, 19–20 and, generally, pp.

1–23, a tendentious account; cf. C. Tyerman's review, *English Historical Review*, 121 (2006), 1437–9.

26 J. V. Tolan, *Saracens: Islam in the Medieval European Imagination* (New York NY, 2002); *idem, Saint Francis and the Sultan* (Oxford, 2009); J. Pryor, *Geography, Technology, and War* (Cambridge, 1988); *idem,* ed., *Logistics and Warfare in the Age of the Crusades* (Aldershot, 2006); Dickson, *Children's Crusade*, subtitled: *Medieval History, Modern Mythistory*; R. Ellenblum, *Crusader Castles and Modern Histories* (Cambridge, 2007); *idem,* 'Frontier Activities', *Crusades*, 2 (2003), 83–97; D. Pringle, e.g., *Fortifications and Settlement in Crusader Palestine* (Aldershot, 2000); B. Z. Kedar, 'The Jerusalem Massacre of July 1099 in the Western Historiography of the Crusades', *Crusades*, 3 (2004), 15–75; P. Edbury, e.g., *John of Ibelin: Le livre des assises* (Leiden, 2003); *idem,* 'The French Translation of William of Tyre's *Historia*', *Crusades*, 6 (2007), 69–105; J. Rubinstein, 'What is the *Gesta Francorum* and who was Peter Tudebode?', *Revue Mabillon*, n.s. 16 (2005), 179–204; F. Cardini, e.g., *Studi sulla storia e sull'idea di crociata* (Rome, 1993); E. Bellomo, *A Servizio di Dio e del Santo Sepolcro: Caffaro e l'Orient latino* (Padua, 2003).

27 K. Leyser, 'Money and Supplies on the First Crusade', in *Communications and Power in Medieval Europe*, ed. T. Reuter (London, 1994), ii, 77–95; C. Morris, 'Geoffrey de Villehardouin and the Conquest of Constantinople', *History*, 53 (1968), 24–34 [later of the University of Southampton and the author of a string of seminal articles on crusade ideas, experience, miracles and propaganda]; J. Prestwich, 'Richard Coeur de Lion: Rex Bellicosus', in *Riccardo Cuor di Leone nella storia e nella legende* (Academia Nazionale dei Lincei, Rome, 1981), pp. 1–15; H. E. J. Cowdrey, *Popes, Monks and Crusaders* (London, 1984) includes an early selection, including the famous 1970 article on Urban II's preaching, *History*, 55 (1970), 177–88; H. Mayr-Harting, 'Odo of Deuil, the Second Crusade, and the Monastery of St Denis', in *The Culture of Christendom*, ed. M. C. Mayer (London, 1993), pp. 225–41; M. Keen, 'Chaucer's Knight', in *English Court Culture in the Later Middle Ages*, ed. V. J. Scattergood and J. W. Sherborne (London, 1983), pp. 45–63; E. Christiansen, *The Northern Crusades* (2nd edn London, 1997); R. Rogers, *Latin Siege Warfare in the Twelfth Century* (Oxford, 1992); S. Lloyd, *English Society and the Crusade* (Oxford, 1988).

28 In his obituary in the London *Times*.

29 *English Historical Review*, 72 (1957), 687; J. Riley-Smith, reviewing a reissue of Runciman vol. i, *Crusades*, 6 (2007), 216.

30 From the 1984 symposium on colonialism in the kingdom of Jerusalem published in *Horns of Hattin*, ed. B. Z. Kedar (Jerusalem, 1992), p. 347. For Riley-Smith's career, see the appreciations, *Experience of Crusading*, i, 1–10 and ii, 1–8.

31 They include, as undergraduate and graduate pupils, P. Edbury, A. Luttrell, J. Riley-Smith, E. Lourie and the author of this book, who was Butler's last DPhil student.

32 J. Riley-Smith, *The First Crusade and the Idea of Crusading* (London, 1986); *idem, The First Crusaders 1095–1131* (Cambridge, 1997). Among his published pupils are P. Edbury, N. Housley, J. Phillips, S. Tibble, M. Bull,

W. Purkis, R. Rist, C. Smith, M. Lower, T. Asbridge, I. Fonnesberg-Schmidt, C. Marshall, N. Coureas, C. Maier, J. Bronstein and E. Siberry. The cohesion of the group was furthered by mutual examination of theses, as pointed out by Housley, *Fighting for the Cross*, p. xiv, and is evident in their mutually supportive footnotes. See also. www.crusaderstudies.org.uk/resources /historians/profiles/rileysmith.

33 Riley-Smith, *What Were the Crusades?* (3rd edn 2002), p. xii.

34 *Experience of Crusading*, i, 3. Riley-Smith included a photograph of himself as a Knight of Malta serving at Mass, *Oxford Illustrated History*, p. 390. Cf. two other crusader historians proclaiming the influence of their Christian faith, D. Queller and T. Madden, *The Fourth Crusade* (2nd edn Philadelphia PA, 1997), p. x.

35 Riley-Smith, 'Erdmann', pp. 17–29; *idem, The Crusades*, pp. 300, 303–4, 308–9.

36 Mayer, *Zwei deutsche Kreuzzugsgeschichten*, p. 10, note 18.

37 For example the use as if accurate or true of wholly tainted and unreliable statements from the trials of the Templars, untrustworthy because of the nature of the legal procedures, torture and the threat of torture, J. Riley-Smith, 'Were the Templars Guilty?' and 'The Structures of the Orders of the Temple and the Hospital in c. 1291', in *The Medieval Crusade*, ed. S. Ridyard (Woodbridge, 2004), pp. 107–24, 125–44. A desire to excuse or justify papal or official church policy is suggested.

38 Mayer, *Crusades* (Eng. trans. 1st edn 1972), p. 281.

39 E.g. C. MacEvitt, *The Crusades and the Christian World of the East: Rough Tolerance* (Philadelphia PA, 2008).

40 W. Urban, 'The Frontier Thesis and the Baltic Crusade', in *Crusade and Conversion on the Baltic Frontier*, ed. A. V. Murray (Aldershot, 2001), pp. 45–71; L. White, Jnr, 'The Crusades and the Technological Thrust of the West', in *War, Technology and Society in the Middle Ages* (Oxford, 1975), pp. 97–112.

41 Constable, 'Historiography', pp. 3, 18 and refs.

42 Y. N. Harari, 'Eyewitnessing in Accounts of the First Crusade', *Crusades*, 3 (2004), 77–99; P. Nora, *Realms of Memory* (New York NY, 1996); M. Carruthers, *The Book of Memory* (Cambridge, 1990).

43 E.g. J. Folda, *The Art of the Crusaders in the Holy Land* (Cambridge, 1995) and D. Pringle, *The Churches of the Crusader Kingdom of Jerusalem* (Cambridge, 1991) and *Secular Buildings in the Crusader Kingdom of Jerusalem* (Cambridge, 1997).

44 E.g. *Gendering the Crusades*, ed. S. Edgington and S. Lambert (Cardiff, 2001); S. Geldsetzer, *Frauen auf Kreuzzügen* (Darmstadt, 2003); N. Hodgson, *Women, Crusading and the Holy Land in Historical Narrative* (Woodbridge, 2007).

45 A. Bernau *et al.*, *Medieval Film* (Manchester, 2009), esp. pp. 22, 75–6, 215, 217; C. Kelly and T. Pugh, *Queer Movie Medievalisms* (Farnham, 2009), esp. pp. 45–59 and 61–78.

46 E. Sivan, 'Modern Arab Historiography of the Crusades', *Asian and African Studies* , 8 (1972), 109–49; cf. C. Hillenbrand, *The Crusades; Islamic Perspectives* (Edinburgh, 1999), pp. 589–616.

47 Sivan, 'Arab Historiography', 112; A. Maalouf, *The Crusades Through Arab Eyes* (London, 1984), p. 265.

48 Quoted Sivan, 'Arab Historiography', 112.

49 Above, pp. 208–9.

50 Sivan, 'Arab Historiography', 142.

51 Sivan, 'Arab Historiography', 148.

52 H. Lazarus-Yafeh, 'An Enquiry into Arab Textbooks', *Asian and African Studies*, 8 (1972), 1–19, at pp. 7, 10, 11.

53 Among western scholars, mention might be made, for example, of M. Lyons, P. M. Holt, P. Jackson, D. S. Richards, R. Irwin, P. M. Cobb, N. Elisséeff, A. M. Eddé, R. S. Humphreys, C. Hillenbrand.

54 E. Said, *Orientalism* (London, 1978; new edn 1995), e.g. pp. 58, 75, 101, 168–72, 192. For a sustained rebuttal of Said's often tendentious arguments, R. Irwin, *For Lust of Knowing: Orientalists and their Enemies* (London, 2006).

55 Maalouf, *The Crusades*, *passim*; for quotations and individual points, Foreward; pp. ii–iv; 90, 180, 261–6.

56 B. Smalley, 'Church and State 1300–77: Theory and Fact', in *Europe in the Late Middle Ages*, ed. J. Hale *et al.* (London, 1965), pp. 41–2; cf. Tyerman, *Invention*, p. 89 and note 261.

EPILOGUE

There have been two reasons for this book. One is that it tries to shed light on how the crusades, one of the prominent historic features of western Europe, have been perceived by literate and academic commentators over the centuries. It is thus a modest footnote to the history of European civilisation and civility. The second reason is rawer, more demotic, but possibly more important. It is clear that the crusades, or, to be precise, perceptions of the crusades, now matter beyond the shades of academe. An end note of autobiography may illustrate this. In 2006 I published a long book covering the crusades as a whole. It appeared on both sides of the Atlantic. The reaction revealed patterns of engagement and partisanship to rival the most extreme earlier examples of distortion. In general terms, academic commentators and writers in print tended to assess the work – positively and negatively – on its own terms of intellectual and historical merit. Elsewhere, mainly but not exclusively in North America (and not excluding some professional scholars), and especially on the internet, the work was more frequently judged according to what readers perceived as its stance in the great contest of cultures. It was simultaneously praised for depicting Islam as a threatening creed that justified violent opposition to it and condemned for minimising the Islamic threat in the middle ages and, by no leap of imagination, today. Either way, the litmus test was the crudest form of the already crude 'clash of civilisation' theory, itself a heated-up version of Cold War propaganda. The debate formed a cocktail of debased Enlightenment positivism, ignorant cultural supremacism and historical illiteracy. The past was imagined as providing a parallel commentary and guide to the present and therefore, in a sense, not past at all. Past and present were being collapsed into each other, the consequent rubble providing the material for convenient tendentious polemic in ways similar to certain strands in contemporary Muslim historiography. Such obsessive First World judgementalism depends on an absence of historic perspective constituting a severe form of cultural solipsism. Given its potential to cause actual present harm, this inspires profound unease. If nothing else, this book has sought to demonstrate that history, the critical study of the evidence that remains from the past, is not fixed. Ultimately, its truth lies in the eye of the beholder. The vision can be shared and agreed widely, it must be directed by evidence, but it is neither absolute nor unchanging. History cannot, therefore, be used as a given certainty, universal fact, immutable interpretation or timeless moral lesson. As the great F. W. Maitland wrote: 'if history is to do its liberating work, it must be as true to fact as it can possibly make itself; and true to fact it will not be if it begins to think what lessons it can teach'. All serious views on the crusades are contingent and will be challenged and modified in the future as in the past. What none will prove is that the medieval crusades have direct lessons for the modern age. To claim otherwise is to cheat the past and corrupt the present.

SELECTIVE GUIDE TO FURTHER READING

The full bibliography can be found in the notes, as can references to the texts under discussion. What follows merely sketches some salient secondary historiographical studies.

General

A. S. Atiya, *The Crusades: Historiography and Bibliography* (Oxford, 1962)

E. Barker, *The Crusades* (Oxford, 1923)

J. Burrow, *A History of Histories* (London, 2007)

G. Constable, 'The Historiography of the Crusades', in *Crusaders and Crusading in the Twelfth Century* (Aldershot, 2008), pp. 3–43

S. Edgington and S. Lambert, eds, *Gendering the Crusades* (Cardiff, 2001)

C. Hillenbrand, *The Crusades: Islamic Perspectives* (Edinburgh, 1999)

R. Irwin, *For Lust of Knowing: Orientalists and their Enemies* (London, 2006)

R. Irwin, 'Orientalism and the Development of Crusader Studies', in *The Experience of Crusading*, ii, *Defining the Crusader Kingdom*, ed. P. Edbury and J. Phillips (Cambridge, 2003)

D. Knowles, *Great Historical Enterprises* (London, 1963)

T. M. S. Lehtonen and K. V. Jensen, eds, *Medieval History Writing and Crusading Ideology* (Helsinki, 2005)

H. E. Mayer, 'America and the Crusades', *Proceedings of the American Philosophical Society*, 125 (1981), 39–45

H. E. Mayer, *The Crusades* (Eng. trans. J. Gillingham, 2nd edn Oxford, 1988)

E. Peters, 'The *Firanj* Are Coming – Again', *Orbis* (Winter 2004) (online resource www.fpri.org/orbis/4801/peters.firanj.html)

J. Richard, 'National Feeling and the Legacy of the Crusades', in *Palgrave Advances in the Crusades*, ed. H. Nicholson

(Basingstoke, 2005), pp. 204–22

J. Riley-Smith, *The Crusades* (2nd edn London, 2002)

J. Riley-Smith, 'The Crusading Movement and the Historians', in *The Oxford Illustrated History of the Crusades*, ed. J. Riley-Smith (Oxford, 1995)

J. Riley-Smith, *What Were the Crusades?* (3rd edn Basingstoke, 2002)

C. Tyerman, *God's War: A New History of the Crusades* (London, 2006)

C. Tyerman, *The Invention of the Crusades* (London, 1998)

Medieval

N. Bisaha, *Creating East and West* (Philadelphia PA, 2004)

P. Edbury and J. G. Rowe, *William of Tyre: Historian of the Latin East* (Cambridge, 1988)

R. Hiestand, 'Il cronista medieval e il suo pubblico', *Annali della facolta di lettere e filosofia dell'università di Napoli*, 27 (n.s. 15 1984–85), 207–27

B. Z. Kedar, *Crusade and Mission* (Princeton NJ, 1984)

A. Leopold, *How to Recover the Holy Land* (Aldershot, 2000)

E. Siberry, *Criticism of Crusading* (Oxford, 1985)

P. Throop, *Criticism of the Crusades* (Amsterdam, 1940)

[Much historiographical material and commentary may be found in the introductions to the various primary sources for the medieval crusades.]

Pre-1800

N. Edelman, *Attitudes of Seventeenth Century France towards the Middle Ages* (New York NY, 1946)

L. Gossman, *Medievalism and the Ideologies of the Enlightenment* (Baltimore MD, 1968)

A. Grafton, *What Was History? The Art of History in Early Modern Europe* (Cambridge, 2007)

M. J. Heath, *Crusading Commonplaces* (Geneva, 1986)

J. G. A. Pocock, *Barbarism and Religion* (Cambridge, 1999–2005)

Nineteenth century

J. R. Dakyns, *The Middle Ages in French Literature 1851–1900* (Oxford, 1973)

H. Dehéran, 'Les origines du *Recueil des historiens des croisades*', *Journal des Savants*, n.s. 17 (1919), 260–6

G. P. Gooch, *History and Historians in the Nineteenth Century* (London, 1913; 2nd edn. 1952)

K. L. Morris, *The Image of the Middle Ages in Romantic and Victorian Literature* (London, 1984)

K. Munholland, 'Michaud's *History of the Crusades* and the French Crusade in Algeria under Louis Philippe', *The Popularization of Images: Visual Culture under the July Monarchy*, ed. P. Ten-Doesschate Chu and G. P. Weisburg (Princeton, NJ, 1994), pp. 144–65

E. Siberry, *The New Crusaders* (Aldershot, 2000)

Twentieth century

T. S. R. Boase, 'Recent Developments in Crusading Historiography', *History*, 22 (1937), 110–25

J. Brundage, 'Recent Crusading Historiography', *Catholic Historical Review*, 49 (1964), 493–507

R. Ellenblum, *Crusader Castles and Modern Histories* (Cambridge, 2007)

N. Housley, *Contesting the Crusades* (Oxford, 2006)

A. Jotischky, *Crusading and the Crusader States* (London, 2004)

J. L. La Monte, 'Some Problems in Crusading Historiography', *Speculum*, 15 (1940), 56–75

A. Maalouf, *The Crusades Through Arab Eyes* (London, 1984)

J. Prawer *et al.* 'The Crusading Kingdom of Jerusalem: The First European Colonial Society?: A Symposium', in *Horns of Hattin*, ed. B. Z. Kedar (Jerusalem, 1992), pp. 341–66

D. Queller, 'Review Article: On the Completion of *A History of the Crusades*', *International History Review*, 13 (1991), 314–30

J. Riley-Smith, 'Erdmann and the Historiography of the Crusades 1935–95', in *La primera cruzada*, ed. L. Garcia-Guijarro Ramos (Madrid, 1997), pp. 17–29

E. Sivan, 'Modern Arab Historiography of the Crusades', *Asian and African Studies*, 8 (1972), 109–49

INDEX